To my darling husband.

# Mikis Theodorakis

# Mikis Theodorakis

## Music and Social Change

GEORGE GIANNARIS

*Foreword by Mikis Theodorakis*

London · George Allen & Unwin Ltd
Ruskin House   Museum Street

First published in Great Britain in 1973

© 1972 Praeger Publishers, Inc.

ISBN 0 04 920038 0

Printed in Great Britain
by William Clowes & Sons, Limited
London, Beccles and Colchester

*To Julia*
who has loved Greece and this book

# Contents

# Foreword

I believe it would not be an exaggeration to say that the modern movements in symphonic music are more *musical-literary* than purely musical. One has only to think of how much literature has been written since the time of the composers of the dodecaphonic movement, and how much creative work finally survived. Consequently, it is the music critic and the musicologist who today create the modern musical climate, and not the composer whose work ends up being almost a pretext for the writing of bombastic newspaper columns and analyses. Every unsuccessful young composer or performer becomes an authority on musical criticism for innumerable magazines, newspapers, and all sorts of other publications. A flood of verbiage inundates our era with ivory-tower fabrications and sterile theories. Thus, we have arrived at this peculiar situation where two parallel musical drives exist: one aiming exclusively at the music critics and a few of the "connoisseurs," the other at the people.

I believe that I write music for the people, and that is why I was truly surprised when I heard that a sophisticated person was seriously concerned with my work. Up to this point, I was accustomed to the love of the public and the silence of the specialist, so that I consider Giannaris' initiative revolutionary in the accepted practice—ethics and customs—of modern musical life. Note that, to all my art and pop music works, from the song cycle *Epitaphios* (1959) onwards, the Greek "specialists" have devoted hardly two or three responsible pieces of criticism. Throughout this period, there have appeared in the Greek press double- and triple-column articles, devoted to analyses and critiques of compositions that were performed only once before an audience of barely a hundred people, and that have never aroused the slightest interest in anyone, except, of course, the creators themselves. Whereas my work, although it has drawn the attention practically every day of millions of Greeks and foreigners alike, has not concerned the specialists up to now. The same thing happened recently even in England, where, within the last few months, although I have given three concerts at the Royal Albert Hall, and several more in various other British cities, I have not been honoured with being told what the specialists think of my work. On the first tour, I presented the première of the oratorio *March of the Spirit*, based on the homonymous poem by Angelos Sikelianos, for soloists, a chorus, a symphonic orchestra, and pop instruments, with the participation of the London Symphony Orchestra. On the second tour, I presented the world première of the *Myth-istorema*, based on the poetry of the Nobel prize–winner George Seferis, and the *Survivor*, based on the poetry of Takis Sinopoulos. I do not, naturally, count the "performances" of the works that were given in the prisons and in exile, where I was kept from 1967 to 1970. Both these works, like the oratorio *March of the Spirit*, belong in the category of the new type, which I call "metasymphonic music." The people came, as they always do. The specialists, of course, did not come—or, rather, they came and, as usual, kept silent.

That is why I greet not only with emotion but also with a certain awe, I would say, the work of Giannaris. I believe it will play a significant role in the efforts of many modern Greek composers (and my work constitutes a part of these efforts).

It is my firm belief that in our country we have struck a well from which we can draw rich nourishment. Beyond the raw material of music, we have advanced on other paths, such as form and composition, that lead, in my opinion, to a possible way out of the contemporary crisis and impasse to which the followers of French impressionism and Austrian dodecaphonic practice have led modern musical art.

Personally, I begin with a fundamental principle, which is that Art must at every moment communicate with the masses. Consequently, there never has been, and never can exist, a genuine artistic work only for the few—the connoisseurs, the specialists, or whatever you may call them. Artistic creativity is a full circle. It begins (as an idea, impression, climate, tradition) among the people and the times; it passes through the sensitivity of the creator, who gives it his own expression and form, and continues on to attain completion there where it began, that is, amidst the people and the times. If this circle is interrupted, or if a segment is missing, then we cannot have a true and viable artistic work. We have, in the best of circumstances, an attempt—an experimentation and investigation, as it were.

In Giannaris' book, the various stages and landmarks of my creative work and effort are developed with clarity and accuracy, namely, in its detailed unfolding of *action*. Between the years 1960–67 (and, to a degree, from 1967 to 1971) the cycle of creativity was completed. The work was begun with, and returned to, the people. Naturally, we are still in the first stage, which was cut off violently by the military junta right at the most critical moment of our effort: when we were becoming conscious of the content and the style of metasymphonic music and were ready to engage in a new and greater artistic adventure hand in hand with the Greek public.

One of the first measures that the militarists took was to ban my music, a ban which still stands. This fact places starkly before us the relationship between music and politics, which is to say, art and politics.

Search as one may in the poetic texts that I have used, one will not find any political slogans. One will find neither obvious nor hidden propaganda concerning specific political viewpoints. Consequently, the politicization of my art is exclusively the result of two causes: (a) its forthrightness, and (b) my personal commitment. This is the consequence and the cost that springs forth from my basic principle—that art ought to communicate at every moment with the people. In

other words, it ought to involve the masses. The masses, however, are not something abstract but are, on the contrary, totally concrete. For instance, "masses" for me are the Greek
people who today live under certain conditions that produce
specific problems, expectations, ideologies, ideals. From its
historical past, this people has inherited particular traditions,
principles, customs, sensitivity, learning, and a specific intellectual and cultural foundation. Hence, in order to converse
with this people, at this moment, and in order to give it—
with the form of an artistic work—aesthetic truths that will
concern it, the artist himself, as well as his work, must be immersed in this historical reality. This means that he must be
sincere as his work, too, must be sincere. This is the essence
of the issue of the politicization of my work. There is, however, something else. Creative expression is, above all, an act
of freedom. I create means I am free—I become free. The
message of art is a message of freedom. Therfore, the art that
wants to express faithfully and sincerely a people that
struggles for its freedom aspires to win not only the love of
this people but also the hatred of its enemies. It is a great, a
consummate, aspiration, which I do not hide; I have pursued
it with all my heart!

Now I am uprooted from my homeland. Far away from
my people, I feel small and useless. I gave concerts in Europe only to realize, finally, that the cultural movement that
we created in our country is unique. The audiences here are
classified: symphonic music, light music, variety, opera, etc.
Nonetheless, there is no dearth of vast musical movements
like pop-music. These, however, have not been able to sur-
mount the barrier of spontaneity and to create complex
works that would aspire to embrace more than the senses and
the heart—the mind, imagination, intellectuality, the aesthetic deliverance, and, finally, the moral and spiritual eleva-
tion, the internal liberation.

To achieve this, the composers of pop-music ought to do
what we did. That is, they should collaborate with the great
modern poets and writers of their countries, so that they
could marry their musical sensibility, which is full of life,

with the poetic visions and the messages of the living poetry of our era. In this way, they would avoid resolutely the threatening danger of repetition and superfluity. The elevated poetic content would reinforce their musical creation and compel it to develop into more complex forms, always speaking face to face with the broad masses of world youth.

If Giannaris' book helps in this direction, it will be of great satisfaction to us who are forced to live outside of our homeland. And for this we suffer, perhaps the more so because so many valuable creative forces do not reach the right target. That is to say, they do not end up creating *art for the masses* of our times. Meanwhile, the masses thirst and continue to wait for the thinkers and creators, not only to express them and liberate them intellectually, but also to take the lead and show them the WAY OUT of this horrible human crisis into which they have been driven by technocracy, lust for power, and intoxication with authority.

Today, the mediocrity of the establishment takes its revenge on the liberal, irrepressible originality, leading humanity to the edge of despair. Man, however, with his faultless instinct of creativity guiding him on, slowly but steadily turns his face towards the creators and waits for their voice, in order to be armed, to survive, and to win. For there is no greater armour than the *Word,* the *Colour,* and the *Sound.*

MIKIS THEODORAKIS

# Preface

It is not easy to write about the life and work of a man of extremes—a man torn between artistic creativity and political activity, a "cultural hero" who evokes emotions of intense hatred and fanatic love. It is even more difficult to write of such a man when he is still alive, burning, moving, changing, creating, and affecting the lives of many thousands. Yet, such has been my task in writing about Mikis Theodorakis, covering all three facets of his life—music, society, and politics.

I have been driven to this task by the conviction that his life embodies the essence of the life of his country, Greece. His vitality, his heroism, and his constant struggle against oppression and backwardness have also characterized Greece. The country's struggle to achieve national autonomy and to raise the economic and cultural standards of the Greek people has been his struggle. No matter what the slogan, no matter what the means, foreign intervention has always been at the root of every major tragedy in the life of the country. Mikis himself has suffered the consequences of four of these catastrophes: the disaster that followed the Greek defeat in Asia Minor in 1922, forcing his parents to leave Smyrna and seek a new life; World War II, which resulted in the bloodiest tragedy in modern Greek history—the Civil War (1944–49); and the present repressive regime of the colonels.

It was as a student of world music, especially folk and pop, that I was first attracted to Mikis Theodorakis. I was irresistibly drawn to the dynamic, masculine, and haunting melodies and rhythms of his works. Above all, I was deeply moved by the beauty and power of the tragic and heroic poetry he had chosen to set to music. His music captures the essence of the Greek soul in all its tragedy. The picture it paints is full of anguish and passion, as if it were an archaic performance enacted against the craggy mountains and the eternally grieving sea. From the early 1960's, not only did I buy all his albums, but I began to collect clippings about him and his works from every newspaper and journal I could lay hands on on this side of the Atlantic. Then, in the summer of 1963, just after the assassination of Grigoris Lambrakis (Z), a member of the Greek Parliament and Mikis' closest friend, I had the opportunity to visit Greece and witness the phenomenon of this revolutionary musician for myself—the electric enthusiasm and total dedication of the young, who have always been the focal point of his musicocultural movement. Wherever I went, Mikis' music poured out of juke boxes, radios, tavernas, and homes. Something new was going on that I did not fully grasp at the time but could very well sense.

I went to all the concerts he conducted—pop as well as classical—and to musical revues. Finally, I met him personally: From that moment on, his youthful energy, his zest for creative action, his open-heartedness and childlike enthusiasm have remained with me. I was to meet him again on many occasions seven years later, in both Europe and the United States, following his release, and to work with him on every aspect of this book.

Mikis' movement has been truly revolutionary musically and socially. He abandoned a brilliant career in classical music and devoted his creative energies to the folk and pop tradition, in order to create new forms of composition and performance. He set his music to first-rate poetry and utilized unorthodox means, such as the "low-class" *bouzouki* instrument, and vocalists who had no formal musical training to perform these works before a public totally unaccustomed to art music, as such. He turned to the young people, in whom he saw the hope of a reborn Greece, and this sparked the first vigorous outpouring of a youth culture. Ron Hall, writing for *The Sunday Times*, said about this paradox: "It was as if Benjamin Britten had set verses by Auden to be sung by the Archbishop of Canterbury—and the records had pushed the Beatles out of the charts."

Mikis attracted the youth, because he gave them a purpose and a cause, so to speak, to which they could relate, clearly revealed in both his music and his politics. Such a movement was diametrically opposed to the apolitical and nihilistic existentialism popular in the West in the early 1960's. What characterized Western youth trends was a deliberate departure from materialism and a search for new attitudes in life—clothes, hero-images, and a new music. Such inclinations could help a confused generation find a meaning in life. Mikis' slogan, "back to the roots" of Greece, gave a positive meaning and a fixed goal to the youth; with his music, he inspired in the people a cultural awakening and instilled in them a pride for what was truly theirs. At the same time, by developing their social consciousness, through traditional rhythms and the poetic message, his music prepared them emotionally for politics. His numerous speeches and articles were directed towards this goal, but, since the majority of them appeared in the left-wing press, it was primarily with his music and his brave defence of Greek culture that he was able to reach a wide audience and to win many hearts.

He won enemies, too. For it was inevitable that a movement seeking to break down traditional social barriers, and to goad the entrenched authorities into progressive action with regard to education and the archaic clientage system of politics, should engender hostility. What was shocking was the violent form this enmity took, from both the militant Right and the dogmatic Left. Not only did he suffer vitriolic abuse at public gatherings and concerts, as well as in the press, but he was also the target of physical attacks from the police and planted agents of the authorities. The extreme Left tried to discount him by generally ignoring the existence of his movement. But Mikis was, and still is, stubborn. To him, social responsibility springs from historic necessity and a law of life, and being free means being responsible. The young generation that had come through the war felt the need for a break through the suffocating cultural and political stalemate with new ideas, and Mikis, part of that generation, accepted the responsibility as his own.

Throughout his thirty years of struggle, his strength and perseverance have sprung from his creative genius, which is as open and genuine as his ideas are public and frank. Moreover, every real creation, as he sees it, is a revolution—an anticipation of styles of life, structures of feelings, for which we do not yet have means of expression. Every real creation offers a foretaste of the human potential. Thus, Mikis, like every original artist, has stood out against political oppression and cultural stagnation. He cannot, therefore, condone the Moscow-oriented, hard-line faction of the Greek Communist Party any more than the military regime in Greece. Since he was freed in 1970, he has continued his revolutionary movement, with his concerts and political activity in Europe's capitals in his efforts to unite all the Greeks against the colonels with his "politics of unity"—a revolution with a revolutionary aim for a Greek whose character in disunity is legendary.

This book does not pretend to offer an exhaustive analysis of Mikis' music; that is the task of the musicologist. It does, however, hope to show that his creativity can be understood only within the complex framework of Greek, as well as European, society and politics. It therefore deals not only with aesthetics but also with history and politics—forces, people, and events that have both inspired and hindered the creative artist. My desire has been to convey the paradox that is Mikis Theodorakis to a reading public little acquainted with Greece and Greek ways.

The Appendixes include a complete list of Mikis' works, a discography of his original recordings, and an English translation of his "Manifesto of Music." I have also found it essential to include documents that expose the all-pervasive nature of parastate organizations that have undermined cultural progress and political freedom in Greece since World War II. Lastly, I have included the text of the "Manifesto of the Lambrakis Youth," in which Mikis spells out in detail the programme of sociocultural activity of the largest youth movement ever born in Greece, a movement that he led.

I am greatly indebted to so many people for countless items—photographs, clippings, documents, reminiscences, encouragement—that it is impossible to thank them all individually. I would, however, like to mention a few. Chief among them are Mikis' father, Yiorgos Theodorakis; Mikis' lawyers, Nicholas Paschos and Christophoros Argyropoulos; Maria Vamvas, Maria Farantouri, Peter Zevas, Andreas Lentakis, Manos Hadjidakis, Vassilis Tsitsanis, and Yiannis Papaioannou; and T. K., D. K., and Albert Levy.

GEORGE GIANNARIS

*New York City*
*March, 1972*

# Early Life and Works

# 1

# Formative Years

I woke with this marble head in my
hands;
it exhausts my elbows and I don't know
where to put it down.
GEORGE SEFERIS in *Mythistorema*.

## A CHILD'S WORLD

Chaos reigned everywhere in the city of Smyrna in the early
days of September, 1922: on the roads leading to the city,
over which the shattered remnants of the Greek Army ran,
hobbled, and crawled as they sought to flee the relentlessly
pursuing Turks; and in the city itself, where waves of terri-
fied Greek civilians, joined by confused, demoralized soldiers, surged en masse to the harbour, fighting with and scram-
bling over one another to get on the few small boats avail-

able to take them to the nearby island of Chios, and to safety. Among the fortunate few who managed to escape were Yiorgos Theodorakis, a Cretan youth of twenty-six, and his fiancée, Aspasia Poulakis, aged seventeen, with her family. The Turks entered Smyrna hard on their heels on September 9, 1922, and, after slaughtering the remaining inhabitants, set the city on fire. Within five days, the once-thriving cultural metropolis became a deserted mass of charred ruins. The Greek Army was cut to shreds. The ensuing rout was so grim, so tragic, that it has been known ever since in the annals of Greek history as the Asia Minor Catastrophe.

Years later, Mikis Theodorakis, a child of that catastrophe, incorporated the story into his musical drama, *The Ballad of the Dead Brother:*

> May God forgive me. . . . I did meet the Turk in the heart of Turkey. If you didn't bother him, he wouldn't bother you. We lived our whole life together in peace. They were honest, hardworking, and weren't any different from us. Except that they weren't Christians. But even so, what differences did we have to settle? We had our churches, and they had their mosques. Then, one day, the Greek Royal Guard came forth from home and we unfurled the Greek flag. We opened our homes to them and the Turks shut them . . . the wretches. They didn't have a tear to drown their shame. No girl was left untouched, no mosque unviolated. For this reason, we saw the eye of the Turk turning red.[1]

The Asia Minor catastrophe is at the focal point of Greek nationalism. It was the result of an undying, fervent desire, born in the previous century, to unite the Greek people and the territories inherited from Byzantium and ancient Hellas, which had been cut apart by Turkish and Western domination. That desire had been given the name of "Great Idea," meaning a greater Greece.

Greece had become a political entity as a result of the War of Independence against the Turks (1821–28). Britain, France, and Russia, which had intervened in behalf of both

[1] Mikis Theodorakis, *The Ballad of the Dead Brother: A Musical Drama* (Athens, 1962) 25-26.

Greece and Turkey, ratified Greece's independence through the Protocol of London (1829) and drew up the boundary line a year later. But the new nation, thus carved out, consisted of only a part of present-day Greece; namely, the main peninsula, or Central Greece—a rocky, unfertile region—and a few of the neighbouring islands. At the time, the whole area contained barely 800,000 people and was not the centre of Hellenism. The most important regions—all of northern Greece, the Asia Minor territories, Crete, and the majority of the Aegean Islands, including the Dodecanese and the Ionian Islands, with a total Greek population of over 2.5 million—were still under Turkish and Western dominion.

With the consent again of the Great Powers, Greece had acquired the seven Ionian Islands in 1864 and Thessaly in 1881. But Crete, the fourth largest island in the Mediterranean, had remained under Turkish domination, despite the abortive attempt at liberation forced on the Cretans by the Greek King in an effort to turn the rising tide of discontent in Greece. If Crete could be joined with the mainland, the Great Idea of a united Greece, free from Turkish domination, would have been given a tremendous impetus, thus increasing the popularity of the palace, which at that time was at a particularly low ebb because of a serious economic crisis. But the poorly equipped Greek Army had been no match for the Turkish Army, newly reorganized under German officers. The ensuing fiasco, known as the "Shame of 1897," had unexpected results. Crete remained under Turkish suzerainty, although the second son of the Greek King had been made governor of the island, with the idea of eventual union with Greece. More importantly, however, the people had become aware that a profound structural reorganization of the military was essential if the Great Idea were to be realized. Everyone had been blamed for the disaster—the palace, the army, the politicians. In 1905, because no steps towards union with Greece had been taken, the Cretans, under the leadership of Eleftherios Venizelos, a young lawyer and fighter, finally rebelled against the policies of the palace and declared union with the mainland. Four years later, after a military coup, staged by the many unsatisfied young officers, Venizelos was entrusted by the army with the nation's leadership. The following year, he was formally elected and formed a cabinet, inaugurating a period of much needed reorganization and reform.

Such political turmoil is typical of the centuries-old history of Crete. From Roman dominion to Saracen, Frankish, Venetian, and Turkish, the mainstay of the people of the island was fighting—as mercenaries in the armies of foreigners or as defenders of their own land. Their rugged individualism is proverbial, and their virile, often pugnacious, character is reflected even in their music and dancing. Yet, Crete produced the paintings and school of El Greco and Kornaros' epic poem, *Erotokritos,* the fountainhead of modern Greek poetry.

Mikis Theodorakis is descended on his father's side from a long line of Cretan fighters, chieftains, and politicians, all of whom had fought for Greek independence. In addition to Mikis' father, Yiorgos, who was born in Kato Galata, a village near Chania, in 1896, Michalis and Ekaterini Theodorakis had three other children—two girls, one of whom died young, and another son. The story of Mikis' surviving aunt is typically Cretan. She had been abducted by a doctor, whom she married, and taken to Athens, thus creating a vendetta between the two families that exists to this day. Mikis' uncle, Petros, like his aunt, had a childless marriage and died on the island he had never abandoned—except to fight in the Balkan Wars in 1912—in 1970, at eighty-four, leaving behind an adopted daughter. One of Yiorgos' most prominent relatives on his mother's side was Eleftherios Venizelos, who, after his initial success in 1905, rapidly rose to a position of leadership in the Greek Government.

In the winter of 1912, the two brothers, Yiorgos and Petros, aged sixteen and twenty-six, respectively, ran away from home with youthful and patriotic fervour to join the Cretan Battalions of the Greek Army, which was led by Venizelos, fighting with the Turkish Army in the Balkan peninsula. In these wars, Greece, in coalition with Serbia, Montenegro and Bulgaria, fought against Turkey and subsequently with Serbia against Bulgaria. The fighting had reached an all-time high when Yiorgos Theodorakis, immediately upon his arrival on the battlefield, was gravely wounded in a bloody battle at Byzani, on December 8, 1912. Lying half-dead among the hundreds slaughtered by the Turkish armies, he went unnoticed and thus, by good fortune, avoided certain death. As the Greek Army counter-attacked, Yiorgos was picked up and sent to a hospital in Preveza, a town in northern Greece, and then to Athens and on to Chania, in Crete. Petros remained in the war to the end.

The Greek Army under Venizelos came out victorious; after the Treaty of Bucharest (1913), the wars were concluded, and Greece acquired Crete, Epiros, most of Macedonia, and the Aegean Islands, except Imbros and Tenedos, the two gates to the Hellespont straits, as well as other areas claimed by the Greeks. This triumphant hour for Hellenism came about after a century of bloody wars, primarily with Turkey. At the end of World War I, Greece was rewarded for its participation with additional territories. Indeed, it would seem that war was essential for the fulfilment of the Great Idea that had become a slogan associated with the policies of Venizelos. Under the Treaty of Neuilly (November 27, 1919), Greece received Western Thrace from Bulgaria. Under the Treaty of Sèvres (August 10, 1920), it acquired Eastern Thrace, the Turkish islands of Imbros and Tenedos, and the administration of Smyrna under a League of Nations mandate. The mandate also included the neighbouring area of the interior, with the proviso that in five years a plebiscite take place in which the population would determine its national affiliation. The Great Idea seemed within grasp, for it was a foregone conclusion that the choice would be union with Greece. Although the Turkish inhabitants were in the majority in the hinterland, the Greeks were far more numerous in the towns, particularly in the thriving commercial centre of Smyrna. The Greeks were the merchants, artists, writers, bankers, technicians, scientists, and educators, just as they had been since the seventh century B.C. Throughout the centuries of Persian, Seleucid, Roman, Saracen, Frankish, and Turkish domination, they had succeeded in maintaining their identity as the intellectual and economic well-spring of Greek culture by preserving their heritage of language and religion, song and dance.

Such was the tradition and cultural milieu of the harbour city where Yiorgos Theodorakis went in 1919 to live for three years. After his recuperation from the wound in the Balkan Wars, he went to Athens to study law. Upon graduation, in 1916, he joined the staff of the Cretan Aristidis Stergiadis, the High Commissioner of Ioannina, in Epiros. In October of 1919, both Stergiadis and Theodorakis were sent to Smyrna, in Turkey. It was there that Yiorgos met Aspasia Poulakis, a girl from an educated and established family that had moved from the coastal village of Tsesmes, where she was born in 1905, to participate in the fuller cultural life of Smyrna. Just as Yiorgos Theodorakis' family tree is characteristic of Crete, so Aspasia's is typical of Asia Minor Greeks, who had distinguished themselves as merchants, artists, and musicians. Aspasia's brother, Antonis, tried his hand at various professions but finally became a musician and composer, thus carrying on the long musical heritage of the Asia Minor Greeks.[2]

History, however, intervened to prevent the usual outcome of the meeting of two young people from taking place. The Turkish Government had never actually accepted the provisions of the Treaty of Sèvres. For two years, Mustapha Kemal —or Ataturk, as he was later called—had been building up his nationalist movement in defiance of the treaty's terms. King Constantine, hoping to undermine the popularity of Venizelos and the Great Idea of his Liberal Party, decided to take matters into his own hands. He dispatched a Greek army to Asia Minor to take the offensive against Ataturk. Once again, as in 1897, the palace had completely underestimated the strength of its foe.

---

[2] One proof of the strong inspiration of this musical tradition is that four of Modern Greece's most important composers were born in Turkey: Manolis Kalomiris (1883–1962), Petros Petridis (b. 1892), Yiorgos Poniridis (b. 1892), and Argyris Kounadis (b. 1924).

The Asia Minor Catastrophe ended King Constantine's essays at irredentism. It also spelled the end of King Constantine. For, on September 22, 1922, a group of officers, sobered by the recent defeat, revolted on Chios under the leadership of General Nicholas Plastiras, with the knowledge, if not the explicit support, of the island's governor, George Papandreou, who had by then become known as Venizelos' young protégé. Six days later, the King abdicated in favour of his eldest son, George II, and fled the country. The Great Powers, once again, intervened. This time, however, Greece lost rather than gained as she had in 1897. The Treaty of Lausanne, which officially ended the war with the Turks, forced Greece to return Eastern Thrace, Smyrna, Imbros, and Tenedos to Turkey and to give up all hope of seeing the Italians leave the Dodecanese and the British yield Cyprus.

A separate agreement between Greece and Turkey, negotiated by Venizelos, called for the exchange of ethnic minorities living in the two countries. Half a million Turks left Greece, and 1.5 million Greeks emigrated from Asia Minor and Bulgaria. The exchange, however, was disastrous from an economic point of view. In the urban centres where they settled in clusters, the refugees from Asia Minor could look forward only to a future of homelessness, joblessness, and starvation. Many joined the ranks of the already large numbers of urban poor, forming a subclass that fanned the fires of political and social unrest. Indeed, the refugees soon became the chief agitators for social change. On the one hand, they proved a cultural boon to Greece, for the vast majority of them had constituted the hard core of the intellectual, scientific, and artistic community of Turkey. In general, Greeks in the Diaspora and on the islands, as well as the seafarers who come into contact with other peoples, are more cosmopolitan and more sensitive to the arts than the Greeks of the rural areas. Some of Greece's most talented artists, musicians, and politicians are from Asia Minor and Crete; George Seferis, the Nobel prize–winning poet who painted the Asia Minor Catastrophe so powerfully in his *Mythistorema* and other poems, was an immigrant from Smyrna. Theodorakis has been inspired throughout his life by the works of Seferis and the Cretan Nikos Kazantzakis.

Two months after the safe arrival of the refugees from Smyrna on Chios, Yiorgos Theodorakis was transferred to Syros. Aspasia Poulakis joined him there, and, on October 8, 1924, they got married. The chief problem for Yiorgos from now on was finding a job and a home for his family. This search took them, like migrating sea birds, from island to island in the Aegean—Chios, Syros, Limnos, Lesbos, Crete, and back to Chios. The happy event took place on July 29, 1925; a son was born to Yiorgos and Aspasia. The child was baptized Michalis by his uncle, Antonis. (The name Mikis was given him years later by his fellow artists.) Yet, in spite of his financial difficulties, Yiorgos, with parental pride and wanting the child to "touch" the Cretan soil and be admired by the relatives, took him to his village, forty days after the birth. From then on, Mikis was to spend every summer and all the eventful movements of his childhood in Chios, among the Smyrna relatives. Born into the inhuman circumstances in which the refugees from Smyrna were forced to eke out their existence, the memories of the holocaust and flight became a part of the boy's life forever. The visits to the relatives reinforced the memory. Moreover, Mikis loved to visit his grandmother, Stamatia, who made a strong impression on the boy. Like most elderly Greeks, Stamatia was devoted to the church, which constituted an integral part of her life. In the flight from Smyrna, she had taken away icons, church books, and other religious items with which she converted any room she occupied, no matter how temporarily, into a kind of church, with her impressionable grandson as an "acolyte." But most attractive to the child was his grandmother's chanting of the liturgy, which she knew by heart. As a result, Mikis was initiated at a very early age into Byzantine music. From his mother, he first heard the melancholy tunes preserved in the folk songs of Smyrna, Pontos, and Constantinople; and from his father, the harsh, salty rhythms of the Cretan *rizitika,* the songs that were sung at the "roots" of the mountains of Crete. One may conclude that Mikis is the product of Ionian lyricism and the

austere Doric modes of Crete, transmitted through the Byzantine world.

Until he was six, Mikis knew only the islands. Then, in
1931, Yiorgos was appointed general secretary to the governor of Epiros. This was his first official position with political
duties since his departure from Smyrna, and it meant remaining two years in the small provincial city of Ioannina. Eventually, he became under-secretary to the Ministry of Public
Works and responsible for planning roads, schools, and other
public buildings and getting local residents to volunteer labour. His success was such that, in early 1932, Venizelos visited
Ioannina and dined with the family as an expression of his
appreciation of Yiorgos' work.

In Ioannina, another boy, Ioannis (Yiannis), was born to
Yiorgos and Aspasia on September 22, 1932. Mikis acquired
a companion. But much more important to his immediate
life and later career as a musician was the encouragement he
received from the local bishop to participate in church services. Since he was drawn by the grandeur of liturgical music,
and already knew many of the hymns, thanks to his grandmother, it was not long before he was made a boy cantor.
Thus began his lifelong interest in Byzantine music. In addition to church music, he became exposed to the peculiar melodies and dances of Epiros, and foreign songs, with Greek
words, which he had to learn in his first years of school.

But peace and stability were not to last for very long at
any period in Mikis' life, reflecting as it does in microcosm
the whole tragic history of modern Greece. In 1932, when the
Populist party of the Monarchist leader Tsaldaris won the
elections, Venizelos and those under his protection fell from
power. Liberal forces were purged from the army and civil
service and replaced with royalist sympathizers who would
work for the return of the king. Yiorgos Theodorakis was one
of the first to lose his job. But a year later, he was reap-
pointed by the government and sent to Argostoli, capital
of the nearby Ionian island Cephalonia. Once more, the family was forced to pick up their meagre belongings and move.

The move to Argostoli had one good side to it for Mikis.

The people of the Ionian islands loved music, and in Argostoli one could hear Italian-inspired city songs, Western
tangos, and local folk songs. The municipal orchestra performed on Sundays in the public square, and a number of
choral groups, sponsored by various guilds and associations,
vied for the best talent and the largest audiences. Mikis was
fascinated by all this interest in live music. He continued to
serve as cantor, as he had in Ioannina, and before long was
selected to sing, as first cantor, the "Epitaphios" (the traditional hymn at the Sepulchre of Christ) during the Good Friday services in the cathedral.

During the Christmas holidays of 1935, he went around
from door to door with a group of children, singing Christmas carols. With his share of the money collected, he was
able to buy a book on solfeggio. This was his first music
book, and he would pore over it for hours trying to decipher
its notes and symbols. At school during this time, he was engaged in all sorts of extra-curricular activities. With the Pu-
pils' Club of Argostoli (MOA), which he helped organize, he
was always planning games and picnics, and took an active
part in athletics.

While young Mikis was preoccupied with music, studies,
and games in Argostoli, political turmoil and popular discontent were steadily increasing on the mainland. Since 1922,
successive governments had been blithely promising more
jobs and housing, without, however, delivering either. Unemployment had reached an all-time high since the migra-
tory hordes had flooded the land, and workers, clerks, and
peasants were constantly demonstrating for higher wages and
civil liberties.

During the spring of 1936, the tobacco workers struck.
The government had signed an agreement with their union
in 1924 but had never bothered to carry it out. On May 9,
1936, the tobacco workers organized a rally in Thessaloniki,
the second largest city of Greece. The Greek Royal Gendarmerie—the State police, called out to deal with the situation—
was brutal. In its clash with the demonstrators, thirty people were killed and hundreds wounded. Yiannis Ritsos, one

of Greece's greatest living poets, outraged at the killing of young workers, immortalized the event in his moving threnody, *Epitaphios,* which was to inspire Mikis with the song-cycle with which he began his musical revolution twenty-four years later. The events in May precipitated a crisis which, over the next few months, grew steadily worse. In August, the King, who had returned to Greece a year earlier, declared the country to be in a state of emergency, dissolved Parliament, and gave his prime minister, Ioannis Metaxas, unlimited powers to deal with the situation. For the next four and a half years, Metaxas ruled Greece as a dictator, and jailed thousands of his political opponents.

Mikis was eleven when the dictatorship began—too young either to understand or to care about its implications. Music was his chief interest, and his greatest desire was to have his own violin; but because of the chaotic economy of Greece at the time, a violin was priced far beyond the means of a poor civil servant like his father.

Immediately after the beginning of Metaxas' dictatorship on August 4, 1936, Yiorgos was reassigned to Ioannina, where he remained until the summer of 1937, when he went to Patras, the capital of the district of Achaea, as director of the Prefecture.

For twelve-year-old Mikis, Patras was at first just another provincial city. But it turned out to be an important milestone in his musical career, for it was there that he was finally able to handle a real musical instrument for the first time. The gymnasium he attended had a music teacher, George Papavassiliou, who gave him lessons on a violin he supplied and taught him the meaning of the mysterious symbols and notes in the book on solfeggio. At Papavassiliou's insistence, Mikis was eventually enrolled in the Patras Conservatory of Music, where he pursued his violin studies in earnest. But Mikis made little progress in his other musical studies. Papavassiliou, who is now living in New York, remembers that he often rapped his young student on the knuckles because he was "withdrawn and would not concentrate." On the side, however, Mikis tried to compose songs to teach to a student

group that he organized along similar lines to the one he had
started in Argostoli. When his father gave him a harmonica,
he became even more interested in writing tunes for the
group.

In June of 1939, the family moved from Patras to Pyrgos,
farther along the main coastal road of the Peloponnese. Mikis
was at an age when one begins to feel the pressures of adoles-
cence—that peculiar, awkward awareness of oneself as no
longer a child but not yet quite an adult. He was especially conscious of his height. The fourteen-year-old boy already towered over his father and could feel people staring
at him when the family went for walks on Sunday afternoons.
Easily spotted wherever he went, he soon became the butt of
jokes from other children. So shaken was he by all this that
he refused to go to the seashore at all during that summer.

More and more, he withdrew into himself, isolating himself in the realms of music and poetry. Since there was no music school in Pyrgos, he could study music only on his own.
So, with a borrowed violin, he began testing the strings to
find out what the notes sounded like and began experimenting in writing his first musical exercise. With no knowledge
of the scales or the signs for the keys, he would write down
for the same sound *do* sharp one time and *re* flat another,
but finally he composed a short work which he simply called
*Concerto for Violin*. At the same time, he became interested
in the greatest of Greece's 19th century and 20th century poets, most of whom came from the islands: Ioannis Polemis
from Syphnos, Aristotle Valaoritis from Lefkas, Kostis Palamas from Missolonghi, Yiannis Gryparis and Kostas Had-
jopoulos from Agrinion. He set many of their poems to music, and in order to hear them sung, and indulge his terrible
need for companionship, he organized a group of friends to
sing his pieces privately, though they occasionally performed
in public. Here, Mikis found an outlet from his isolation.

Meanwhile, the Metaxas dictatorship began to weigh heavily on Greeks, especially the young. To strengthen his hold
over the country, Metaxas held before the people the glow-
ing vision of a "Christian Greece," or, as he called it, the

"Third Greek Civilization." And, like Hitler and Mussolini, he organized young people into military cadres to inculcate in them the Fascist and Nazi doctrines which were to come in greater force with the Italian and German occupation.

Fourteen-year-old Mikis' first reaction to the activities of the disciplined Metaxas Youth was to bury himself in his father's diaries. He devoured Yiorgos' vivid description of his youth in Crete and his Balkan adventures as other children devour the adventures of *Robinson Crusoe*. Eventually, constant reading of the diaries with their strong patriotism of the early twenties and the incessant Metaxas propaganda in school to return Greece to "the glory that was" led the impressionable adolescent out of his isolation. Inspired by a "literary" group his father had created in his youth in Kato Galata, Mikis now formed a third group which had more serious aims, like collecting books for the creation of a library and participating in political activities.

The young idealist thus became caught up in the net of Metaxas' slogans of Nationalism and Christianity. Together with his friends, he joined the National Youth Organization (EON). He was enticed by the promises of a greater Greece and the goals of a disciplined life. In a ferment of patriotic fervour, Mikis even composed a song celebrating the coming glories.

Thus, as the family left Pyrgos for Tripolis in July, 1940, two things began to preoccupy Mikis—music and politics.

## FROM ARCADIA TO RESISTANCE

Tripolis, the capital city of Arcadia, lies in the heart of Peloponnese. Built in the 14th century on a high plateau surrounded by mountains, for centuries it provided a natural defence against the Turks. During the Revolution of 1821, it became the centre of action, with its famous son, Theodoros Kolokotronis, as the chief leader. In the early part of the 20th century, it grew into a thriving commercial community whose agricultural commodities, local festivities, and excellent climate attracted visitors from far and wide. Of all the provincial cities in which Mikis had lived, this was the most flourishing. Yiorgos, who as assistant to the Nomarch of Arcadia, became closely associated with the local officials and educators. As a result his family achieved its first stability and a certain standing in the community.

As his family became settled in its new surroundings, Mikis, now fourteen and bursting with adolescent energy and ambition, became active in the youth movement (EON) popularized by the Metaxas regime. A para-military organization, EON sought to instill in Greek youth discipline, frugality, and patriotism in the form of unquestioned obedience to church and state. Only through adherence to such Spartan principles, declared Metaxas, would Greece be delivered from the "double bondage of Communist tyranny and the paltry tyranny of parties."

As his first act upon joining the movement, Mikis, along with other youths, had his hair cut very short—a symbolic act by which the members of EON set themselves apart from the *malliaroi,* or "long-hairs." For, since the turn of the century, writers and intellectuals who used the demotic, or vernacular, rather than the purist *katharevousa* artificially derived from the classical Greek, had been ridiculed as long-hairs and *ipso facto* Communists, and were now especially anathema to the Metaxas regime.

Before long, Mikis was wearing the dark-green uniform of the movement's company commander (*lochitis*), learning to use firearms and taking his company out for target practice in the fields. Since one of the chief duties of the movement was to help "rid Greek society of parasites," Mikis and his company were given the task of rooting out the locally active brigands (*listes*). This pleased Mikis because twice in the past brigands had tried to kidnap him and hold him for ransom. In the spring of 1940, he and his company went on an excursion to Chryssovitsi, some ten miles outside of Tripolis, to show their strength, and for a while afterwards they were successful in chasing the *listes* out of the area. Mikis' family, however, looked with particular dismay upon these dangerous activities, and urged him to give them up. But Mikis, glorying with adolescent pride in his mission, would not listen to them. One day, after a heated argument, he ran away from home to stay at EON headquarters. From there, he and other members of the movement, whom he had organized into a group called Friends of the Mountain, put on social events and nationalistic poetry readings, and continued their excursions, dressed all the while in their uniforms and bearing arms. One day, the *listes* reappeared on the hills outside Tripolis where the boys were camped and chased them back into town. This was the last straw for the boys' parents. With the tacit approval of the authorities, they stopped their sons from going on any more guerrilla-like excursions.

By the summer of 1940, the course of the war in Europe had created considerable tension in Greece. On the one hand, Metaxas, whose police state closely resembled the Axis regimes, was nevertheless more sympathetic to the Allies, particularly the British, while, on the other, the palace advocated neutrality or should the need arise, intervention on the side of Germany. On August 15, as the country celebrated the Feast of the Assumption, the most solemn religious holiday in Greece next to Easter, an Italian submarine torpedoed the Greek cruiser *Elli,* off the island of Tenos. Metaxas, hoping to avoid being drawn into the war, refrained from any direct protest, and the press, restricted as it was by heavy censorship, was unable to take a stand. But the people were infuriated. The Italians continued their drive against Greek frontiers. On October 28, Mussolini sent an ultimatum to Greece demanding that the Italians be allowed to enter Greece, whence a campaign could be launched against the British navy in the eastern Mediterranean. Metaxas, conscious of what such a request implied, firmly refused with his famous "Ochi!" (No!). But he had hardly given his reply when Italian troops began streaming across the Albanian frontier into Greece. Hastily mobilized, ill-equipped, and far outnumbered, the Greek army nevertheless succeeded in repulsing the invasion. Within a few days, the Italians, suffering heavy losses, withdrew.

The Greeks' swift victory astonished the world. In Greece, its effect was to rally the nation around its resistance forces in a spirit of patriotic fervour. For none doubted that Mussolini, stunned by his troops' ignominious defeat, would try again, this time with increased vengeance. And, indeed, barely seven months later, on April 6, 1941, the combined forces of Italy, Germany, and Bulgaria (which, nourishing territorial ambitions in northern Greece, had fallen into the Axis orbit in the hope of realizing them) swept across Greece's northern frontiers. In Athens, the government that had succeeded Metaxas (who died in January) suddenly collapsed. Within three weeks, the King, accompanied by members of his government and a group of military officers, fled to Egypt, where they formed a government-in-exile.[3] Those in the government who remained behind followed a course of open collaboration.

Axis occupation had a greater impact on Greece than on any of the other European countries. Each of the victors was rewarded: The Bulgarians took Eastern Macedonia; the Italians, the Peloponnese and Central Greece; and the Germans, all the other strategic areas. Executions became a daily event, especially in areas where the invaders encountered resistance. Hunger struck the capital and other cities. Greek law and government disappeared completely from almost all regions. Schools were closed and formal education was replaced by makeshift classes run by teachers for small groups of youngsters.

Sixteen-year-old Mikis was lucky to live in the provinces, and had the good fortune to attend classes by Evangelos Papanoutsos. A strong personality, Papanoutsos had earned an estimable reputation with his writings on Plato, Aristotle, and Kant, and was known as one of Greece's most progressive educators. His ideas, though, had never been accepted by the Athens University archaic system. They were considered too modern. Faithful to his credo on education and culture, Papanoutsos created the cultural centre Athenaeum in Athens

[3] The *New York Times* of January 30, 1941, reported the King's declaration of the continuation of the dictatorship after Metaxas' death, and it was not until February, 1942, a year after the country had been overrun, that King George, under pressure from the British, announced the official termination of the dictatorship.

(closed by the military regime in 1967) , and served as Secretary General to the Ministry of Education under George Papandreou. In that capacity he drew up plans to modernize Greece's archaic system of education. Under Papanoutsos' influence, Mikis and a group of friends formed a literary *cénacle*.

Since the makeshift nature of classes allowed the students a great deal of free time, Mikis would spend many hours with his closest friend, Grigoris Konstantinopoulos. Grigoris, four years older than Mikis, was the son of a local cantor, a learned man who possessed a large and varied library, and it was there that the two would often gather to read, discuss, and even try to translate into modern Greek the works of the ancients. Sharing his friend's love of poetry, Grigoris laboured painstakingly over Homer's *Odyssey*, while Mikis, influenced by Papanoutsos, struggled with Plato's *Dialogues,* in whose style he even ventured to compose philosophical writings of his own, while he kept a diary in which he jotted down the happenings.

When Grigoris' father was killed during the first bombing of Tripolis, in the summer of 1941, Mikis, saddened by his friend's bereavement, drew even closer to him, and the two became inseparable. Throughout the summer, they buried themselves in their studies, increasingly enchanted by the world of ideas that was unfolding before them. It was at this time, in fact, that Mikis discovered the poet who was forever to remain a favourite of his, Yiannis Ritsos. On a special rock, which they christened the Rock of Ritsos, they read through his *Moonlight Sonata, Tractor,* and other poems. In Grigoris' home, the members of the *cénacle* read their own poetic efforts; here Mikis read his first poems. A year later, he had them printed in a volume entitled *Siao* and signed with the pseudonym Dinos Mais. The title comes from the Chinese for a musical instrument resembling the Arcadian flute, and *Mais* is Greek for the month of May, which to Mikis symbolized the vigour of youth. Grigoris, who contributed an epilogue to the volume, followed suit with his own book of poetry, also published under a pseudonym.

In the fall, the Germans arrived in the city and stayed over three months. Two soldiers quartered themselves in Mikis' house, and a warm but guarded friendship soon developed between them and the Theodorakis family. The soldiers took a liking to Mikis and Yiannis, and would often tell them how Greece and Germany were bound culturally, and if they would only work together, they would make Europe the greatest power on earth. Mikis would respond with stories of the Greek struggle against the Turks, and other tales of heroism. But one night, as the Germans came in after a battle, in full armour and with horror on their faces, Yiannis was frightened and wouldn't go to sleep. The family joined Mikis in singing a lullaby. The soldiers learned that Mikis was a composer, and brought records for him to play, one of which was Beethoven's *Ninth Symphony*.

By the fall of 1941, famine was raging across Greece. In Athens, thousands had already died of starvation; hardest hit were the children, and in some areas, the infant mortality rate had risen to 90 per cent. In order to reduce the number of deaths that would undoubtedly occur in the winter months ahead, the National Mutual Aid (EA), a group supported by the Resistance, arranged for children from the capital to be sent to the countryside, where food could still be found. In November, a truckload of children arrived in Tripolis. When the driver stopped in Areos Square and asked for the mayor, to inform him that the children would be discharged there, the peasants who had gathered curiously around the truck immediately scattered and disappeared. The children, however, driven by hunger, scampered out of the truck and started running from house to house, begging for food and shelter. But the peasants, having barely enough food for their own families, chased most of them away.

Mikis and his friends, outraged at such cruelty, quickly organized a group of youngsters to go to surrounding villages and compel the peasants to give food for the hungry children. They also forced every student in their class to bring food for those who had none.

With all of these activities, Mikis nevertheless continued

his work in music. He and other youths formed a choir called *Chorodia Ethnikon Skopon* (Choir of National Aims). When not singing together, the choir members would go around playing their harmonicas to collect food and clothing for the refugee children. And, when not occupied with these projects, Mikis spent his afternoons with athletic clubs. The Italians, taking notice of this active youth who seemed always to be organizing something, began calling him in to the local *carabinieri* for periodic questioning; for by now the Resistance movement was growing daily, and the Italians were certain that he was a part of it.

In spite of his seemingly outgoing and active nature, Mikis was actually deeply withdrawn, and unable to share his doubts and troubled feelings. On the one hand he felt drawn to religion, to its strange and alluring mysticism, and was inspired especially by the spiritual and physical power of the Christ figure. On the other hand he deeply admired the free and enquiring spirit of classical Greece, of which he and Grigoris were now beginning to acquire a clearer and more mature appreciation.

For Mikis, the church was both a sensual and a social enticement. The church's enveloping interior tranquility, its awe-inspiring cupola, the warm atmosphere, the smell of burning wax, votive tapers and incense, the visual splendour of the icons of the church martyrs and saints, with their agonies captured so powerfully on their faces by the anonymous iconographers of Greek Orthodoxy, all dominated the boy's mind and transported him to another world, far beyond daily realities. But the part of church experience which gripped him most intensely was the music and the performance of the liturgy itself, the mystic and dramatic re-enactment of the eternal passion and sacrifice of Christ.

As for its social attractions, the holidays of the church, particularly that of Easter, were the most happy events of the year for a child. The long weeks of fasting, the dramatic reliving the Passion, Crucifixion, and carrying out of the sarcophagus in the Burial, culminated in the day of happiness, the Resurrection. After the joyous greeting, "Christ is risen,"

everyone would disperse in a hurry to taste the wonderful
Easter soup and get his brilliant red Easter egg. As a child
Mikis could not understand the timelessness of this celebration preserving into the modern era so many of the features
of the ancient spring Dionysia, when the great poets presented as tribute to Dionysos, the god of the "then," and the
"now," their tragedies, the re-enactment of the Greek myths,
the heritage and experience of the race. The boy could catch,
however, the spirit of excitement, and the thrill of spring.
Furthermore, the church was the place where boys and girls
had fun exchanging furtive amorous glances. Mikis along
with the other youngsters would go to church in his Sunday best to see, and be seen by, his friends and, of course, the
local pretty girls. This was how he fell in love for the first
time. The girl, Elli, was attractive and liked him too, but
Mikis felt shy with girls. Their relationship lasted over three
years—holding hands, exchanging poems, secret looks—and
nothing more.

Mikis was drawn to the church, but he also soon began to
be aware of its duplicity. With youthful fervour he served as
an acolyte and cantor, only to realize that the same priest who
preached love of Christ and the church was all too quick to
strike him or another boy with the thurible, or even to spit
on them, curse them, and chase them away on the slightest
pretext. Mikis began to see that Christianity, far from fulfilling his utopian ideas, proved wanting when it came to imminent social problems. Most clearly lacking were answers on
how to combat the occupying forces which were sapping the
spirit of Greece. So he turned to literature, particularly Ibsen's plays. Through the strong determination and sacrifice
of Father Brand, Mikis derived his own understanding of
Christianity—as sacrifice and duty. Father Brand's strong determination to erect a vital living church, effective in man's
daily life, made an indelible impression on Mikis' sensitive
spirit.

He became a soloist and director of the choir at St. Barbara's Church. He composed *The Lord,* an oratorio for four
voices and strings based on the long poem by Grigoris Kon-

stantinopoulos, which was performed at a large public gathering in March, 1942. Selecting from his own volume *Siao* a number of poems, he composed a song-cycle titled *Grievous Nature* and set to music several poems by Kostis Palamas.

At this time, Mikis' church held a competition for a short *troparion*, or hymn, in honour of a saint, offering a prize to the winning composer. The mere announcement of the competition, however, created a stir, for the Italian authorities had expressly forbidden putting up posters and public assembling; but permission was soon obtained when the nature of the contest was explained. Mikis submitted his *Troparion to Kassiani* and won.

Yiorgos was pleased to see his son immersed in his musical studies and in literature. He gave Mikis money to rent a harmonium, with which he continued to practise his solfeggio exercises. Between the church and pondering over the solfeggio, Mikis made significant progress, but he could not accomplish much on the harmonium. In the winter of 1942, Mikis began piano lessons with a music teacher named Papastathopoulos, but he soon realized that he would never develop the technique required of a pianist. It seemed that every time he sat down to play a scale, his hands would involuntarily slide into a song. His talents seemed to lie in the direction of a composer rather than a performer. Eventually, Mikis gave up his lessons with Papastathopoulos and began studying on his own in the home of Yiannis Meindanis, a wealthy Greek-American who invited him to use his piano as much as he liked. He bought a book on harmony and immediately began trying to put what he learned from it to use in his compositions. In the spring of 1942, his *Sonatina for Piano,* completed in Meindanis' house, was performed there by the pianist Dora Apostolakou and greatly impressed the circle of friends who had gathered to hear it.

Excited by this success, Mikis asked his father to show the composition to Philoktitis Economidis in Athens, so that he might register at the Athens Conservatory. Economidis was the most powerful figure in the Greek musical world. One of the founders of the Athens State Conservatory, he was at that

time the director of both the Athens Choral Ensemble and
the Athens Conservatory Orchestra, which under his guidance became the government-subsidized State Orchestra. He
had become a close friend of Mikis' uncle Antonis Poulakis,
who was now working as Inspector of Finances in the Ministry of Economics and who was trying to help him see the
Conservatory through a difficult financial period. Mikis had
heard a great deal about Economidis through correspondence
with his uncle.

Yiorgos went to Athens where uncle Antonis invited the
great teacher to dinner so that they could talk about Mikis'
musical aspirations. Economidis examined carefully all of
Mikis' compositions which Yiorgos presented to him and
asked about the boy's technical knowledge and training. But
in the end, he said that he would have to speak to the boy
himself before deciding whether or not he should go to the
Conservatory. When Yiorgos told Mikis of his meeting with
Economidis, the boy was so disappointed that he decided to
devote less time to music and more to other activities.

By August, 1942, when the Germans occupied Tripolis for
the second time, the Resistance movement that had sprung
up a year earlier had taken strong root among the people.
The National Liberation Front (EAM), the most active group
and, since its founding in September, 1941, the chief organ of
Resistance, called on all Greeks to take up arms against the
Italians and Germans through the People's Army of Liberation (ELAS). But when the EAM began to organize the resistance in Tripolis, Mikis was not asked to join, even though
he was one of the most active and best known of the youths
in the city. This was probably due to the jealousy and hostility that he incurred because of his father's position as a civil
servant. For a long time, Mikis brooded over this exclusion,
but when EAM announced that an all-Greek Resistance Day
demonstration would be held on March 25, the anniversary
of the War of Independence against the Turks, he decided
that he would take part in it, even if he had to do so on his
own.

On the day of the demonstration, he went to the designated site at ten o'clock in the morning and was the first person to appear at the cenotaph in Kolokotronis Square. A few minutes later, as more people began to arrive, Italian soldiers and the gendarmerie charged from all sides. The demonstrators fell back, but Mikis remained calm and tried to stop them from dispersing in panic. Standing up on a bench, he appealed to them to stay and fight. A large group did remain, and Mikis shouting at the top of his voice, "Long live the Resistance!" "Long live the Allies!" "Long live Greece!" gave the signal to march to the town hall. The Italians charged into the group and a bloody hand-to-hand struggle began. Mikis and several others were taken off to the *carabinieri*. As soon as they arrived, Mikis was singled out for questioning. The Italians were convinced that he was a member of EAM and knew the names and whereabouts of the men who had planned the demonstration. In an effort to make him tell they began beating him first on the head and then on the back, and the more he protested that he knew nothing about EAM, the more violent they became. They even rubbed salt on his wounds. But through all of this torture, the boy refused to give his tormentors the satisfaction of hearing him cry out. The next day, Mikis and a few others were forced to parade before the people as an example of what was awaiting them. On the third day the demonstrators were handed over to the police who rounded them up in an open-air theatre to hear a talk from the Prefect of Arcadia, who told them that unless they stopped such activities the Italians would set fire to the whole city, and warned them that order would be maintained at all costs. He then ordered the police to set the demonstrators free.

The demonstration, arrest and torture had a great effect on Mikis. For the first time, he considered the possibility of a Greek spiritual rebirth through national struggle. Alone or with others, he began reading Lenin's biography and Marxist literature and participated in secret discussions of Marxism. Finally he was asked to join the Resistance group, and, in a short while, he became the representative of the National Liberation Front in his school.

On March 25, 1943, a year after the first demonstration organized by EAM, Mikis put on a pop festival with shows, poetry readings and patriotic speeches, while Resistance leaflets and pamphlets were circulated all over town. A few days later, Mikis found General Festuccio, military commander of the area, waiting for him as he crossed Areos Square on his way from school. When Mikis approached, the General greeted him with the Fascist salute and then arrested him and took him to the police station.

At the station, Festuccio suddenly became very friendly. He told Mikis that he knew all about his activities in the Resistance and asked him to stop before it was too late. He even sang *"La donna è mobile,"* to show how much he, too, liked music and to persuade Mikis that his vocation should be music, not Communism and the Resistance. The Mussolini regime was coming to an end, he said, and the Germans, who were about to replace the Italians in Tripolis, would not be as friendly as he was. He then told Mikis that he was on the list of those to be shot immediately.

Festuccio's warning did little to cool the boy's revolutionary ardour. In June, when the people rose to protest the militarization of the country as the Italians and the Greek state police tried to organize ex-policemen and collaborators into Security Battalions, Mikis was in the front lines of the demonstrators. Festuccio's information was accurate, however, for shortly afterwards, the Germans flooded the whole peninsula, killing and burning whatever they thought was a source of resistance. Mikis, having just graduated from high school, left for Athens barely in time, for when the Germans arrived in Tripolis, ten of those who had been arrested with him a year earlier were hanged in Areos Square.

These events marked the conclusion of Mikis' childhood and formative years. Life in Athens was to prove far different from life in Tripolis. In Athens, he would be on his own as a man and an artist, but mainly as a fighter against foreign occupiers and their Greek collaborators.

# 2

# The Undefeated Foe

And I said: I know, yes, I know, that
your Gods, too, the Olympians, have become the earthy foundation; for we buried
them deep down, lest foreigners find them
and the whole foundation was twice and
thrice stablished with as many bones as
our enemies piled up one upon the other.
. . . And still I know that for the libation
and offerings of the new Temple which
we dreamed of for you, O Greece, for days
and nights, more brothers were slaughtered among them than lambs have ever
been sacrificed for Easter. . . .

ANGELOS SIKELIANOS, *March of the Spirit*

## THE BLOODY DECEMBER AND ITS AFTERMATH

Still smarting from his brutal experiences in Tripolis, Mikis
arrived in Athens in July of 1943 and went to live with his
uncle Antonis in Nea Smyrne, a suburb of Athens. His father and uncle had already decided on his future. It seemed
obvious to Yiorgos, a lawyer, that his son should follow in his

footsteps. Antonis agreed with Yiorgos and urged Mikis to keep music as a hobby, as he did. By and large, the profession-oriented Greek middle class saw no future in the arts.

Mikis yielded to these pressures and took private lessons in Latin, ancient Greek, and history in preparation for the entrance exams to Law School. But he continued to work on music on his own, and with other young people involved in the United All-Greek Youth Organization (EPON) remained active in the Resistance.

In September, he persuaded his uncle Antonis to take him to see Economidis. The professor gave them a warm reception and asked Mikis to play and sing some of his compositions. But when the boy finished, Economidis grimaced and told him he must forget all he had written and start afresh. Nevertheless, he was convinced that Mikis had genuine ability and he told Antonis that he would take Mikis on as a pupil. Thus, with Economidis' approval, which neither Yiorgos nor Antonis would dispute, Mikis began preparing for the Conservatory.

Mikis passed the entrance exams for both the Law School and the Conservatory in early October, and Economidis, enthusiastic with his new protégé, took him into his composition and harmony courses and made him a member of the Athens Choral Ensemble. Yiorgos, who in the meantime had brought the rest of the family to the city and found a house, was overjoyed at his son's success. One day he invited some friends over to celebrate. Among them was the Altinoglou family which had three daughters. Mikis was immediately taken with Myrto.

Myrto Altinoglou, who had just passed her entrance exams for the Medical School of the University of Athens, was an active member of the United All-Greek Organization (EPON) in Nea Smyrne. When the partisan[1] she was engaged to was

---

[1] Myrto's fiance, Phaedon, fought with EDES (Greek National Democratic League), a rightist group headed by General Napoleon Zervas; it served as a link between Greek rightists and British intelligence. The major victory of EAM-EDES and the British was sabotage of the Gorgopotamos bridge on November 29, 1942. Shortly thereafter, there was a parting of the ways, and Zervas cast his lot with the British and the Greek royalists.

killed in action, in the fall of 1943, her world was shattered. But Mikis visited her often, and their long talks about the interests they shared helped divert her thoughts from her dead fiancé. Eventually Myrto stopped working for the EPON in her neighbourhood and became more involved in political and academic activities at the University. There she and Mikis were able to talk to each other more freely than at home, and gradually they became good friends.

Mikis spent the early months of the fall semester of 1943 immersed in his studies. When he was not attending classes, he would sit for hours on end in the Conservatory library, poring over the works of Franck, Bach, Schmidt, Mozart, Beethoven, Wagner, Berlioz, and even a composer as modern as Hindemith. Economidis, seeing his great potential and drive, appointed him assistant choir master at the Conservatory and of the Choral Ensemble.

The relationship between Mikis and Economidis grew closer as each day passed; and as mutual respect developed between teacher and student, Economidis invited Mikis home, and talked to him about famous artists, many of whom he knew personally. The older man had rarely established such a rapport with any of his students, and a whole new vista opened up in Mikis' mind.

Mikis' family, newly settled in Athens, was beset by financial difficulties. Although Yiorgos was employed at the Ministry of Interior, his monthly salary barely covered two weeks' expenses. Besides that, malnutrition took its toll in the family, and Yiannis' health deteriorated to the point where he had to be hospitalized. Mikis had to get a job. His uncle found one for him at the Greek Tobacco Industries Association, copying the minutes of the proceedings. This was an exacting job that demanded perfection, since ink and ledger were exorbitantly expensive. So, when Mikis made an error in copying, he was quickly demoted to assistant to the guard in charge of transferring daily receipts to the National Bank of Greece, a job he held for a year and a half until the Tobacco Association was disbanded at the end of the occupation. Though not a job with much status, it was important.

Money was changing in shape and value almost every day, and depositors had to rush to the bank as soon as they could. Employees now were paid at the end of each day, but the continuous monetary fluctuation could change the value of their wages overnight. Transfer and deposit had to be made fast before another devaluation occurred. Every day, Mikis would haul huge bags of currency to the bank. Afterwards, he would lock himself up in an executive bathroom his co-workers had helped him to find, and study his music, opening the door only when he heard the special code he and his friends had devised. His evenings were spent at rehearsals and performances of the Choral Ensemble and the Conservatory Orchestra.

But his commitments went beyond music and his job. He soon became an active member of the All-Greek Youth Organization of Nea Smyrne. In the spring of 1944, he and a student from the Polytechnic School were assigned to distribute leaflets and deliver explosives to a centre in Athens. The other boy walked in front, pulling the cart; Mikis walked behind. Suddenly, they were stopped by an SS patrol. The Polytechnic student, questioned first, denied any involvement with an underground group and swore up and down that he had no connection with Mikis, and didn't even know he had been following. In a rage, the Germans beat him so mercilessly that he fell down in a coma and was left on the street, where he died a few hours later.

Mikis was taken to SS headquarters for more thorough questioning. When one of the Germans, struggling with the Greek on Mikis' ID card, discovered that he was a student at the Conservatory, the blows suddenly stopped and Mikis was dismissed and told to return the following day. The next day, Yiorgos came with his son and testified that he was only a student. Mikis was released.

As the Germans began to feel the pressure of Allied power, brutalities increased. Dismembered bodies and rows of heads, displayed in mockery, were not unfamiliar sights; and from every corner of the land, there was news of collaborators and Resistance fighters butchering each other. This chaos and slaughter plunged Mikis into a terrible crisis which he could only meet with passivity and non-violence, and a return to the idealism and religion of his days in Tripolis. He embraced a utopian humanism which would achieve the salvation and unity of mankind through beauty created by art, and developed a theory of metaphysical escape which would deliver man from violence and turmoil. Music would be a substitute for religion. Man would be placed in an area isolated from material needs and daily happenings, surrounded by such means and objects 'as would sharpen his senses, and direct his attention to the function of the inspiring force that would affect both vision and hearing. These thoughts eventually found their musical outlet in Mikis' oratorio, *Sinfonia,* which was completed in the fall of 1944, along with other choral sketches.

Along with such "metaphysical" problems, Mikis struggled with the awful violence that had erupted between resistance fighters and collaborators. The treatment of captives and hostages tormented him, and he expressed his agony in three essays to which he gave the general title *Evangelia pros tous Synanthropous* (Messages of Goodwill to Our Fellow Men) . He had read Malraux's *La Condition humaine* (Man's Fate), and saw in that account of the Communist uprising of 1927 in Shanghai striking similarities to the Greek situation of 1944. It seemed to him that Mao Tse-tung's policy, as described by Malraux, of having captives live side by side with the revolutionary army, in order to experience at first hand the feelings of their foes, was a tactic that could be applied in Greece. Vehemently opposed to the spirit of revenge that characterized the treatment of hostages and captives in Greece, he reasoned that, whether collaborator, Communist, or German, the captured foe should be tried by due process of law. Above all, he emphasized the need for love, not a passive love, but a fighting, positive force, based on brotherhood and justice and opposed to violence and killing.

There was a lull in Athens, and in the rest of Greece, before the terrible storm, as almost the whole country had been slowly liberated and placed under the control of the National

Liberation Front, the People's Liberation Army, and the All-Greek Youth Organization. The people began to hope that, at long last, they would have a say in the government, for a Political Committee of National Liberation (PEEA) had been created on March 10, 1944, and was now working hard to prepare the road for a normalization of political life and a truly socialist society. People poured into the streets, singing and dancing. They could be seen kissing the British soldiers and embracing each other. Mikis and Myrto, who had become very close, shared the joys of that summer. They would walk to the beach at Kalamaki with other friends or their family, savouring to the full those idyllic moments—swimming and playing in the clear blue Saronic Gulf, or singing the romantic songs of the day. It was on such an outing, on a Sunday afternoon in July, that they confided their love to one another.

But their romance was not without its difficult moments. Myrto was a dedicated intellectual whose entire existence revolved around science. Most of her friends were students in the applied sciences and professional schools, and her whole milieu was one of calm rationality. She and Mikis seemed to disagree on almost everything they discussed, whether it was their own specific problems or those that were troubling their generation. Mikis was the dreamer, the uncontrollable free thinker and optimist. Myrto was guided above all by logic and realism. Her career as a doctor promised her a secure future, whereas Mikis' profession offered no certainties as far as job, money, and home were concerned, except for the possibility of a job as a music teacher in some provincial city. Even politically, Myrto was more orthodox than he, dutifully obeying the EAM line, while Mikis acted rather according to his own emotions and enthusiasm.

Mikis pressed her to marry him, but Myrto had a very different view of her future. She wanted to make her own life as a scientist. Her profession came first, and she had no desire to be saddled with children and a household routine. She was very adamant about her ambitions and even went as far as not wanting to change her name. She insisted that Mikis change his instead and become "Mikis Altinoglou."

As the summer days drew to a close, the lull in the conflict, too, approached an end. The Germans, making their
last stand, concentrated all their efforts around Athens, and
the bitter clashes started up with greater intensity than before. Partly because of the daily happenings and partly because of his disagreements with Myrto, Mikis came to realize
that his search for justice would require more than mere phi-
losophizing. He did not want to kill, but he felt that action
was needed and was eventually drawn to active participation
in the struggle almost in spite of himself. One day in Kallithea, a district of Athens, he came upon a street skirmish between an ELAS unit and several German soldiers supported
by *tsoliades*. With the ELAS group was a friend of his from
Nea Smyrne who cried out to him to help them. Unarmed,
Mikis hesitated, but someone threw a gun to him, and, finding himself suddenly a soldier, he joined his comrade. After
the Germans and their Greek collaborators were dispersed,
Mikis walked with the ELAS unit back to headquarters.
From then on, he fought as an EPON reservist.

Having gained complete control of the country, the Germans and their Greek allies began fostering Greek collaborationist groups oń whom they could depend. The best known
and most active of such groups were the *tsoliades* (Royal
Guards), the *bourandades* (armoured police battalions led by
Bourandas), and the "X" activists, a terrorist band headed
by General George Grivas. In addition, there were the Security Battalions and other terrorist groups. But the EAM-
ELAS victories in the countryside forced the Germans to
mount a counter-offensive in Athens and neighbouring areas.
Guided by EAM, the people began to confront openly both
Greeks and Germans in the cities. Beginning on August 22,
1943, EAM and the labour unions staged continuous strikes.
Ioannis Rallis, the quisling Premier, responded by calling on
Greek civilians and ex-policemen to join the Security Bat-
talions. A new phase in the national struggle had begun:
Greeks were to fight Greeks.

On the night of October 12, during the final evacuation of
Athens, the Nea Smyrne EPON assigned Mikis to guard duty
at a warehouse that the Germans had used to store ammuni-

tion and other spoils of war. Warily, Mikis circled the building, which was fenced off with barbed wire, all the while
looking for the approach of the Germans. Suddenly, he came
across a Greek youth trying to cut the barbed wire and get
into the building. Mikis helped him cut a hole large enough
to get through, and the youth dashed for the basement, gathered up as many cameras and other items as he could carry,
loaded them on his motorcycle, and disappeared into the
night. Alone again, Mikis went outside, and suddenly found
himself staring into the muzzle of a German machine gun.
Smiling at the challenge, Mikis made as if to shoot. The German, embarrassed by Mikis' bravery and seeing that he was
not going to fire, turned his own gun away. Each one, deathly
still, waited for what seemed an eternity. Then the German
walked away; and Mikis put his gun down, seized by a strange
pity for the German, who, he felt, would never make it back
to his homeland.

Not long after that incident, a band of looters rushed the
building. Mikis could not possibly keep them away all by
himself. He was soon joined by another guard who had come
to investigate, but the two were no match for the greedy
mob, who burst into the basement where Mikis and his fellow Resistance fighter had retreated, and made off with all
the guns, clothes, shoes, and goods they could handle. In the
corner of the boiler room, they came upon an Italian officer
hiding in terror. Over Mikis' desperate protests, the vengeful
mob dragged him out and, a few blocks away, riddled him
with bullets. Seeing more and more people on their way to
loot the building, Mikis decided to frighten them away by
firing a few shots in the air and warning them that an explosion was about to go off. This had the desired effect and the
crowd dispersed. Once again, the building was in Mikis'
hands. He felt as if the spoils by now belonged to his EPON
group, but he was to be disappointed. One of the top officers
in the Resistance, Vassilis Zanos, whose jurisdiction was the
whole area, appeared on the scene with some other ELAS
officers. After a few moments of heated dispute as to whom
the building and its spoils belonged, the supplies were di-

vided between the ELAS men with Zanos, and the Nea Smyrne EPON unit.

Behind the escalation in hostilities between Right and Left lay months of planning by the British to return the monarchy as part of the postwar Greek Government. The situation was complicated, because, while the British were negotiating with the right-wing groups, the Germans were arming staunch rightist collaborators in a desperate attempt to defeat EAM-ELAS. In spite of the power of EAM-ELAS, the British would communicate only with groups that could be counted on to support the monarchy. Churchill would have nothing to do with the mutinous units of the Greek Army in Egypt, who were protesting the refusal to include EAM in the new government of national unity. To the British, the EAM-ELAS forces, who had been starved, tortured, and killed in their heroic resistance against the Germans, were no more than "banditti," while the brigades of the Cairo Army, who wanted a government that would include all political parties, were "ambitious émigré nonentities." Eventually, the British succeeded in purging the Greek Army, for the mutinous units surrendered, and approximately 200,000 men were sent to concentration camps in Libya and Eritrea. Those left behind were obviously pro-British.

The British next had to settle upon a premier who would play their game. They selected George Papandreou, a liberal republican with whom they had been in contact for some time. He was sworn in on April 26, 1944. Instead of working for unity, he set about attacking the EAM-ELAS with such venom that the people could hardly believe it was the same once liberal Papandreou. In his book *Triumph and Tragedy,* Churchill reports cabling to Foreign Secretary Anthony Eden, "We cannot take a man up as we have done Papandreou and let him be thrown to the wolves at the first snarlings of the miserable Greek Communist banditti."

Papandreou was well aware of his slim support among the leftists. Realizing that, without British support, he could not maintain his position, he cabled Churchill early in September that political means were no longer sufficient for handling the situation. It was an open invitation, but the British were still consolidating the "direction of Greek affairs," as Churchill put it. It was decided that there would be a conference of all factions at the Villa Caserta in Italy, where the palace and Papandreou's cabinet had moved from Cairo in August. By the Caserta Agreement, as it came to be known, each party was supposed to give a little. EAM agreed to join Papandreou's provisional government on two conditions—that units of the Cairo Army and all guerrilla bands, whether of the right or of the left, be dissolved and a new national army formed from the groups; and that the Security Battalions be considered enemies. The new national army would be placed under the supreme command of British General Scobie, and the British would be allowed to land troops in Greece after the German evacuation to prevent a power vacuum.

While the Germans were evacuating Athens in early October, Stalin and Churchill were meeting in Moscow to decide the fate of the Balkans. Greece was to come under British influence, and Russia was to take the rest of the Balkans and Eastern Europe under her wing. Neither power was to put its hand in the other's dish. All of this was to have fateful consequences for the future of the left-right struggle in Greece. But, on October 12, the average citizen of Athens knew only that the Germans were finally evacuating the city, fighting every inch of the way.

It is impossible to give a picture of Athens during those bleak October days. Each neighbourhood was its own little country, with barricades and boundaries that had to be crossed like frontiers. Between Mikis' house and the centre of Athens, a distance of over three miles, there could be from three to six such barricades, depending upon the route, each fortified by either a few units of partisans, by right-wing groups, or by British reinforcements. One never knew where a lone German sniper might be hiding, or when a mine would go off. Whether it was this complete anarchy, this lack of unified purpose, or the sheer terror of those days of slaughter, or both, that led Mikis to join the Communist Party, is hard to say. Certainly, it was through his involvement with

EPON that he became familiar with, and attracted to, Marxism. Moreover, he had not failed to notice and become profoundly impressed by the sharp contrast offered between the leftists' sacrificial concept of nationalism, on the one hand, and the Metaxists' expedient collaboration with the invaders, on the other. As Greece was becoming dangerously polarized in this period between the Left and the Right, the choice grew clear and unequivocal to him. In October, having already met the Secretary of the Communist Party through his EPON activities, Mikis became a member of the local bureau of Nea Smyrne, KOB (Party District Unit).[2]

Years later, in trying to assess the importance of the contrasting attitudes of the Left and Right, as seen by those immediately involved, he said: "Those [the Metaxists] who had talked to us about national pride and Christian brotherly love were the first to come to terms or actively collaborate with the Germans. It was an immense blow to my entire intellectual and emotional existence. Then, when I had my first contact with Marxists, I cried tears of real passion because I knew they were right—yet at the same time they were tearing apart the entire world that the ideals of my youth had created within me. But what finally convinced me was not so much the ideas as the personal examples being set by the Communists. They demonstrated by their actions that they would sacrifice their lives for their ideas. When they were executed by the Germans—as so many were—they died singing the 'Internationale' and shouting slogans about Greece and the people. So you can say that I entered Marxism through the door of nationalism and patriotism."[3]

Mikis was appointed second secretary of his local KOB and served as an information officer and as head of the local army command post. In his first capacity, Mikis came in contact with all the publications of the leftist groups and Radio

[2] The first Marxist party in Greece was created in 1922—the Greek Socialist Party. In 1924, it accepted the doctrines of the Comintern and became the Communist Party of Greece. Because of the Asia Minor Catastrophe, it gained many members among the refugees and the industrial workers.

[3] Don Heckman, "Mikis Theodorakis: I Am a Symbol of Power," *The New York Times,* Sec. 2 (August 16, 1970).

EPON, which, at the beginning, had been a pirate station but by the end of 1944 had become officially recognized. He did not, however, participate in the KOB Bureau's official meetings, preferring, instead, to devote his time to the youth work of EPON.

By November 1, the Germans had evacuated almost all of Greece, with the exception of a few islands. But, if Greece was free from the Germans, she was not free to decide her own government. Churchill's attitude toward EAM-ELAS had hardened, and General Scobie, in charge of the British forces in Athens, was instructed to consider EAM-ELAS forces bandits. Papandreou's attempts to pull the groups together in compliance with the Caserta Agreement failed, for no one was able to agree on how the new united army of Left and Right should be organized, how many units of each sector should be included, who should be the officers, and who should have the high command. Since no formal agreement could be reached on these essential points, the guerrillas refused to disband. Day after day, ELAS began bringing more and more of its units into Athens as the few militant leaders assumed control of its policy. On November 7, Churchill cabled to Foreign Secretary Eden: "In my opinion, having paid the price we have to Russia for freedom of action in Greece, we should not hesitate to use British troops to support the Royal Hellenic Government under M. Papandreou. This implies that British troops should certainly intervene to check acts of lawlessness. Surely M. Papandreou can close down E.A.M. newspapers if they call a newspaper strike. I hope the Greek Brigade will soon arrive, and will not hesitate to shoot when necessary. . . . We need another eight or ten thousand foot-soldiers to hold the capital and Salonika for the present government. . . . I fully expect a clash with E.A.M., and we must not shrink from it, provided the ground is well chosen."[4]

The disagreement over the disarmament of guerrillas and the composition and leadership of a national army finally erupted into a political crisis; EAM resigned from Papan-

[4] Churchill, *Triumph and Tragedy* (Boston 1953), 286-287.

dreou's government of national unity and called for a mass demonstration of protest on Sunday, December 3. Informed of the pending rally, Papandreou gave his permission but withdrew it at the last minute under British pressure. The demonstration nevertheless went on as scheduled.

Mikis who took part in the events of this "Bloody Sunday," as it came to be known, recalls it thus.

On Saturday, we were making preparations for a peaceful demonstration. I remember perfectly the orders we had been given by the organizers. Bearing arms was strictly forbidden. Only a few dozen cadres, charged with keeping order, had been authorized on this point, in order to avoid all provocation. One must remember that the gendarmes, the police, the collaborators had not been purged, and that there were incidents continually.

We were supposed to gather at first by neighbourhoods and to move toward Constitution Square in procession. The group from Nea Smyrne had its rendezvous on Syngrou Boulevard. There were women, children; we sang Resistance songs. It was a beautiful day, but still cold. A light fog hovered over the streets.

We marched on peacefully, waving our placards that called for the integration of the Resistance into a national army, unfurling Greek and Red flags. We were shouting "Papandreou resign!" "Democracy!" "No new occupation forces!" "Roosevelt!" We must have been in the tens, in the hundreds of thousands. As we reached Constitution Square, I saw through the fog, near the Tomb of the Unknown Soldier, British soldiers and Greek gangs, all armed. The Square, the neighbouring streets, were packed with crowds.

With a sudden staccato, gunfire exploded. From the roof of the old Parliament Building, the police were using machine guns. We hit the ground. Everything was in a panic. No one had any idea that they were going to shoot at us. We retreated about a hundred yards or so into the National Park. The procession regrouped, and we started again toward the Parliament Building and the Grande Bretagne Hotel, which was the seat of the government and the British High Command. We were advancing towards the tanks. I saw the British soldiers pointing their guns at us. Then, once again, the machine guns sounded from the Parliament Building. Police were shooting in cold blood. It was horrible. This time, they shot directly into the crowd. Hundreds were wounded; the dead lay all over the place. The pavement became red with blood. It was the first time I ever saw so much blood.

I grabbed a Greek flag. I soaked it in the blood and stood up again. The soldiers were laughing stupidly. The square was empty. An American photographer took a picture that later appeared in the world press. Then I caught sight of my father, fallen in the middle of the wounded. But he was all right. He shouted to me to stop. I was walking with a young blonde girl. We were joined by a soldier who had been disabled at the Albanian front. We kept saying to each other: "This time, for sure, we are going to our deaths." We crossed the whole square in dead silence. Not a shot was fired. We saw the police about to open fire behind the iron railings of the Grande Bretagne. Someone shouted out: "Don't come any closer! You'll be shot!" We began to sing the national anthem and answered back with the slogans of EAM: "Roosevelt!" "Stalin!" "Democracy!" The square filled up again. The dead and wounded were carried away. From a balcony of a building opposite the Grande Bretagne—the one which today belongs to Olympic Airways but which was then the seat of the Communist Party—the Party's secretary-general, Siantos, made a speech denouncing provocation.

The tanks moved in to disperse the crowd. An English soldier hit me with the butt of his gun and I fell a distance of two or three yards headlong into the bushes. I picked myself up and started for home, covered with blood, my clothes torn in shreds. Halfway there, I met my mother, who had come looking for me, crying. My father, who had returned distraught and in a state of shock, had sent her for me. She was afraid that I was dead.

The next day, EAM called a general strike so that everyone could attend the funeral of the twenty-eight killed on Sunday. Over half a million thronged to the service, held in the same area as the killing. A deathly silence prevailed. As the crowd began to drift away in groups of stunned and weeping families, they were fired upon by the "X" gangs of General Grivas, the Security Battalions, and others. Deaths were four times those of the first. And, as if in support of such policies, Churchill, in the early hours of December 5, cabled to Scobie: "Do not however hesitate to act as if you were in a conquered city where a local rebellion is in progress. . . . We have to hold and dominate Athens . . . with bloodshed if necessary."[5]

And bloodshed there was. The Security Battalions, which, according to the Caserta Agreement, were enemies, were increased to thirty units of five hundred men each. "They proved very useful in rounding up armed hostile civilians and guarding areas cleared by our troops."[6] Occasionally, the "hostile civilians" rounded up the others. In one such episode, Mikis had taken up his gun and, leading the Nea Smyrne EPON in search of three collaborators who had been reported hiding in the vicinity, attacked the local police station. Half of the policemen gave themselves up; some joined the attackers. The rest began to shoot, meanwhile turning on the warning siren that signalled the British to send support. Mikis' group was reinforced by people from the neighbourhood, who rushed into the station and grabbed guns. Mikis and his group then secured the station. After a brief debate about what to do with his hostages, Mikis decided to let them go. The officer in charge of the precinct trembled in fear of what would happen to him at the hands of the partisans if he were to leave the building; Mikis asked a comrade to accompany the officer to his house.

In spite of the imposition of martial law, ELAS units achieved a series of successes in the weeks following "Bloody Sunday." One of these victories, which succeeded in penning the British in the very centre of Athens, was in the Battle of Makriyianni. The district of Makriyianni, an ELAS stronghold, lay between the upper end of Syngrou Avenue and the Acropolis, and was one of the most contested points in Athens. Mikis and his group participated in the struggle; and an American journalist photographed him running in front of his squad. American journalists were everywhere; they were accepted and appreciated by the Resistance fighters

5 *Ibid.*, 289.
6 *Ibid.*, 287.

for their fair reportage and frequent condemnation of British policy in Greece.

By now, however, as more and more British troops kept pouring into Athens, the tide had begun to turn against ELAS. As the British strength increased, the People's Liberation Army and the All-Greek Youth Organization units received orders to attack them behind the lines. Mikis' Nea Smyrne group was assigned to areas surrounded by the British. Such an offensive policy in the face of overwhelming odds seemed like sheer folly to Mikis and his unit, but their district leader warned that disobedience would be punished by death or imprisonment.

At Barchami cemetery, one of the designated areas, a conference was held between the fighters and EAM-ELAS captains. One of the men in Mikis' group declared that they would no longer obey their district leader and demanded directives from headquarters. After discussing this insubordination, all the captains decided that Mikis and his group would be condemned to death. At first, the men laughed at such a ridiculous sentence, unable to believe that it was meant seriously. But when the others remained silent, they drew to one side, in close formation, and fired a few shots, threatening to shoot anyone attempting to carry out the order of arrest. The gunshots brought British troops rapidly to the scene and a bloody fight broke out.

Mikis escaped and dashed into the first house he saw. It was inhabited by an old widow and her son who had lost his mind after seeing a human body severed at the waist, lying face up in the street, staring at him with lifeless eyes. When Mikis burst into the house so suddenly, the boy let out a howl. Mikis locked him in the bathroom, but the damage had been done. Two men of the Security Battalions rushed into the house. Mikis jumped out of the back window into the garden, with bullets whizzing wildly over his head as the men followed in hot pursuit. Doubling back through the British lines, Mikis managed to make his way back to Smyrne Street, as if driven by some blind instinct. There, he hid himself in a dry well until night.

When it got completely dark, he went back to the house of the two elderly spinsters he was living with at this time, having moved out of his own home because of disagreement with his family over his activities. Since he knew the rightists had discovered his address and would be waiting to seize him as soon as he appeared at the house, he jumped in through the window. His two maiden landladies, who were accustomed to a quiet existence revolving around French and piano lessons, were nearly frightened out of their wits, but there was nothing they could do but hide him; so while one watched the street, the other, trembling and crying, pretended to be giving him piano lessons. As Mikis sat down to play, the French teacher whispered that an armoured car full of Security Battalion men was passing. When she signalled that it had passed, Mikis darted out the front door and almost fell in front of its wheels. He dashed back into the house and out the back door, through the yard, and ended up at the kitchen door of his own home. His mother greeted him in a state of panic, and said that he must get out immediately, because the British were guarding the house. Mikis ran to the second floor to find his father. A girl placed there as a guard by the British challenged him, and tauntingly told him that, while he was out endangering his life, his beloved Myrto was down in the basement enjoying herself with a British soldier. Mikis tore down the stairs and discovered the two, together with Myrto's two sisters. Myrto looked at Mikis as though she had never seen him before, so as not to betray him to the soldiers. Mikis checked himself from saying anything just in time and was going back up the stairs when a Greek Army officer who had worked with his father in the Ministry of Interior rushed in to tell Yiorgos that the British knew that Mikis was home and were on their way to arrest him.

Yiorgos quickly decided that they should all leave before the British arrived. One by one, all the members of the family slipped out the back way and regrouped at Syngrou Avenue, which was under partisan control. Within a few minutes, they were strolling down the avenue, on their way to their relatives in Makriyianni. At a check-point at the beginning of the Makriyianni district, almost on the very spot where the clash had occurred a few hours before, they met a captain of the Greek Royal Gendarmerie, who had known the family in Tripolis. Mikis asked what had been happening, and why all the commotion? The captain answered that there had been bloody fighting all day long and said that it would be safer if he personally escorted Mikis and his family to their relatives' house. The whole family remained there for a few days, until they felt it was safe for them to go back to Nea Smyrne. Mikis, who was the object of an intensive search, stayed on. But it was not long before the police tracked him down. One day, they burst into the house and placed him under arrest. But as they were carrying him off to the police station, Mikis managed to escape and make his way to another relative's house in Kallithea.

Such incidents as these in Mikis' life were typical all over Athens, after the Bloody December. Neighbourhood clashes and bloodshed became a way of life.

Churchill, however, consistently maintained that it was not his purpose to secure any particular government in Greece. In his speech before the House of Commons on December 8, he reiterated: "Whether the Greek people form themselves into a monarchy or a republic is for their decision. Whether they have a government of the Left or Right is a matter for them. *But until they are in a position to decide, we shall not hesitate to use the considerable British army now in Greece to see that law and order are maintained.*"[7]

His emphasis on "law and order," however, came under heavy attack at home. *The Economist* declared: "It must be proved that the Papandreou government is supported by men who have genuinely resisted the Germans and who hope for a democratic and progressive future for Greece, and not only by Royalists, Right-wing guerrillas, and the timid centre of all those who desire no more than law and order, whether it is the Germans or the British who provide it for them."[8]

[7] From Churchill's speech before the House of Commons, quoted in *The Economist* 106 (December 23, 1944) 838. [Italics added.]
[8] Comments in *ibid.*

Clearly, it was the British who must provide law and order, and Churchill flew to Athens on Christmas Day to bring it about. The first conference was little more than a grand opportunity for Churchillian eloquence, and a chance for all the factions, including three Communist representatives—who, to Churchill's surprise, "were presentable figures in British battle dress,"[9]—to get together and talk. The conference went on for two more days with attacks and counter-attacks by all sides. In keeping with Churchill's dislike of EAM-ELAS, he refused to meet privately with the Communist delegates, although he spent several hours in private consultation with Archbishop Damaskinos of Athens, whom he decided the King should appoint as Regent. On January 1, 1945, the Archbishop formally accepted the mandate of the King, given under Churchill's instance. Papandreou, now made expendable, resigned, and on January 4 General Nicholas Plastiras was selected Prime Minister.

A truce signed on January 1 was followed by a general amnesty, but the reign of terror was far from over. The *tsoliades,* Security Battalions, and "X" gangs outdid the British in their brutality. Mikis remained in hiding with his relatives in Kallithea as long as he could, but by the beginning of February, the police had traced him to his new hideout with a whole dossier of charges against him. They took him to the police station and had just begun torturing him when his father arrived, protesting his son's treatment and demanding a military trial. At the trial, Yiorgos used all his legal skill to defend Mikis and succeeded in getting him off with a brief jail sentence.

On February 12, the famous Varkiza Agreement was signed in a small village on the seacoast of Attica. The leaders of the National Liberation Front and the People's Liberation Army agreed to give up their weapons on the condition that elections be held, in which all political parties would have a voice. The Communist Party was officially recognized for the first time since 1936, and the National Liberation Front was promised parliamentary representation. As reported in *The Economist* on February 17, 1945,

9 Churchill, *op. cit.* (supra n.4) 316.

On Monday last the Greek government and EAM signed an agreement which brought the civil war in Greece to a definite conclusion. . . . The Athens agreement provides for the preservation of democratic liberties, the cessation of martial law, the release of hostages, and the amnesty for EAM. A national army is to be raised, there is to be a purge of collaborators and Metaxists from the Administration, and finally provision is made for free elections and a plebiscite on the future of the monarchy.

But the utopian hopes of reconciliation faded rapidly in the face of reality. The attitude of Mikis' professor of music, Economidis, was a good example of why. When, during the temporary lull in fighting resulting from the Varkiza Agreement, Mikis decided to register for courses again at the Conservatory, he found Economidis' feelings toward him completely changed. He had brought along his *Sinfonia*, the oratorio reflecting the bloody December Days, hoping that it could be performed by the Athens Choir. But Economidis would not even consider the work; in fact, he told Mikis that what had passed between them had better be forgotten altogether. He said that Mikis should have followed the example of two other students at the Conservatory. Both had participated in the National Liberation Front–People's Liberation Army Resistance, but they had since renounced their behavior, apologized, and promised to refrain from any further active participation. Mikis tried to explain his thinking, but to no avail. Economidis had suffered personal losses at the hands of the leftists and was in no mood to forgive or understand. The house of a relative of his in Kiphissia was razed to the ground because of the man's involvement with the rightists. Economidis told Mikis not to expect anything; he was not going to perform any of his works, take him into the Choir, or even let him participate in the Athens Orchestra.

The break seemed complete and irrevocable. Mikis decided not to register in any of Economidis' classes. There were other teachers, with more modern techniques and training. When Mikis told his father of his decision to leave Economidis, Yiorgos was taken aback. He told his son that

Economidis was the "alpha and omega" of the music world in Greece, and that, without his protection and favour, Mikis could never hope to get anywhere. He might as well abandon any hopes for the future. Becoming more and more persuaded by his own arguments, Yiorgos finally forbade Mikis to abandon his old teacher. But Mikis was equally adamant, and registered with other professors.

In spite of his outward show to his father, Mikis was not totally happy that he no longer would see his former professor. He had worked very hard on his own compositions in the months since the dreadful December Days and had wanted to show them to Economidis. In March, 1945, he completed a work inspired by the "Bloody Sunday," for which he wrote both the music and the words, entitled *Third of December*. That same month, he wrote an oratorio, *Night March Toward Makriyianni,* for piano, strings, and chorus. Since he did not know any of the new professors too well, he hesitated to show his works to them. *Third of December,* however, was performed at the EPON centre with Karafotias as the baritone soloist.

In the spring of 1945, as the armed conflict built up again, and arrests and wanton violence began to reach enormous proportions, Mikis, without abandoning the Conservatory, began attending the Marxist preparatory school. One day in May, during a lecture at the secret preparatory school, he heard strains of Schubert's *Unfinished Symphony* coming from a radio across the street. As soon as the lecture was over, he went to the Party office and told EPON leaders that he could no longer concentrate only on the military aspect of the movement. He wanted to develop his musical talent, and to spend more time on his studies. The leaders made him the head of a newly established cultural centre in the centre of Athens, where most of the intellectuals and young writers of the Resistance and EPON met and organized their activities.

It was around this time that Mikis, who was still trying to clarify his own political, military, and social beliefs, became involved with the youth of the various districts in Athens. With other EPON members, he took a census of what the young people of Nea Smyrne had been lacking for so many years. Other EPON members conducted the same investigation in other Athens and Piraeus districts. They were anxious to find out what the neighbourhoods needed in the way of schools, vocational training, sports, and cultural activities. The members of EPON would go out to the different districts and get the youth to help clear away the war debris, rebuild schools, and fix up recreation areas. Life began to take on new meaning for the young people in these war-torn sectors. During all the years of the war, no one had ever done anything specifically for them. For Mikis, working with the youth was the real humanism he had sought so long. At the same time, because of his interest in literature, he and a group of writers who were to become Greece's greatest poets and writers created the Young Writer's Association.

Meanwhile, the time of examinations was approaching at the Conservatory. Economidis had given him the cold shoulder the whole semester and now, when he had to take the finals in harmony, Mikis was worried—Economidis was on the examining committee. The old professor still bore a grudge against him, and when the time came he saw to it that he flunked. Mikis was deeply hurt. Not only did Economidis' reaction affect him emotionally, but he knew that, without official sponsorship and professional recognition, he would never be able to get a job. He tried to avoid becoming depressed by burying himself in his musical compositions and expending his energies at the EPON centre.

One day at the movement's headquarters, he heard about a young composer who had participated in the December battles and who, rumour had it, would not go along with the increasingly aggressive and violent policies of the EPON leadership. Curious, he asked to be introduced to him. The composer's name was Manos Hadjidakis, and their first meeting took place at the centre. When Mikis arrived for his appointment with Manos, he found a slim, sensitive, short fellow, with a childlike smile, sitting on a bench in the corner, poring over music sheets. Manos and Mikis opened their hearts to each other and discussed their problems for hours.

Manos had composed a number of songs and often played the piano for friends and some of the upper-class families in Kolonaki. He had another circle of friends, besides those at the EPON centre, at the United Artists Theatrical Company, for whom he had composed background music and done arrangements. Several days later, as a token of friendship, Manos and the United Artists invited Mikis to write a musical score for them. Mikis was unable to accept because of his heavy schedule at the cultural centre, but he asked Manos, in turn, to give him some songs to perform with the EPON choral group. Manos gave him a series of his songs, which Mikis then presented several nights in a row. These same songs were later included in Manos' song cycle, *For a Little White Seashell.*

Also participating in the EPON cultural group was the composer Yiannis Xenakis, who, in addition to studying music at the Conservatory, was also studying architecture. He had been wounded so seriously by the bullets fired from a British tank that his left cheek and eye still bear scars. In 1947, his citizenship was taken away and he was condemned to death *in absentia*. Xenakis is a typical example of a Greek composer whose music is a living re-enactment of the December Days. As he himself said years later: "In my music there is all the agony of my youth, of the Resistance, and the aesthetic problems they posed with the huge street demonstrations, or even more, the occasional mysterious, deathly sounds of those cold nights of December, 1944, in Athens."[10]

Mikis wrote many songs during the years of war and resistance. He always carried music sheets with him wherever he went, no matter what the adventure. Whether in battle or at meetings, social events, demonstrations, school and parties, he would jot down an idea as it came to him. Many of his songs were written and distributed on the spot. But most of them were not "successful," for the leaders of EAM did not consider them in keeping with the desired military "spirit." They preferred other songs, based on European or American

[10] Donal Henahan, "Xenakis: How a Man Defines Man," *The New York Times,* March 17, 1968.

marches, to Mikis' own, which were drawn from Greek thematic material. Many of his songs, however, were used the next few years during the civil war. One of his compositions received national recognition when the National Liberation Navy (ELAN) made it their anthem.

An indication of how important the Resistance deemed such songs could perhaps be found in the proclamation issued by the Joint Chiefs of Staff of ELAS in 1943. It asked every Greek to compile all the Resistance songs he knew, both lyrics and music, and send them as best he could to the nearest ELAS office. One song in particular, "The March of ELAS," with music by Tsakonas and lyrics by the poetess Sophia Mavroidi-Papadaki, won a prize in April, 1944, in a contest sponsored by the Writers and Musicians Division of EAM, a group to which Mikis also belonged. Although some of the best known Resistance songs were based on foreign tunes, the majority were original.

In spite of the strong interest shown by ELAS and the valiant efforts of scholars and poets in Greece and other countries at the time, little has been done with the Resistance songs. Although many of them are still remembered and sung secretly, the songs have never been recorded and their composers remain anonymous.[11]

Mikis did not want to be part of the fighting cadre of EPON, but he knew that something must be done to stop the terrorism of the "X" gangs, the police, and other right-wing fanatics. The situation had become so desperate that on June 5, 1945, all the recent prime ministers—Plastiras, Sophoulis, Kafandaris, Mylonas, and Tsouderos—signed a protest that said in part: "The terrorist organizations of the extreme right, which had been armed by the Germans and had collaborated with them, have not been disarmed or prosecuted, but have allied themselves to the security forces in order to strangle completely all democratic thought."[12]

Their protest had little effect. The terrorism of the police

11 Mikis himself sings four such songs in an LP record, *Canti della Resistenza Europa 1933–63*. Discografiche D.N.G., GLP 81003-4-5.
12 C. Tsoucalas, *The Greek Tragedy* (London 1969) 93.

and "X" gangs spread beyond the universities to all areas of life, including art and the theatre. In the middle of June, theatres were invaded on three different occasions by armed gangs in search of leftists. At the Hermes Theatre, they entered and began shooting indiscriminately at the stage and the audience, wounding two actors seriously in the chest. At the Lyrikon, during a performance of *Julius Caesar,* another gang climbed on the stage, shooting and clubbing actors and audience alike. After destroying the sets, the gangs stood up on the stage and sang royalist songs. At the Ethnikon Theatre, where the *Merchant of Venice* was playing, a third group rushed in, shooting in all directions. In all these episodes, the police served as escorts for the gangs.

Before long, committees of artists and intellectuals had sprung up in all quarters to protest these outrages. On June 23, one committee went to the Ministry of Justice to register written and oral protest, but after waiting several hours without seeing the Minister, they left and decided to circulate their protest to the governments of the U.S.A., U.S.S.R., England and to the various European universities. Among the 85 signatories were Nikos Kazantzakis, Angelos Sikelianos, Marios Varvoglis, A. Tassos, and Yiannis Ritsos, figures who represented the whole mind of modern Greece.

Mikis could not continue working at the EPON centre without a job, for having failed his course in harmony, he had lost his scholarship and the small income it provided. Fortunately, the conductor Menelaos Pallandios took an interest in him and found him a temporary position teaching music in a secondary school. Since this did not take up all of his time, he was free to continue his own music projects and his work at the EPON centre. But more important, the position gave Mikis a feeling that his training could be put to some use and that there might be a future for him as a music teacher, at least.

During the fall months, he composed *The Duo for Violins on a Greek Theme,* a *Trio* for piano, violin, and cello, a *Sextet* for flute, piano, and strings, and the song-cycle *Love and Death.* He also worked on several other compositions to which he returned in later years. His most important work of this period was a symphonic piece, *The Feast of Assi-Gonia,* the first version of which he completed the following spring. It was inspired by his father's descriptions of the feast of Assi-Gonia, a little village in Crete. Mikis himself had never gone to the festival but he wanted to pay tribute to the Cretan blood in his veins. Another work begun during this period was the *Oedipus Tyrannus* for full orchestra.

Mikis liked his teaching job but he could only remain at the school one semester without a diploma from the Conservatory. When the semester was over, Mikis found himself again without an income. He could not expect assistance from his family because his father's salary barely covered the most pressing necessities. So, with the help of a boy at the EPON centre who sold newspapers, he got a job doing the same thing. Though not "proper" employment for the son of an official of the Ministry of Interior, it was easy work and, besides bringing in money, however little, it left him time to study for readmission to the Conservatory. He felt that to make progress in the world of music, he must have a degree.

On the political level, things were not going smoothly. As a result of the Left's regroupment of forces, the hardliners took over the positions of leadership. Although he willingly adhered to the Left's political line and carried out his duties faithfully, Mikis could never behave in the manner the party thought proper for its leaders. To the hardliners, he was the *"pallikaraki,"* the young tough, who would run ahead and fight, do and say interesting things, but not leadership material, not one of the mainstays of the party.

At the January Panhellenic Conference of the All-Greek Youth Organization, Mikis was granted only ten minutes to make his report on cultural work among the youth. But a group of younger people made so much noise, chanting "More time! More time, for Mikis!" that he was finally permitted half an hour. During his talk he denounced the Left's cultural policies for allowing foreign elements to intrude into the people's culture and accused ELAS of taking Russian songs to create Greek Resistance songs and even taking a tune from Texas for the EPON Anthem. The leaders replied that they ought to be, above all, "internationalists" in their struggle. The meeting soon developed into a riot, and many sided with Mikis, pressuring him to become a candidate for the Executive Committee. He was elected but declined to serve, saying that it would take him away from his work at the cultural centre.

The one really bright development for Mikis at the beginning of 1946 was his readmission to the Conservatory and his acceptance in one of Economidis' classes. One day, shortly after the semester had begun, a classmate who worked in the American Library took him to the library's music section and arranged for him to borrow records and scores. It was the first time that Mikis had seen scores of works by Stravinsky and Schoenberg, and as a result, he began training himself in the twelve-tone technique.

Meanwhile, terrorism and violence increased. By March, 1946, the number of arrests had reached 85,000, and the "X" gangs continued to raid the countryside in search of more victims.[13] The increased ferment was attributed to the elections that were scheduled to take place on March 31. The Sophoulis government wanted them postponed until a more normal situation prevailed in the country, but British Foreign Secretary Ernest Bevin would not hear of it. Sophoulis, who realized that any elections held under such conditions would be a sham involving only right-wing extremist participation, finally resigned, and Communists and Centrists decided to abstain.

The most important issue of the election was the September plebiscite on the return of the monarchy. Because of the withdrawal of the Centre and the Left, more than half of the Greek population was not represented. On March 26, the day after National Independence Day, the people poured into the streets of Athens to protest the elections. Businesses were closed, and virtually everyone took part in the demonstration. Mikis again was in the front lines. The human waves were singing his Resistance songs, while the focus of

[13] Tsoucalas, *op. cit.* (supra n. 12) 98.

attention turned to Greek dances. The throngs marched
down Panepistimiou, heading for Omonoia Square. Across
the street from the university, as chain-lines of police bore
down on the demonstrators, an officer pointed out the tall
leader in the crowd and told his men to concentrate on him.
Mikis was immediately surrounded and beaten mercilessly.
He tried to fight back but finally fell to the pavement unconscious. Looking like a corpse, he was taken to the morgue
and officially listed as dead. A few hours later, in spite of the
many dead and wounded, an official communiqué gave out
false statistics: a few wounded and one dead. This was for the
benefit of an International Commission that was present in
Athens to supervise the elections.

When Mikis came to, he found himself in the morgue,
barely able to move. He tried to lift his arms and legs, but
each movement brought excruciating pain. His head was
throbbing, and as the smell and taste of dried blood flooded
his senses, he choked back an overwhelming wave of nausea.
Looking around in terror, he suddenly realized that he had
been left to die in that horror chamber. In agony he forced
himself to crawl inch by inch to the door, and managed to
get it open at the very moment when his friends from EPON,
who had combed every hospital in the city, were passing
down the corridor. Without waiting for official authorization,
they made a stretcher with their hands and carried him to a
clinic, where he underwent an emergency operation for cra-
nial fracture. As a result of the fracture on the left side of
his skull, caused by the beating, the vision in his left eye
was permanently impaired. Mikis stayed in the clinic two
months.

While he was in the hospital, the elections took place as
scheduled. Out of a population of 7,000,000, only 1,121,246
voted. Of these, only 1,108,473 votes were valid. The elections put the United Nationalist Party under Poulitsas in
power on the strength of a mere 610,995 plurality.[14] The
September plebiscite on the return of the King showed similar results. Only 1,661,060 voted; 1,136,289 in favour of his

14 J. Meynaud, *Les Forces politiques en Grèce* (Montreal 1965) 80-82.

return; and 524,771, opposed. The International Commission of observers listed the abstentions as 15 per cent, whereas the calculations of Mikis' father, who was in charge of co-ordinating the results at the Ministry of the Interior, listed the abstentions at 38 per cent. When he gave this figure to an American reporter, he was immediately attacked by the press of the extreme right and denounced as the "father of the partisan." He was subsequently dismissed from his post and was to remain unemployed for many years. Other sources put abstentions as high as 50 per cent.[15] Thus, British policy triumphed; George II, who had been responsible for the appointment of the dictator Metaxas in 1936, returned to the throne he had so ignominiously fled at the outbreak of the war. It was the final blow. The polarization of forces between the armed Left, which depended on the Communist world, and the armed Right, with its British and American backers, was complete.

It was several months before Mikis was able to get over the horror of that March day, and its aftermath, and return to his music. By the fall, however, he managed to complete the *Sonatina No. 1* for piano and violin in the dodecaphonic style, which he had started in the spring. He also wrote a work for orchestra and chorus based on Nikiphoros Vrettakos' poem, *Margarita*.

A wave of enthusiasm for the possibilities of modern music, choral combined with dodecaphonic technique, swept over Mikis. He thought up the idea of forming an association of young musicians who would study the modern forms, perform their compositions for each other, and criticize, much like his youthful literary cenacle. He convinced some of his fellow composers, young and zealous like himself, pointing out that only in this way would they be on their own, free from dependency upon the older established composers and music professors, and their political factions. His idea caught fire; the Association of Young Musicians was born. It was unanimously agreed that Mikis should assume the presidency. Two other aspiring young composers, Sissilianos and

[15] Tsoucalas, *op. cit.* (supra n. 12) 97.

Kounadis, became vice-president and general secretary. Significantly, another creative composer, Hadjidakis, though well acquainted with the group and urged by Mikis, did not join. As was to be expected, however, youthful zeal of a tiny few for new cultural developments could hardly have an effect among a people hungry, ill-clad, poverty-stricken, and deprived of political freedom.

In the early months of 1947, Mikis found himself in a debate with Manos concerning the progress of music, in particular, and their personal ideologies, in general. Manos declared that EAM had, to all intents and purposes, lost the struggle, and that they, therefore, as creative artists should adjust themselves to the new situation. If they still wanted to effect a cultural rebirth, then they needed a symphonic orchestra, theatres, the radio, records—all of which were in the hands of the new forces. EAM and all the fighters would eventually go underground and everything would be lost. Mikis, however, insisted that EAM would fight and win. The argument, of course, achieved nothing. Each continued in his own path. Not much later, Manos accompanied the United Artists Theatrical Company to Larissa. At the performance, Fascist gangs, who had learned that many of the artists that had fought with EAM were present, attacked the theatre. Manos was hit violently across the mouth with the butt of a gun. The blow knocked out his front teeth, and, to this date, he has not replaced them.

### LIFE IN HELL

The story of the Greek concentration camps, from the Metaxas days to the years of their full capacity after the Second World War and during the Civil War, has long been buried along with those who died there. The stories of the Nazi concentration camps with their gas chambers, the subhuman treatment of the American and Chinese prisoners of war by the Japanese, the forced labour mines of Siberia have all been told in detail. But the horrors of the Greek concentration camps, the vicious brutality reserved for political prisoners, the diabolical ingenuity of the torturers, have been the most forbidden secrets of modern Greek history.

The camps were located in various areas all over Greece, but especially on the islands, since they could be easily isolated. The most infamous during the Metaxas terror were Anaphe, the southernmost island of the Cyclades, and Gavthos, a solitary island in the Libyan Sea off the southeastern end of Crete. Leros in the Ionian Sea; Yaros, in the Cyclades; Ikaria, near Samos and Turkey; Makronissos, off the coast of Attica; Aegina, forty minutes by boat from the port of Piraeus, and Psitalia, the tiny, barren rock between Aegina and Piraeus, became famous in the years of the rightist terror after 1945. But before the Civil War, the prisoners had broken out and escaped to fight in the Resistance. It was the survivors from among these groups, as well as thousands of new faces considered dangerous to the public order, who now filled the prisons.

When the struggle between leftists and rightists increased because of British insistence on restoring the monarchy, following the German withdrawal in 1944, the concentration camps began to fill up with new political prisoners, victims of the "X" gangs and the Security Battalions. As the guerrillas became more successful in the rural areas, the armed gangs and the royalist police intensified their reign of terror in the cities.

In January, 1947, a British parliamentary report recommended that a new government comprising all political parties, with the possible exception of EAM, be formed in Greece, and that the special security decrees be cancelled and political exiles permitted to return home. It also recommended that new elections be held with modern registration methods, and that British troops go home.[16]

The royalists became concerned: Was not Greece the only outpost against Communism in an area where Russia was creeping ever closer? Guerrilla warfare increased all over the country, particularly in Macedonia, Thrace, and Crete. West-

[16] L. S. Stavrianos, *Greece: American Dilemma and Opportunity* (Chicago, 1952) 180-181.

ern aid was essential to safeguard democracy. On January 16, the Tsaldaris coalition collapsed, and a new one under Maximos, the former head of the National Bank of Greece, was formed. Britain officially pulled out on February 24. The cold war was daily becoming more serious. Thus, on March 12, 1947, the United States assumed the responsibility of keeping Greece from Russia's clutches. President Harry S. Truman told Congress:

> I believe it must be the policy of the United States to support free people who are resisting attempted subjugation by armed minorities or by outside pressures. . . . The very existence of the Greek state is today threatened by the terroristic activities of several thousand armed men, led by Communists. . . . Assistance is imperative if Greece is to survive as a free nation.[17]

From March to July, the bloodshed and carnage by extremists of both sides was so horrible that the memory still haunts every Greek today. There were mass butcheries in the villages and mass arrests in the capital in retaliation. At the beginning of July, in order to prevent aid to the guerrillas from their sympathizers in the cities, General Napoleon Zervas, the Minister of Public Order, announced that all persons suspected of being "dangerous to the public order" would be arrested. On July 5, nearly 10,000 persons were rounded up in Athens alone. Mikis was one of them.

After he was arrested, he was thrown into the fenced-in enclosure on the huge, barren rock, Psitalia, an island just between Piraeus and Aegina. There was no water, no verdure, no living creature on the island. All the water had to be brought in by boat. The torment of the first two days' heat and thirst was made somewhat bearable by singing and the feeling of togetherness it engendered. But the intense thirst continued for fifteen days. Whenever the ship came with the tins of water, there would be a near riot to get one, for there was never enough to go around. Finally, on the fifteenth day of this martyrdom, an arms-transport ship arrived, and the prisoners were herded on board. Two days

17 Cited in *ibid.,* 182.

later, they were unloaded on the island of Ikaria, the island
that received the body of Icarus in mythological times, when
he flew too close to the sun and the wax holding the feathers
of his artificial wings melted.

Mikis was on the first shipload that was let out at Agios
Kyrikos, a rocky hamlet on the eastern shore of the island. As
the prisoners were discharged, they rushed in every direction
to find water. But there was no water to be found, and it was
only late at night that each prisoner received one potato to
eat. Fenced in by barbed wire, they were forced to sleep out
in the open on the bare ground, infested as it was by snakes,
thorns, and vermin. Sleep became impossible, and, hungry
and thirsty, the prisoners began to collapse. In the midst of
all this suffering, Mikis noticed one man tranquilly sharing
his potato with another prisoner and showing others where
they could settle down for the night. He recognized him as
Vassilos Zanos, the ELAS officer with whom he had captured
the German arms in Kallithea in October, 1944. The two
spent a few hours together talking, but eventually they were
separated by the guards.

A few days later, Mikis and many other prisoners were
transferred to the west coast of the island and discharged at
the village of Vrakades. On one side, the area was bordered
by a rocky mountain, and, on the other, the Aegean extended
endlessly before it. The largest building in the village was the
heavily guarded police station. Immediately upon arriving,
each prisoner was assigned to a militia unit in charge of the
forced-labour tasks. They would have to report to these units
every day on the progress of their jobs. Certain liberties were
granted to them. They were allowed to move from one place
to another; they were permitted to arrange their own quarters
as best they could on their own. But "arranging" their lives in
the barren camp was no easy task, for they had to clear the
rocks to make a level space. Then, they could build a little hut
to protect themselves from the dry heat and searing winds.
They were given some food and water, but, as for the rest, they
would have to shift for themselves. A little later, another ship
packed with prisoners arrived at Vrakades. When Mikis

spotted Vassilis Zanos stepping off the boat, he found himself smiling for the first time in three weeks. Zanos, too, was happy to see Mikis; from then, they spent every minute they could manage together. On a big rock overlooking the sea, they would sit and talk about the fate of Greece. Always, they ended up talking about music. Mikis would sing his works, simulating as best he could the parts of the flute, the violin, or the piano. Innumerable "concerts" were performed this way. Mikis would also show his latest short pieces, all written on scraps of waste paper. Zanos was erudite, with a professional knowledge of music; moreover, he was a fierce fighter—all of which attributes Mikis admired.

On the boat coming to Vrakades, Mikis had heard, for the first time, a striking pop song dating from the Metaxas days, "Captain Andreas Zepos," which told of the heroic and adventurous character of a sea captain. He wrote down the tune, and the tunes of hundreds of other sea and mountain songs that the prisoners sang. It was here that he sketched the *Greek Carnival,* based on many of these themes, including one on a song his uncle Antonis had composed, and eventually performed six years later.

Coincident with Mikis' arrival on Ikaria, the American Mission for Aid to Greece, headed by Dwight Griswold, arrived in Athens. Griswold was responsible for administering American aid without meddling in internal politics. But he soon discovered that this could not be done in Greece. It was useless to put a factory back into working order with American money, only to have it burned down the next day by guerrillas. Funds were needed to build up the government troops against the guerrillas. But the government troops were all extreme rightists, while the rebels were all considered Communists.

The Maximos government collapsed in August, having failed to make any headway against the guerrillas. The Americans were convinced that a new government should include liberals as well as royalists if there were to be any progress towards a solution of the crisis. The chief of the State Department's Office of Near Eastern Affairs, Loy Henderson, arrived in Athens to warn the Greek political leaders that they must form a coalition government if they wanted any more dollars. Thus, on September 7, Sophoulis formed a government with Tsaldaris as deputy premier. The royalist Stratos held on to his post as Minister of War. The following day, Sophoulis read a magnificent-sounding proclamation to Parliament, in which he invited the guerrillas to lay down their arms peacefully. If they did so, an amnesty would be granted to all those imprisoned or deported; if they did not, the government had no choice but to declare all-out war.

The guerrillas refused. How could they have confidence if the rightists controlled the army? There had been talks of amnesty for years. The promises were never kept. Thus, the Civil War was to be a fight to the death. But the government could not fight the guerrillas by itself. By December, the U.S. Military Mission had assumed leadership of a joint U.S.-Greek military staff. The Greek National Army was greatly enlarged, particularly by small guerrilla units. It received supplies of artillery, napalm bombs, tanks and aircraft, and repairs were made to roads, airfields, bridges, and other strategic points of communication. The Communist Party, in retaliation, increased the guerrilla offensive of the Democratic Army, and on December 24, created a "provisional government." Three days later, on December 27, both EAM and the Greek Communist Party were outlawed by Decree 509, and remained so ever since.

Meanwhile, the Greek issue had become a subject of discussion at the U.N.'s Human Rights Commission. Appeals were made through various legal and humanitarian associations for the release and more humane treatment of prisoners. A committee of attorneys and judges arrived on the island of Ikaria to investigate the charges concerning the concentration camps. Then, rumours circulated that the Communist Party had decreed that to appear before the committee was tantamount to signing an oath of loyalty to the King and the National Army. This evolved when the authorities of the concentration camp pressured the prisoners to present themselves to the judges. The situation was very confused, for the committee itself was split in two. A few of the stronger members had been appointed by the government; they wanted merely to report on the welfare of the prisoners with no questions asked. But the others wanted to hear the prisoners' complaints and appeals for release. The prisoners, however, hid to avoid the officials, and the committee finally left. Concurrently, the U.N. increased its pressure and the authorities had to make a gesture of goodwill.

In October of 1948, when the government granted a partial amnesty to a number of exiled prisoners in order to show the U.N. that things were at least returning to normal, Mikis and Zanos were released and shipped back to Athens. But this proved a fate worse than exile. Unhampered by the restrictions or rules applied in concentration camps, the police were freer to act in the capital. By now, they had a most efficient system of espionage and control, and, despite the amnesty, they sought out anyone who had participated in the Resistance as a "dangerous Communist." Consequently, Mikis' arrival was marked by a cat-and-mouse chase. He could not stay at home, since the police could enter and search any house at any time, so he went into hiding, sleeping in a different place every night. The underground helped him make arrangements to see Myrto and his family in secret. Myrto would bring him food, bread, cheese, whatever she could get, along with the most delicious of all, the *"myrtietes,"* as Mikis called it, a concoction she would make with chocolate and biscuits. His mother would meet him twice a week and bring him clothes. They would enter a cinema separately, meet in a dark corner, and exchange news. Mikis would take the package of clothes from his mother and slip into the toilet, where he would change as quickly as possible. Then, they would kiss again and each would take off in a different direction. Once in a while, his father and Pavlos Papamercouriou, a friend also in the underground, would meet him, and all three would go to a cheap taverna on Athena Street, where they would try to remain inconspicuous among the workers.

After weeks of being constantly on the move and sleeping out of doors on cold, winter nights, Mikis came down with pneumonia. He and Myrto set up a sleeping schedule, so that she could give him medical attention several nights a week in the homes of different friends. One night, with a printer's family, another at the house of Konstantinopoulos, Mikis' boyhood friend from Tripolis, and a third at the house of George Sissilianos, the composer with whom Mikis had established the Association of Young Musicians in 1946. But he had to spend the remaining three nights of the week in abandoned buildings, in open lots, or among the ruins, often hiding with Papamercouriou. This situation lasted through the winter and spring of 1948.

In the spring, having successfully eluded his hunters, Mikis finally dared to emerge in public. A violinist friend got him a job at the Town Theatre of Piraeus, where Melina Mercouri and Elsa Vergi were starring in a play. Mikis played the piano, or the tympani, backstage and orchestrated the background music for one of the productions, but he had to be always ready to run at the first appearance of the police. During intermissions, he would work on his music studies or rearrange parts of his *Assi-Gonia*. Once in a great while, with utmost caution, he would go to the Conservatory to practice on the piano and attend chorus rehearsals. Despite the great risk involved, the doorman would always let him shave and freshen up backstage, so that he would not appear suspicious to the students.

When he received his first pay at the theatre, he was so happy that he decided to risk everything and take Myrto out to dinner. He took her to a restaurant by the seashore and ordered the best meal the house had to offer. For several hours, as he and Myrto feasted like a fairy-tale prince and princess, he forgot his problems; he prolonged the idyll until all that was left of his "fat" salary was a few coins for Myrto's bus ticket home and his back to his place of hiding.

One weekend, alone and sick with hayfever, he got on a bus and rode aimlessly. Without realizing it, he had taken the route home. When the bus passed his house, he instinctively jumped off and ran in. His parents were getting ready for a trip to Crete, where his father's sister had been taken ill. Mikis insisted on going with them. Safety was no longer important to him; he was tired of leading the life of a fugitive. After hesitating, his parents finally agreed to take him along. By the time they reached the harbour, it was pouring rain, so they ducked into a coffee house to dry off and have some tea. Mikis' mother, seeing that he was shivering and realizing that his hacking cough would attract attention, insisted that he allow her to take him to his father's cousin, Petros, a medical officer in the army. Petros, a rightist, had an English son-in-law who had served with the British in Greece, and his house was full of all sorts of guns. It was impossible for Mikis to hide in such a setting. Forced to leave, he decided to hide out in a vacant lot. But, furious and tired of being constantly on the run, he changed his mind and one night took the bus home. He arrived at eleven o'clock at night. His family, having just returned from Crete, was shocked to see him arrive at that hour, especially since it was April 30, the day before May Day.

Early the next morning, the police started a house-to-house search in the neighbourhood. Soon enough, they got to Mikis' house; the first police officer to walk in was the same one Mikis had set free and ordered a comrade to escort home when they had captured the precinct in 1944. Mikis just happened to be in the house during the spot check and was picked up on old charges. He was taken to Asphaleia (security police) headquarters and thrown into a cell with fifteen others, most of whom he knew; they had been involved in a recent sabotage plot and were caught on the spot. Several days later, when more prisoners arrived, the original fifteen were put in other cells, where they remained for two months, in a state of constant tension, awaiting trial before a military tribunal. The trial came at the end of June; the fifteen accused saboteurs were all convicted and sentenced to death. Since there was no evidence that Mikis was involved in the sabotage plot, he was condemned to exile, on old charges. The exiles, handcuffed in pairs, were taken to Piraeus. Mikis was intentionally tied to another prisoner who was half his height, so that he would have to bend towards the shorter. They were all put aboard an American Liberty Ship and sent back to Ikaria. At that time of year, the sea was very rough; a few days before another ship of prisoners had gone down taking all aboard with it. The captain would come around to inspect and remind the handcuffed prisoners of the ill-fated ship, adding that they, and all "Commies," deserved to die. When their ship finally made it to Ikaria, they were taken to a camp in the village of Daphne, on the northwest coast of the island.

At first life seemed more rigid on the island than it had been at Vrakades during his first exile there. The prisoners had to spend hours at forced labour under the supervision of brutal guards. But, slowly, they adjusted to the monotony and frustrations. Occasionally, they would get together and openly discuss the theories and writings of Marx and Lenin or learn history and languages from each other. Mikis often told stories and jokes to amuse his fellow prisoners; and, as in his previous jail experience, he taught some of them music. When the authorities saw what a calm effect this had on the prisoners, they allowed him to have music sheets. He laboured on works by Beethoven, Stravinsky, and Debussy, while composing pieces of his own. The prisoners liked to be around him and would participate in the choral singing of works he taught them.

One day, a new group of prisoners was added; among them was the musicologist Phivos Anoyiannakis. As in his previous exile with Zanos, Mikis again found a companion. Together with Anoyiannakis, he worked on serious problems of composition and style. But, as the two talked, Anoyiannakis happened to mention the death of Vassilis Zanos. He had been in the same cell with Zanos, he said, on the night before he died. They had spent several hours discussing music and culture in general and concluded by singing Byzantine chants. On the following morning, Zanos was shot. He had been condemned to death for his part in the shooting of Ioannis Ladas, then Minister of Justice, who himself had ordered the shooting of thirty prisoners in Aegina on Easter Sunday, 1948. The news of Zanos' death affected Mikis profoundly. A few days later, he wrote the *Elegy and Threnody for Vassilis Za-nos,* a composition for strings, in memory of his dead friend.

This second exile in Ikaria proved most productive for Mikis. During the months that he spent at camps, first at Daphne and later at Evdilos, he added two more art songs for Myrto to *Love and Death,* which he had written in 1945, thus making it a complete cycle of four songs for voice and piano. He sketched the *Passacaglia on a Theme of the Islands* for orchestra and completed the *Preludio-Penia-Choros,* a prelude and dance for percussion, strings, and celesta, the theme for which was born from the melodies he had heard the prisoners sing. In addition, he also wrote some essays on musical problems and compiled, as well as analysed, over one hundred pop and folk songs. It was his resistance to the punishments.

December of 1948 was extraordinarily cold, and icy blasts swept over Ikaria. One day, a thunderstorm broke, tearing the prisoners' tents to shreds. Mikis' belongings—his papers and music sheets—were scattered all over the area, caught in the barbed wire or floating in puddles of water and mud. But this seemed minor in comparison with the fearful wind of news that blew over the island. All who were of age for military service were now to be transferred to the lowest point of hell—the island of Makronissos, which was already filled with political prisoners. Among the thousands of prisoners were women, children, professionals, and artists, one of whom was the poet Yiannis Ritsos.

Makronissos is a rocky, desolate island located in the strait between the island of Kea and the mines of Lavrion on the Attic coast, off Cape Sounion. Its shores are covered on all sides with stones, while the interior of the island rises sharply in a north-south mountain range. It has come to be known as "the cursed island." It was ideally suited as a prison. The ostensible reason for the establishment of a concentration camp on Makronissos was the "rehabilitation" of those who had deviated in their political loyalties. It was run as an autonomous body with the pretentious name "Institute of National Re-education." The head of "operation Macronissos" was the infamous Colonel Bairaktaris, who had spent the occupation years with royalists in the Middle East suppressing the mutinous regiments of the Greek armed forces in 1944 and imprisoning the majority there. Right after December, 1944, he appeared as head of the Makronissos concentration camp. Having acquired British training and experience in the organization of detention camps, he combined these with his native shrewdness to coordinate his "institute." Under Bairaktaris, in charge of the youth and soldiers-to-be, was the notorious officer Vassilopoulos.

The journey from Ikaria to Makronissos at the close of December, 1948, took one whole night. As soon as Mikis and the others landed at their new camp, they were rounded up under heavy guard and assigned to a regiment. The most infamous of all the regiments were the AETO, BETO, and CETO. Each of the six barbed pens was given a letter of the alphabet and subdivided in squares, each square, with its own military tents, housing fifteen men. Each letter section signified its own classification of prisoners. The first regiment consisted of the most unyielding; the second, of those who were beginning to show signs of submission; and the third, of those who had signed and were ready to defend the country against the Communists. The last were forced to convince the others, employing the same methods that had "swayed" them. Mikis was placed in the first section.

From the first moment of their arrival, all the prisoners were presented with duties and unfinished work. They were assigned to open roads, break up rock piles, build walls, and use whatever skills or vocational training they had in re-creating the "Golden Age" of Athens. This revival of ancient culture devised by the camp authorities included miniature replicas of the Parthenon, the Acropolis, and ancient theatres. They were also forced to erect buildings to house their keepers, and chambers designed for their own torture. One such quarter was built to house the most deplorable of all the Athens Military Prisons, SFA, as it was called. The guards assigned to the Athens military prisons and to the "Isolation Block" were the most barbaric in the camp. Most of them were former prisoners who had foresworn their old beliefs and had signed oaths of loyalty. In order to prove their loyalty in deed as well as in word, they became the torment-ors of their former comrades. In addition to the building of dorms and walls, each was assigned a rock that he was sup-posed to keep for his daily "exercise" periods, when he was made to walk back and forth, chain-gang fashion, carrying it on his back. These exercises would last until the "recruits" would drop from exhaustion.

But the purpose of Makronissos was not merely punitive. A series of inhuman torments was devised to break the pris-oners' spirit and make them "repent," by signing a loyalty oath condemning Communism or, if that failed, to kill them in the process. One of the most effective was deprivation of sleep. The whole island was kept ablaze with light day and night. It was practically impossible to sleep, and, if one were lucky enough to get a few moments of rest, one would imme-diately become an object of harassment by the guards. After the fitful night, the prisoners would be summoned to reveille. Lined up, half-naked or dressed according to the day, each one would be forced to say how much he liked the island. The question was usually, "Isn't the island beautiful?" to which the expected response was, "Yes!" If a prisoner replied otherwise, he would be removed from the line and tortured for "lying." Then, one by one, they would be called upon to read aloud what was written on the hills at either side of the camp: "Long live the King!" and "Long live Makronissos!" Often, an illiterate prisoner would confuse the slogans. As punishment for this, he would be tied by the genitals to an-other prisoner who had made an error. A kick to one of them would cause the other to fall and be mutilated or paralyzed with pain.

Every hour, the loudspeakers would blare out a message from the authorities. Often, it would be a speech written by those who had "repented." Another way to convince a pris-oner to atone for his "mistakes" was to make him stand at attention in a specially drawn square for twenty-four hours. If he made the slightest move, it was to be interpreted as a sign that he had changed his mind and wanted to sign. But, if he still refused to sign, he was punished for not standing as ordered. There was no end to the sadism; for, if a prisoner survived the punishment and would still not agree to the authorities' demands, he would be taken to the "theatres" to be tortured before the others. Meanwhile, the Communist Party had spread the word that anyone who signed loyalty papers would be stigmatized and completely denounced, which denunciation, in the case of many, resulted in death.

In January of 1949, close to five thousand "recruits" were gathered in a ravine for a "conference." The others were forced by the guards to fence them in all around and watch as the guards opened fire. Then, in the midst of the dead and wounded, they had to listen to a "lecture" on how wrong they were to have remained Communists, and were warned that the same fate awaited them if they did not sign the oath. When no one came forward to sign, the guards fired again. Those running for cover behind the rocks were fired upon by military police stationed nearby or from an airplane. Having no cover, they fell on each other and were asphyxiated. Some thirty prisoners survived the massacre. Of these, fifteen were condemned to death and shot on the spot. The whole regiment was decimated in one day. It was unbelievable: In that one week in January, close to five thousand men were mercilessly slaughtered. The regiment was built up again with new arrivals.

In February, the authorities began working on Mikis' regiment. Here, a different method was used, an extended three-month plan. In the early hours of the morning, the guards would bring in a victim who had signed the oath after being subjected to the most abominable tortures imaginable. The guard would yell out to all to listen, and the new "convert" would scream: "I have a message for you. They will torture you the way they tortured me. Sign! They will kill you all!" A few hours later, they would all be forced to come out and march in single file to an area behind the encampment. A lieutenant would begin the lecture with insults, curses, and vitriolic attacks on the Resistance and the "Commies." Then, in his frenzy, he would order them all to sing anthems to the glory of the King. One day, when this order was given, there was dead silence. The gendarmes fell upon the prisoners, hitting them with their cudgels. The line broke and the men started running in every direction, most of them heading south towards regiment A some five miles away. Others remained behind and were taken to the Isolation Block. A group of guards from regiment B bore down on the men escaping south, blocking their path at gunpoint. The fugitives, gradually encircled, crushed together in a headlong flight.

They reached a hilltop, but other units of guards awaited them. They were outflanked on all sides. The only exit left open to them was the sea. They stopped. A lieutenant came up ordering them, for the last time, to cry out, "Long live the King!" "Down with the banditti!" "Long live eternal Greece!" Menacingly, they were pushed closer and closer to the edge of the cliff. The lieutenant held out papers to sign: "Whoever is ready to sign, come out before it is too late." There was a break in the suspense; twelve men wanted to sign. The torturers welcomed "the new brethren," but no one else would come forth. The lieutenant ordered tortures and executions for the rest and the soldiers rushed at them with guns and bamboo poles from the tents they had just destroyed, driving the men into the sea. Some fell into the water, some stayed on the rock and were knocked unconscious by the blows directed at their heads, backs, genitals, and stomachs. The first shift of attackers exhausted itself and was replaced by new units, which continued the beating for hours. The seashore was filled with blood and human rags.

Mikis was knocked to the ground and almost trampled to death as the others stepped on him and the guards kicked and rolled him on the ground. He was left lying on the ground for several hours, until the guards came to count the dead. Mikis was found barely breathing. When he was dragged back to his tent, the archtorturer, Loris, the terror of the "Institute," arrived and demanded that Mikis sign a loyalty oath and denounce his ideas. When Mikis refused,

Loris had him strapped down on a table, and he started twisting Mikis' legs until finally a shooting pain in his right leg rendered him unconscious. Mikis was then taken to the first-aid station, where a fellow-prisoner placed him on a stretcher. Almost immediately a group of guards rushed in and began to torture him with a hot iron and beat him until he again lost consciousness. When he came to in another tent to which he had been dragged, he was again handed a paper to sign. But his arm was broken and he was unable to move or speak. Brutally the guard picked up his broken arm and forced him to make a cross on the paper with his own blood, yelling, "I'm going to save you, you faggot! Sign! Sign!" Mikis still refused. He was taken to Loris' headquarters where he was forced to wait and witness the torture that was going on. Loris handed the other man a pen with which to sign. The prisoner threw it away. A finger was chopped off. Given a second pen, the man again refused, and a second finger was chopped off, and then the rest of his right arm.

By the time Mikis' turn came, Loris was raging like a maniac, and sweating profusely. Insanely he turned on Mikis and started beating him uncontrollably, mercilessly all over his body. Mikis blacked out completely. An eye-witness account of what followed was recently related to me by a man who had been a fellow prisoner. "I was put far away from the others in isolation. One day I saw some soldiers carrying on a stretcher filled with blood, a man who was unconscious, and whose body was bluish-purple in colour. He was being taken to the morgue. A little while later, the regiment's captain, Vassilopoulos, one of the most expert torturers on Makronissos, asked me if I knew someone called Theodorakis. 'Not personally,' I answered. 'The only thing I've heard is that he is a young man with an exceptional musical talent.' 'How unfortunate,' Vassilopoulos said mockingly. 'He just died today.' "

The doctor sent to examine Mikis found him on the brink of death. He ordered an end to the torture and Mikis transferred to a hospital. Loris, satisfied with the results of his work, consented. A few days later, Mikis was taken to Lavrion, and from there to a military hospital in Athens. Shortly after his arrival, his father's cousin, Petros, a zealous rightist and on active duty as a medical colonel at the hospital, informed Yiorgos of his son's condition.

Mikis' father, unemployed since the 1946 elections, immediately left Crete, where he had taken his family after Mikis had been sentenced to exile. He picked up Myrto in Athens, and headed straight for the hospital. On arriving they found the halls packed with human bodies disfigured beyond recognition. Together the father and his cousin carefully checked all the bodies in the various wings of the building. Their search proved fruitless. On the following day, accompanied by a second doctor, they repeated their search. Desperately Mikis saw them himself, but being unable to speak or move, could not get their attention. Again they left. As a last chance, Yiorgos came back once more, this time alone. Slowly he searched through the building. Suddenly, hearing a faint moaning sound, he turned sharply. Bending down he saw it was Mikis, his jaw smashed, his body paralysed. The shock was almost more than Yiorgos could bear. He realized his impotence to do anything for his son, and silently walked out to where Myrto was waiting. They returned to Athens, and Yiorgos, overcome with profound depression, locked himself in his house for weeks. Mikis was dying. His mother suffered a nervous breakdown and was not to recover completely for over ten years.

Under these circumstances, Yiorgos took the initiative to sign the papers for Mikis and to commit himself orally to the authorities about his son's loyalty. Mikis never forgave his father for that.

It was nearly two months before Mikis was well enough to move around on crutches. His father's cousin did his best to keep Mikis from being sent back to Makronissos but had little success. One day, as Mikis was walking on his crutches, he stopped to listen to a tune a soldier was singing. He recognized it. It was one of his Resistance songs. Pleased and surprised, he asked the man where he had heard it. The soldier replied that he had heard it on the mountains of Northern Greece, sung by some women guerrillas. In the meantime, Yiorgos had been pressuring for a military tribunal to try his son's case, as he had been exiled without formal charges. The trial was held in May, and Mikis once again was condemned to go back to Makronissos. But, this time, he was demoted to the rank of auxiliary because of his poor physical state.

Once more, he took the road back to the island of death. There were four other soldier-prisoners in the same situation. They were handcuffed and taken by train to the military transfer station in Athens. From the train station, they had to go by trolley to Omonoia Square. Myrto had heard that the transfer would take place. So, early that morning, she went to wait for the train. Mikis did not know she would be there. Passers-by stared at the men with curiosity, sympathy, or hatred. As they stood in line to board the trolley, Mikis then noticed Myrto in the front. He could not believe it. She, of course, made no sign but, instead, got on the trolley and took her seat up front. Once the prisoners were safely on the trolley, the guards undid their handcuffs, so that they could grab the straps. All the time, Mikis kept looking at Myrto, and she at him, unable to speak. At the Omonoia stop, the guards hustled the four off and put their handcuffs back on. As they walked down Agiou Constantinou Street, Myrto followed along, on the opposite sidewalk. Suddenly, Mikis heard the poignant melody of one of the pop hits of that year, "We Parted One Evening," sung by the foremost *bouzouki* virtuoso of the time, Manolis Chiotis. Myrto heard it, too, and their eyes met. One of the soldiers, seeing the direction of Mikis' glance, crossed over to the other side of the street and gruffly ordered Myrto to be off.

When they arrived at the transfer station, the guards started to rough them up, beating them with their clubs. Then the four were unchained and pushed down a narrow metal stair into the lower basement of the building. It seemed as if they were going down into hell itself. At the bottom they detected a speck of light, but it turned out to be just a faint reflection of the guard's flashlight in the sewage water that was trickling out of the walls, for it was next to a cesspool. There, imprisoned in that pitchdark hell-hole, Mikis managed to survive for over a month, amidst the rats and slimy water bugs. Once a day, the prisoners had their only contact with the outside world—when the basket of meagre rations was let down from the top. There was never any explanation. of why the prisoners were there, nor how long they would stay or when they were supposed to be transferred back to Makronissos.

One day, without any warning, they were all ordered to come out. The guards shoved them into the brilliant June sun. They had been without light so long that they were almost blinded. The four were handcuffed and pushed onto an open truck, along with six others. Finally, the transfer back to Makronissos was taking place. At Keratea, the truck pulled up at a way station, and deliberately parked in the sun. The midday heat was unbearable as they sat there for hours, waiting for the driver to start up again. On the truck was a young man from Piraeus, who brought Mikis a lemonade. In harsh, Piraean tones, he said, "My name is Grigoris Bithikotsis, and I'm not afraid of anybody. Here, take this and drink it, and don't pay any attention to these shits," he added, referring to the guards. Bithikotsis was in charge of distributing water to the "recruits." He soon became a favourite with the inmates of Makronissos for his wise-guy attitude, for his cocky walk and speech, and, most of all, for the harbour songs he sang for them. Ten years later, Mikis made Bithikotsis his lead singer.

Back on Makronissos for the second time, things were not quite as bad. The guards did not bother the prisoners, and the atmosphere was calmer. A great many of the "comrades," the soldier-prisoners, had given in and the tortures had been suspended. Instead, a new, and much more subtle, method of torture, a kind of diabolical brainwashing, had been devised. The main body of the prisoners lived in tents, in groups of fourteen. Mikis was isolated in a separate area, along with another "incorrigible" Cretan. They were the only two who had been severely beaten and were thus unable to participate in the regular prison-camp programme. Instead, after their morning exercises and a meal of watery black gruel, they were brought to join the others for "Moral Training Class" at eleven in the morning. The guards would order all the captives to come listen to a new "brother" who had discovered the path to truth and light in Makronissos. In public, the "reducible" prisoner would make a speech to the other detainees and guards, condemning all his previous activities in the Resistance and concluding with praise for the King and the National Army as well as with thanks to the Makronissos authorities for guiding him on the path of righteousness. The last line was usually, "I was a Communist, now I'm a Greek. Here I saw the light, I was rebaptized." Then the prisoner was allowed to join the National Army to fight the leftists or, in rare instances, given a one- or two-day leave to visit his family; or, he would be made a torturer of other "fallen" Greeks, his co-prisoners who had not yet repented. These orations were a daily event. During that summer, Mikis had a chance to communicate with his old torturer, Loris, on a human level. One day, Loris saw Mikis standing alone, visibly exhausted from dragging himself around on crutches in the broiling sun. He walked up to him. "How's your leg? You think you will be left crippled?" "I don't think so," Mikis answered. "Come," said Loris, "I'll give you some lemonade, or maybe some yoghourt." He took him to the "Kitchen." The other prisoners were surprised to see this, and started coming closer. Loris shooed them away, and carried on with what he was saying. "This is a bad situation. . . . Nothing can be done. It's been going on too long." Then, looking Mikis in the eye: "What do you think?" Mikis shook his head and said nothing. Loris let him go. Mikis realized years later how insane the man must have been. In his old age, he voted for the leftwing party of EDA.

The psychological torture of the other prisoners was beginning to yield results. The "recruits" were slowly broken. Every day, they were given telephone books and told to send a letter to any address in their native village or in the capital, saying that, in Makronissos, they had found light, were rebaptized, and had become good Christians, good Greeks. "You don't know me," the letter to the unknown receiver would conclude, "but I am telling you that this is a fact. I was a Communist. Long live the King, God bless my brethren-teachers. Yours, in

Christ." Then, the soldier-prisoners would be forced to buy the stamps for the countless envelopes. Each letter was numbered and registered with a guard; the more letters written, the better the conduct report. The letters were first sent to priests all over the country, and the standard ending was, "Believe me, your Eminence." Before long, "Believe me, your Eminence," became a catch-word around the camp, and the prisoners would repeat it in unison.

Mikis now was constantly suffering seizures. He would black out and fall to the ground, and come to hours later, not knowing what had happened. He was given injections to bring him back, but there was no over-all improvement. Yet, in spite of this complication, and his crutches, he persisted in trying to do something with his music. He located a few "recruits" who had instruments, an extraordinarily rare thing in a concentration camp, and, with guitars and violins, he held the first performance of his *Elegy and Threnody for Vassilis Zanos* for his regiment. During this period, he did a musical study of songs and symphonic works and composed some of his own. He thus compiled a large selection of Greek songs and sketches of his own ideas that he worked on and developed years later. Once again, Mikis became the centre of attention in the camp. In addition to their interest in his music, the prisoners, having exhausted their vocabularies in the daily letter-writing, would come to him for new expressions and words.

Besides the letter-writing, the prisoner was supposed to become an orator on the subject of his transformation into a loyal subject of King and country. When the royal family paid an occasional visit to the "Institute of National Re-education," parades and celebrations were organized in their honour, and those who had been "educated" and "converted" participated and were shown off to the other "recruits" and specially invited dignitaries. While these sham procedures took place at Makronissos, hundreds of Greeks were being killed in the mountains. The guards loved to pass on the news of how the Communists were being defeated and all their friends killed.

Mikis' health continued to deteriorate. The seizures became more frequent. His chest now began to hurt; he would often feel weak and dizzy. News of his serious state reached his cousin, and pressure was brought to bear on the director of the Athens Military Centre to get him discharged. On August 1, he was released.

Mikis boarded the transfer boat to Lavrion with fear and disbelief. Was he really leaving that cursed island? He refused to look back. The only thing that was important was to get away as fast as possible. He arrived in Athens, a complete mental and physical wreck. The first thing he did was to look for Myrto. He headed straight for the university. A classmate of Myrto's saw him and let out a shriek at his emaciated appearance. She ran to the lab where Myrto worked, to warn her what a sight Mikis was. Stunned, Myrto rushed out to meet him. Her once tall and handsome "pelican" was disfigured almost beyond recognition. She burst into tears.

After many minutes, she pulled herself together, happy that he was still alive, and they left to find a place for him to stay. Neither she nor his uncle could shelter him without endangering their lives. They went from hotel to hotel, but their search was in vain: No place would take him in with his ID card indicating his Communist affiliation and the frightful sight he was to look at. At last, a musician friend suggested that Mikis use his bachelor flat in the red light district.

After a week in his friend's apartment, Mikis decided to go to Crete, where the climate was healthier and his mother could nurse him. The reunion with his family was like the miracle of Lazarus' resurrection.

# 3

# Recuperation and Creativity, 1950–60

The campaign against the guerrillas and their strongholds in Northern Greece came to an end with a truce on October 16, 1949, but the struggle of the Greek people for freedom and a true share in the policies of their country did not cease. Not a single basic issue, such as representation in Parliament of all parties or abolition of the security measures, had changed, after nearly five years of civil strife. Certainly, no one in any of the governments of that period had seriously reflected on how to modernize the country's political and social institutions so that Greece could rise on its own feet. The United States spent lavishly in Greece under the Truman Doctrine, and Greece became heavily dependent on U.S. subsidies. But, although the failure to recover can be blamed on the drain of the Civil War by those who do not want to face the issue squarely, the real obstacles to recovery lay in the attitudes of those in power. No effort was made to analyse the problems of finance, and of

*78*

genuine representation in the elections, or to check the constant scandals involving public embezzlement. Politicians had one goal: to get into office and to stay there. They had one obligation: to reward those who had gotten them in. An extraordinary document reflecting this attitude is the portrait of Spyros Markezinis, who later was to figure so crucially in the Papadopoulos takeover, given by *Time* magazine May 23, 1949:

> He has a somewhat satanic profile, sports a silver cigarette case with the inscription "Machiavelli," was recently involved in a black market scandal. . . . His ideas on how to straighten out Greece's economy are at least provocative. He once told a U.S. official: "Income tax? Hell, no. It would never work in Greece. I'd go where the money is—for example, the Federation of Greek Industries. I'd say, 'I need 20 million drachmas by next Wednesday'—and I'd get it."

The agony of a decade resulted in the victory of the past.

For nearly six months, Mikis remained on the island of Crete trying to put the past behind, and become a human being again. The brutalities he had witnessed and endured remained vivid in his mind and his thoughts were like an ever-turning kaleidoscope, each shifting pattern more horrible than the one before. He was free of this hell only when buried in his music, working out arrangements for pieces, and writing down his thoughts about what music should be like if it were to be a true product of its times. Slowly he returned to his old self and began thinking about the future. Of first importance was getting a job. For too long, he had been a drain on his father who was finding it difficult to practice his profession in the tiny village of Kato Galata, or even the larger town of Chania. There was no dearth of lawyers established in the area for years, and even though Yiorgos had been born there, his many years away from home and the fact that he had lived for a long time in Athens made him suspect to the traditional village milieu. He had had to sell the little real estate that he possessed, together with family heirlooms, in order to keep the family alive.

After much talking, visiting, interviewing, and many moments of despair, Mikis finally got a job as a music teacher with administrative duties in the Chania Music School. But in spite of the grand-sounding title, "Professor of Music at the Chania Conservatory," the job was a farce. He had only two students to teach. Moreover, the pretensions of grandeur in the provincial town made him sick inside. The people showed how "cultured" they were in their love of the tango, the Italian *canzona*, or the German *Lieder,* while scorning the wealth of their native song. Mikis was particularly incensed by the scorn for the *rebetic*, or city-song, an outgrowth of the hashish joints. Why this scorn for the native music of Greece? Why had the Athens Conservatory never taken note of this music? Why should he be forced to teach, in an insignificant music school, the elements of Western harmony to two uninterested students?

In the fall of 1949, Mikis sat down to write his first articles on Greek music in an attempt to point out the relationship between the people and their music and to trace its history. Three articles, for which he was paid all of 50 drachmas ($1.50) per article, were serialized in the bi-weekly *Simerini Epochi* (Modern Era), in October and November and constituted a compilation of his studies and reflections on the particular Greek type of music of the *bouzouki.* What upset him was the notion that there should be one kind of music for the educated and "cultured" and another for the working man or the peasant in the village. "The people want to sing their sorrows and joys," he wrote, "and since the contemporary composers do not offer them what Schubert and Verdi offered their own countries, they go on singing their own songs. And thus it is that today we have official Greek music for the cultured residents of the large centres and *laik* (music of the people) music for virtually the rest of the Greek population."[1]

He tried to analyse the development of the popular rebetico song from Byzantine times, pointing out the importance of

[1] Mikis Theodorakis, "The Modern Laik Song," *Simerini Epochi* (October 9, October 23, November 7, 1949) reprinted in his collected essays, *Yia tin Elliniki Mousiki* (On Greek Music), Athens, 1961, 157-169.

the melody in this type of music. Melody was the chief contribution of the *laik* song, for the lyrics, he admitted, were
often trivial. Nevertheless, even these were related to the
character of the Greek people, showing their innate gentleness, pride, and dignity. The popular music not only showed
the way to creative assimilation of folk and Byzantine music,
but could provide a new type of genuine Greek music if the
melody and harmony were properly assimilated.

Such revolutionary ideas fell on deaf ears in those days
when the major problem was stabilization of national life and
finding a solution to the havoc wrought by ten years of war.
Bitterly frustrated in his artistic hope in Chania, and rootless
—with only 600 drachmas ($20) in his pocket, the suit on his
back, and his musical compositions—Mikis decided to head
back to Athens to see Economidis, his old music teacher. The
professor was filled with horror as Mikis poured out to him
the whole story of the brutal months on Makronissos. He encouraged his former student to finish the work for the degree
and take his last two exams. Mikis passed with flying colours,
and on January, 1950, he graduated *cum laude* from the
Conservatory.

Economidis had asked Mikis if he had any works ready for
performance, that he could rehearse with the State Orchestra.
Mikis immediately gave him the *Feast of Assi-Gonia*, which he
had started in 1945, and had worked on sporadically ever
since. Having at last completed the orchestration, he was con-
fident that the work was ready to be performed. Economidis
was enthusiastic; but fate was against them. In early February,
without warning, Mikis was recalled to the army, on the
grounds that he had been discharged as an invalid in August,
and had not completed his two years' obligatory duty in the
service.

Back again he went to the Athens Military Centre for re-
assignment. First, he had to sign a statement declaring his
obedience to the established order and renouncing all the
enemies of the fatherland. Mikis refused, however, and was
again assigned to Makronissos, the only place for "incorrigi-
bles." He had two days of grace, in which to say goodbye. In

those two days, Yiorgos worked feverishly to prevent his son
from having to return to Makronissos. There was one string
which could be pulled. It was the eve of elections. The Minister of Justice, General Napoleon Zervas, was running for
office at the head of the National Party of Greece of the National Resistance, as he called it, which he had formed in
1946. Yiorgos went to see a distant cousin of his, who was in
charge of the Supply Base of the Athens Military Centre and
who was on good terms with Zervas. There was just a possibility that, if the cousin went to see Zervas and promised him
votes from Yiorgos' home town in Crete, the Minister would
be willing to help in Mikis' case.

An appointment was set up; Yiorgos' cousin gave the whole
story and begged Zervas to intervene. Zervas agreed, and immediately wrote a letter to the officer in charge of the Centre. The letter produced results. Mikis was released and dispatched to serve with his cousin at the Supply Base.

Since his cousin's military post was not far from Athens,
Mikis could get leave every so often to go into the city. Economidis was determined to perform the *Feast of Assi-Gonia*;
a date was set, May 5. Mikis' enthusiasm knew no bounds.
This was the first time he was to have one of his compositions
played by a whole symphony orchestra—"a mythological
beast," as he called it. On the day of the first rehearsal, he was
given leave. All his musician friends, who had helped in one
way or another to persuade the artists to play for the first
rehearsal, were in high spirits. After giving out the music,
Mikis sat down in the front row, jubilantly awaiting the first
sound of his work. Unfortunately, however, Economidis had
been too busy the previous month with administrative problems and had neglected to look over the score. What followed,
then, was a sight performance by everyone. The arrangement
and the whole orchestration were badly done due to the circumstances Mikis had been working on it all the years in
prison and in hiding. The first rehearsal, despite Economidis'
efforts, was a complete fiasco.

The next day, the old professor begged Mikis to come to
his home to talk the whole thing over, admitting that the

orchestra had not done the work justice. The music had power. he said, and the arrangement was good, but the work needed polishing. The two then sat down and began to go over it, page by page. For two days, they worked at ironing out the problems. The third day, they were ready for rehearsal again.

The fateful day arrived. Mikis remembers that, as he sat waiting for the performance to begin, the echoes of Crete, and of all the years of suffering, went round and round in his mind. "I had to touch the land of Crete. The rhythms and the dances, the figures of the dancers, the *lyra* and *mandola*, the *mandinades*, the scent of wine mingled with honeysuckle and lemon trees, the girls and the sea, a world of its own, free in a space outside of space and time, suspended between the sky and the sea."[2] All the years of work were justified that night; Economidis was at his best, and the performance proved a smashing success. Mikis was inundated with congratulations; the audience urged him to stand up and take a bow. But Mikis demurred—not out of stage fright or emotion, although, to be sure, he was deeply moved. The reason, rather, lay elsewhere: On that very morning, his old, worn belt had suddenly given way; with neither time nor money to buy another, he went to the concert hall beltless, never expecting he would be asked to stand, clutching at his trousers, while hundreds of eyes remained riveted on him. Yet, it is not often one is rewarded with such public acclaim. Bravely, he rose, quickly thanked the audience for their enthusiastic response, and then ducked away. The next day, he was wildly praised by the press. Economidis was overjoyed; his faith in the young composer had been fully vindicated. For Mikis, May 5, 1950, was the happiest day of his life, and 5 (5/5/50) has always been his lucky number in life.

As a result of his musical triumph, the military authorities

2 Theodorakis *op. cit.* (supra note 1) 275. *Lyra* is a small three-stringed instrument kept from ancient times by the Cretans and the Greeks of Pontos. It is played by a bow lying parallel to the human body on the knee. *Mandola*, a string instrument plunked at with a feather, is somewhere between the mandolin and the lute. *Mandinades* are the distinct rhyming songs so peculiarly Cretan. They are sung at a girl's window by her lover and his friends. They are remnants of Venetian songs.

assigned Mikis to direct the military band. But, instead of a pleasure, it turned out to be a torment. The commander of the unit, an unsuccessful musician himself, did everything he could to make life miserable for Mikis. Whenever there was not a musical engagement, the commander would find a pretext to sentence Mikis to KP duty, loading and unloading hundred-pound slabs of ice. In addition to the strain of his back, the muscles in his arms became severely strained, and his fingers lost their dexterity for playing the piano. In view of these circumstances, Mikis asked his cousin to try to have him sent somewhere else. In early October of 1950, Mikis was shipped to Alexandroupolis, a port in Thrace near the Turkish border.

Mikis arrived before his record could be sent to the outpost. The general in charge was delighted to greet someone who appeared a cut above the ex-Communists under his command. He entrusted Mikis with the files on the soldiers and other secrets, advising him to have nothing to do with the men, as they were all Communists who had served prison terms. But, a week later, when Mikis' own file arrived, the general went into a rage. He ordered Mikis' head shaved, and locked him in the stockade until he could be sent back to Makronissos.

In the underground cell, another prisoner who was awaiting the same fate told Mikis that the only way out was somehow to appear deranged, so that he would have to be sent to a mental hospital. The trick was to swallow just enough gunpowder to become totally incapacitated. Mikis didn't like the idea; besides, the fits dormant since the Makronissos trials could occur at any moment. But, when the other soldier went through with the plan, and got transferred, Mikis, unable to bear the prospect of going back to Makronissos, finally decided to swallow a large dose of the powder himself. He passed out immediately. Hours later, he came to in a military hospital in Thessaloniki. At first, he was placed in a clinic with heart patients, since the psychiatric ward was filled to capacity. There, he was placed by himself in a huge room; left alone, he leisurely began to read Dostoyevsky's novel *Crime and Punishment,* which an attendant had given to him. In a few days, however, a patient in the psychiatric ward was shipped out, and Mikis had to move in. He has never forgotten the eerie atmosphere. The attendants, having no other treatment, were beating the patients to keep them quiet. The screams and groans he had to live with caused relapses of his early seizures. But, three weeks later, his father found a doctor to certify that Mikis was mentally ill and should therefore be sent home to recuperate. Yet, instead of being discharged, he was transferred to Firka, the military base outside Chania. Here, his duty was to guard the warehouse, where munitions, gasoline, and wood were kept.

Although still in the service, he at least was not far from his family, whom he was able to see fairly often. At Firka, he would sit for hours staring out at the sea from his sentry post at the top of the hill. The Cretan sea has a specially soothing, mesmerizing effect, in the way the waves wash ceaselessly against the shore, seeming to sweep over the sand with an eternal caress. In these surroundings, he began slowly to recuperate. Moreover, as the Civil War began to die down, conditions at the camp became more and more relaxed. He would even write down music and melodic lines while on duty. One of the more inquisitive sergeants at the base would see him making black dots on lines, when he was supposed to be keeping records of stores. Glancing a mite suspiciously at the pieces of paper on the table, he would ask, "What're you scribbling, eh? Here, what's this black dot with a tail?" Mikis would answer calmly, "Those are the molecules of gasoline." "And what's this vertical line, eh?" "That? The sign for No. 10 oil, of course!" Satisfied, the sergeant would nod and saunter off. No doubt about it, Mikis was a good, diligent soldier.

In his off-duty hours, Mikis would turn in earnest to his music, always, in times of distress, his one solace, and try to improve his earlier compositions. He selected passages from his *Elegy and Threnody for Vassilis Zanos,* which he had written on Makronissos, and developed them, having now acquired a greater understanding of orchestration. Renaming it, simply, the *First Symphony,* he dedicated the work to

Zanos, a leftist, and Makis Karlis, a rightist. Using his own poem, *December and After,* which he had had distributed in pamphlet form under the pseudonym "Lyrolykis," he wrote a work based on those days of struggle. He also wrote a song-cycle, *Five Cretan Songs,* which was performed in Chania later that year. In an amazing way, these songs caught the spirit of Crete—its rhythms and melodies, the fighting tradition of its heroic people, and the wild beauty of its language.

An atmosphere of ease and camaraderie prevailed in the Greek Army following the Civil War years. The rightists and the militarists had won; America was now keeping them afloat; and all they had to do was guard the provisions America sent. In fact, there was a lot of non-guarding done, for supplies were constantly stolen and sold to the people, from which activity many of the soldiers and officers got rich. There were several men in Mikis' unit who had been in the Resistance, and were thus under surveillance. But this was little more than routine. Mikis was often invited to play for the officers' parties, since he was a pianist. Often, soldiers even drove leftist deputies around in military vehicles. Everyone expected an amnesty law would be passed soon, after which reconstruction could begin, at last, after a decade of war and bloodshed.

January, 1952, saw the end of Mikis' tortured years of military service. It was an experience that marked him for life and could not help bursting forth in all his music. He returned to Athens to try his luck once more at a musical career. The problem of finding a job, even with a degree, was no easy matter. Greece was still in the throes of an economic depression, and one with Mikis' political background was among those least likely to be hired, should there be an opening anywhere. But, for the first time since the war, Mikis was at least free of the terror of police and sudden arrest. He began to seek out his old acquaintances in the artistic world, while looking for professional assignments. As his family was still in Crete, he found lodgings with an old friend, Michalis Katsaros. Another friend from earlier days, Rita Boumi-

Papa, offered him a job writing the tunes for her children's poems, which she played on her morning hour radio programme. For each song, he received 50 drachmas. Concurrently, Mikis began compiling melodies for school children, for he believed that children should be trained as early as possible. Through Boumi-Papa's connection, he managed to put on several radio broadcasts of his own about Greek music.

His next break came with assignments to write critical reviews for various liberal and leftist newspapers that were sympathetic to his progressive ideas; they paid him between 50 and 100 drachmas for each review. Mikis wrote many of his articles under the pseudonym "Daphnïotis," as a reminder of the village on Ikaria, Daphne, where he had been exiled the second time in May, 1948. For articles in *Avghi* and the Cretan journal *Kyrix,* however, he used his real name. From June, 1952, to July, 1953, his output was prolific. Fourteen of the most representative of these articles were reprinted in 1961 in a volume of essays on music, *Yia tin Elliniki Mousiki* (On Greek Music); they are a storehouse of knowledge on all aspects of Greek music, from the artists to the critics and to the nature of music itself.

In his early articles, the thrust of his polemics was directed against established musical practices. He attacked the hidebound policies perpetuated by the Conservatory and lingering nineteenth-century attitudes. In an article in *Avghi* on June 23, he attacked the continuing preoccupation of the orchestras and older conductors with romantic Germanic compositions. "We ought to change the title of our Athens State Orchestra to the 'State Beethoven Organization,' so that we could be rid of our illusions and they [the entrenched musical establishment] could be rid of our grumblings."[3] He made it quite clear, however, that it was not Beethoven whom he was attacking but the Greek musicians who should turn to other schools—the French, the Russian, or the American—for their inspiration and repertory. He concluded by saying that even those Greek works that were included in the orchestral repertory had nothing to do with Greece. Mikis

3 *Ibid.,* 33.

suggested that, if Greeks were to create a "National School of Music," then they must perform continuously, en masse, the works of the younger artists. Only thus would it be possible to bring about a necessary self-awareness, to create a fruitful, competitive climate, and hence to attract larger audiences.

To show critics that he could practice what he preached, he began working with the Elliniko Chorodrama, a dance company founded by individual artists, such as Dora Stratou, Rallou Manou, Manos Hadjidakis, and others in 1950. Then, he started to work on the ballet *Orpheus and Euridice*. When the score was ready, Economidis offered him the opportunity of rehearsing it with the State Orchestra, so that he might make any changes he deemed necessary. The work was performed in May, 1952, at Mycenae, choreographed by Manou and directed by Hadjidakis, and was greatly acclaimed.

At the same time he was engaged in these commitments, he was doing consultation work with the National Broadcasting Corporation's orchestra. His talents were discovered by Lykoudis, the director of the National Theatre, who hired him to work on musical arrangements for the staging of ancient drama. He also arranged the background music for Hadjidakis' *Midsummer Night's Dream*, which was staged by Karolos Koun.

In a second work with the Chorodrama, his *Greek Carnival*, which he began sketching in 1948, Mikis, for the first time in his career, incorporated themes from pop songs, one of which had been written by his uncle, Antonis, and another by the melodist Yiannis Papaioannou that told of the legendary adventures of Captain Andreas Zepos. Because of its "folkloric" themes, the work later became especially popular with European audiences. Its loose construction of plot, with different dance groups participating freely in the carnival, permitted Mikis to use melodic elements from all regions of Greece—the folk, the pop, the romantic Athenian *cantada,* and even a theme from Prokofiev.

In addition to these two ballet works, Mikis' *Sonatina No. 1,* for violin and piano, and his *Sextet,* for flute, piano, and strings, both composed during his student days (1945-

46), were performed by the National Broadcasting (EIR) Orchestra. Both works, especially the sonatina, incorporate Greek elements and Western technique.

Among those impressed by Mikis' involvement with the problems of music in Greece was Yiannis Xenakis, who, condemned *in absentia* by a military tribunal, was now living in Paris. He sent Mikis a few of his own compositions, including *Ziyia,* through an acquaintance in Athens, and asked him to make an evaluation of them in his columns. He wanted to know, also, whether there was any possibility of their being performed in Athens. Finally, he appealed to him to see whether anything could be done for his safe return to Greece. Little did he know, though, what problems Mikis himself was having. Mikis, however, did try to do whatever he could but his attempts could not go beyond the leftist artistic circles in Athens.

In the summer of 1953, Mikis' *Feast of Assi-Gonia* was performed by the Athens State Orchestra in the theatre Herodus Atticus, where it was again warmly received. In the audience was a committee of Greek Americans who were so impressed with the work that they asked Dimitri Mitropoulos to speak to Mikis on their behalf. They were anxious to have Mikis perform at the music festival in Salt Lake City. The news of this honour was quickly spread by other jealous Greek composers, and the United States was promptly informed of Mikis' Communist affiliations. Shortly thereafter, the American Consul summoned Mikis and told him that he had received instructions not to allow Mikis to give performances in the United States. When Mikis informed Mitropoulos, the conductor asked Mikis to give him the work, at least, and he would see what could be done. But he could not exert very much influence, and nothing came of the invitation. Thus, the first attempt to export Mikis' work to the United States was thwarted by the State Department.

By now, Mikis had begun to explore another area of the arts—the cinema. In early 1953, he signed his first contract with the Greek American producer, Gregory Tallas, who was then directing *Barefoot Battalion*. This film, with its subject the Occupation years, the Resistance, and the beginning of the Civil War, seemed almost too real for Mikis. There was no problem of writing a score for it. At the same time, he was working on a score for a Greek film, *Eva*. With the money he earned from these two films, he was able, for the first time in his life, to live like a human being. It was then, too, that he finally decided he was secure enough in his profession to ask Myrto to marry him after ten difficult years. On March 18, 1953, Myrto Altinoglou became Myrto Theodorakis (and not the other way around, as she had insisted in her youth). The poet Notis Pergialis served as best man at the wedding, which was attended by many friends and fellow artists. Myrto had just received her degree from the School of Medicine; Mikis was to become her first patient.

He had already made up his mind that it was important for him to study in Europe, for, without foreign study, he felt he would never be able to get beyond the provincialism of Athens. Both husband and wife, therefore, decided to apply to the French Government for scholarships—the one to study music at the Conservatoire de Paris, and the other to specialize in radiology at the Fondation Curie. Both were given three-year grants, but, at the last minute, the Greek government prevented Mikis' departure, planned for December, because of his Resistance activities and subsequent arrests and exile. Economidis was incensed at this rebuff to his favourite student, and he and other influential friends brought pressure to bear on the administration to reverse its decision. At last, in February, 1954, the two were permitted to leave. The new world that lay before them would be filled with events, intense study, new friends, even international fame, but, above all, the discovery of what it was to be Greek.

## PARIS: THEODORAKIS' ARTISTIC RESOLUTION

Upon their arrival in Paris, Mikis and Myrto knew two things: that, having belonged to each other for so many years, they could at last live together in peace; and that their studies would consume most of their time and attention. They moved into a small hotel near the Sorbonne and at once settled down to work. Myrto continued to perfect her French and concentrate on her studies at the Fondation Curie, but, for the most part, she limited her own time and joys in deference to Mikis'. She had the added responsibility of watching Mikis' health closely, since the tuberculosis he had contracted during his exiles required special care. They spent that whole first season feverishly concentrating on their work and adjusting to their new surroundings, not even once going to see a film in that most artistically challenging of cities.

Mikis registered at the Conservatoire de Paris in Olivier Messiaen's class of musical analysis and studied conducting under Eugène Bigot. The composer and teacher, Pierre Ancelin, from the first days of their acquaintance became the couple's closest friend and companion. Not much later, however, they took up temporary lodging in a small apartment on rue Pelleport belonging to a Greek woman, Mme. Theodor, a refugee from Smyrna, who was married to an Englishman. She offered them a place at the pension used by her son, who at the time was studying in England. But here Mikis had no freedom of action; he needed privacy and free time to work, and he soon found the attraction of the Latin Quarter, the centre of Paris' artistic community, irresistible.

Soon, however, the young couple, attracted increasingly to the Latin Quarter and its artistic and intellectual milieu, found a small flat there. Mikis plunged immediately into a hectic round of activity. He began an exhaustive search for his own method and aesthetics of composition and performance. With Pierre Ancelin, he analysed extensively the works of Igor Stravinsky and Bela Bartok, with the purpose of finding their inspiring forces and the aesthetic rules in them. Besides the Russian folk element in Stravinsky's compositions Mikis liked the Russian composer's use of antique subjects and Greek myths, and the heroic manner in which he dressed them in neoclassical garb. Mikis' thorough musical research into the folk music of Bartok, on the other hand, urged him to do the same with the Greek tradition. It was Bartok who em-

ployed various ancient scales and abandoned traditional dia-
tonic systems to indulge in treating the twelve tones of the
chromatic scales as separate entities. Moreover, Mikis found
guidance to his own research and aesthetic in the influence
of ancient folk music in Bartok. The ancient melodic line
and the Byzantine *gamma* (scale) set the foundation for Mikis' interest in the tetrachord and the Greek modes around
the G scale, which gave him great melodic and rhythmic freedom in his own compositions.

But, although he admired the aesthetics of Stravinsky and
Bartok, as well as the French musical techniques, he wanted
even more to vitalize and express the traditional Greek musical soul. He tried writing Greek symphonic works with
Occidental technique. This resulted in a prolific number of
new pieces.

In short, Mikis never forgot Greece. In the spring of 1954
he sent his *Greek Carnival,* completed, to the Elliniko Chorodrama Company of Rallou Manou. A few weeks later, the
company was invited by the Italian Government to perform
this and other works. And, in the winter of that year, the
Greek public heard, for the second time, one of Mikis' most
powerful works, the *First Symphony,* premiered by the State
Orchestra of Athens under the direction of Andreas Paridis.
Although the audience received the youthful and thematically original work warmly, most of the Athenian critics did
not bother to review it. The few who did found it weak.

Mikis' consuming interest in musical creation extended to
collaboration with Xenakis. They began working together,
showing their compositions to each other. Mikis was the first
to be shown Xenakis' *Metastasis* and *Pithoprakta.* The two
worked on technical problems with Chronopoulos, a musician
from Greece whom Mikis had taken in, but what interested
them most was Greek musical education and the creation of a
national style of composition. In 1955, Xenakis wrote a series
of articles for the Athenian leftist periodical *Epitheorisi Technis,* exposing the failure to establish a "School of Greek
Music" and attacking the musicologists and composers who
had failed to investigate the roots of Greek music. But Xenakis

became more attracted to the aesthetics of Boulez and Messiaen and he and Mikis came to a parting of the ways.

In the same year Mikis was debating theories of composition and performance with Xenakis, he made his first public appearance in Paris. In August, 1955, at the Cortot Hall of the Ecole Nationale de Musique, he presented his *Sonatina for Piano,* a small chamber piece that the critics found gentle and a little folkloric. Mikis was not very pleased with the critics' views, for his sonatina was intended to be a product of his research on the Occidental method. He next composed the *Suite No. 1,* for piano and orchestra in four parts: allegro, andante sostenuto, allegro, and calmo. The orchestration was typically Theodorakean: strings, tympani, and woodwinds. The composition, inspired by Cretan musical elements, was the answer the composer had been seeking in his quest for an aesthetic path. Commenting on the idea that inspired the work, Mikis has said: "Crete is a music that advances on rhythms of steel. The rhythms support high in the air melodic schemes, embroidered on an endless multicoloured canvas. And, suddenly, now you hear a scream, and then a sigh. The blood, excited, quickly waters the flowers in vine-props and then feeds on love in the feasts."[4] It was his Cretan inheritance, his "Greekness," that would not leave him, even while writing in the Western scales.

Mitropoulos was in Paris at that time, and Mikis called on him and to show him the composition. Mitropoulos took an immediate interest in Mikis and told him that, since 1953, when the State Department had prohibited Mikis from performing in America, he himself had spoken to various people about his case. Mitropoulos took the suite and studied it carefully. Impressed, he suggested a few possible changes from a conductor's point of view. Then, their conversation proceeded from the piece at hand to the musical problems in Greece, in general. Mitropoulos urged Mikis to go back to Greece. He felt that all the Greek musicians studying abroad were needed more at home, where they had a valuable contribution to make. With a view towards possible collaboration

4 Theodorakis, *op. cit.* (supra n. 1) 275-276.

together, Mitropoulos asked Mikis to meet him in London, where he would be working, when he had some works for him to perform.[5] Mikis, however, had promised the *Suite* to Andreas Paridis, who conducted it in Athens, in April, 1957, with the State Orchestra and Jean Vigné at the piano. It was not received well by the Athenian critics. But it won a golden award for the young composer at the Moscow Music Festival.

On May 7, Economidis, with whom Mikis had never stopped corresponding while in Paris, wrote a very warm letter.

> The creator, beyond his own Truth, which he expresses as he himself perceives it, must await his vindication with the passage of time, and even this is uncertain. . . . That is why I avoided writing to you anything about your last work, *Suite No. 1.* Neither the general clamour (never in my experience as a manager have I received so many cutting letters, with especially the critics in the lead) nor my own opinion, whatever that might be, is of any real importance.
>
> I believe that young people like yourself should not concern themselves with replying to the critics. I consider it a weakness and therefore would never have done it myself. But this is a matter of personal judgment, and, since you decided to do so, you acted rightly. . . . I congratulate you, however, for your faith in your own beliefs. This is a great virtue. Therefore, continue on your path and my wishes are always with you.

In his reply, Mikis admitted his great obligation to his mentor, and, at the same time, declared his future plans vis-à-vis Greece. Then he gave his opinion on critics: "As far as the Greek critics are concerned, my views are diametrically opposed to yours. I'll tell you why. You start with the premise that you are dealing with true critics, but I am positive that they are no more than charlatans."[6] He vowed to return to Greece and fight, adding, "The work will give the answer."

Economidis died in December, 1957. As a tribute to him, Mikis wrote a second version of *Oedipus Tyrannus,* the sym-

[5] They did meet in London, in 1957, when Mikis had gone there to sign a contract for the film, *Ill Met by Moonlight.* But, since both were very busy, nothing concrete came of the meeting. Mitropoulos died a few years later.

[6] Both letters serve as introduction to Theodorakis' book (supra n. 1) 13.

phonic work of 1946. He arranged the new version as a
chamber piece, scored for three violins, one viola, one violon-
cello, and one contrabass. It was an attempt at an interplay
between the ancient mode and Western technique. The
piece fills the listener with an awareness of the tragic element
of the ancient drama. No doubt this is because, in the *Oedipus Tyrannus,* we encounter the expression in music of an
epoch that moved Mikis deeply—the Occupation and the
years that followed the Civil War. The work was the most
personal of all up to now and the most important. For in Mikis' works up to this point, the classical element had been approached through the Byzantine mode and the Greek folk
melody. Yet, perfection and clarity came with the music
written for the ancient drama, and this work served as the link
between the two aesthetics.

Mikis sent the work to the State Orchestra of Athens, which
was going to give a concert in memory of Economidis. Paridis undertook production of the work, giving it a striking interpretation on December 8, 1958. One of the critics who
attended the premiere commented:

> In such a serious programme, suitable for this occasion of
> mourning, the most interesting of all was *Oedipus Tyrranus,* by
> Mikis Theodorakis. . . . It is a serious work, in which the melo-
> dic element prevails, with a Byzantine harmonization, reveal-
> ing the unusual sensitivity of this young Greek composer, and
> demonstrating in a novel manner the originality of his talent.[7]

Then followed the *Suite No. 2,* for orchestra and chorus
(words by Varnalis), written in 1956 and performed in 1958
by the Orchestre National de France. Two more performances took place at the Herodus Atticus theatre, during the
Athens Festival—the first in 1956, and the second, conducted
by Chorofas, in 1958. *Suite No. 3–The Mother,* for orchestra, soprano, and chorus, and drawn from Dionysios Solo-
mos' poem, "The Insane Mother," was completed in the
same year. These were followed by the *Suite No. 4–Images
d'Antigone,* for violin and orchestra, which has never been
performed, another *Piano Concerto,* presented at the Ecole

[7] Avra D. Theodoropoulou's review in *Kainouryia Epochi,* Winter, 1958, 149.

Normale in 1958, and the well-known *Sonatina No. 2*, for violin and piano. The last is one of the most impressive compositions of this period, lyrical in mood, with vivacity and a blithe and merry gusto that echoes especially in the parts where the violin plays melodic rhythms from the Greek islands. During this period, Mikis also completed the first version of *The Cycle*—six demotic songs for piano and voice—and various other symphonic compositions, together with sketches of chamber pieces.

In all these works, he "narrated," in his personal style, the past and his own experiences. Three of the four suites he wrote while in Paris have one predominant theme, that of the "heroic death," which also inspired the *First Symphony*. The composer himself has remarked:

> The "heroic death" is, I think, the problem that has mostly influenced, more than anything else, our generation. Under one or another state, we were forced to confront far more than ten continuous years, in the blossom of our youth, a whole chain of "sacrifices" that often, as a natural and fateful resultant, had this death—the "heroic," that is—the unbelievable and incomprehensible.[8]

The period between 1954 and 1960, when Mikis was wavering between Greece and Europe, was the most productive so far. Twenty-one works were completed in Paris, while twenty-three, in all (seven from his Greek years), were performed.

During those years, as Mikis progressed in his studies, Myrto finished her specialization in radiology and continued to work as an assistant to Dr. Baclaez at the Hôpital Curie. But, contrary to her acknowledged competence (Dr. Baclaez would even trust some of his patients to her care), the job had its disadvantages. It demanded long hours at the hospital every day, after which she would run home in the evening and start her household routine. She would drop off her briefcase full of research notes, do her grocery shopping and errands, and then come back and cook for Mikis. Her social life was virtually nil, as her whole existence revolved around

8 Theodorakis, *op. cit.* (supra n. 1) 276.

the hospital and her home. And, since the couple's combined income—hers from the assistanceship and his from scholarships and loans—was barely enough to make ends meet in Paris, Myrto many times suggested that they return to Greece. Then came the great opportunity from London.

Early in 1955, Mikis was introduced by Mme. Theodor, his landlady on rue Pelleport, to the producers Emeric Pressburger and Michael Powell, who had just come from London with their technicians en route to Crete to shoot the film *Ill Met by Moonlight*. The script was about the Cretan resistance to the Germans in World War II. Pressburger needed a composer capable of handling such a script, and Theodorakis seemed exactly right. Mikis left for London with whatever compositions he had at hand. He was immediately hired and received his first payment of $700 for the film score. It constituted his first employment in Europe, and his joy was shared by Myrto and their friends as well, including Pierre Ancelin, or "Uncle Pierre," as he came to be called by the group. The film met with great success.

Throughout the years of financial difficulties and sustained production, Mikis never forgot his fellow-fighters, who were coming out of Greece in search of a more favourable artistic climate. He tried to help them in their studies and artistic careers as much as he could. He also became involved in a milieu of French artists who had fought in the Resistance. His own professor of synthesis, Olivier Messiaen, had written a *Quartet for the End of Time*—an eight-movement work for violin, clarinet, cello, and piano that grew out of his experience as a prisoner of the Nazis during World War II. It was through the people around Messiaen and Xenakis that Mikis became interested in France during the Occupation. Besides the aesthetic touch of the Paris compositions and those of the Greek Occupation and Resistance, he brought to light, by putting them to music, ten poems of Paul Eluard for voice and piano.[9] Eluard had visited the Greek revolutionaries under General Markos Vafiadis, on Mount Gram-

---

[9] The two song cycles *Les Quatre Eluard* (1955) and *Les Six Eluard* (1958), have never been performed publicly or recorded.

mos in northern Greece, in August, 1949, as the Civil War
was drawing to a close, and there, with the assistance of a
Greek revolutionary poet, he produced a volume of poetry,
entitled *Paul Eluard pour la Grèce.*

In 1958, two ballets, *Le Feu aux poudres,* drawn from the
*Greek Carnival,* and *Les Amants de Teruel,* were performed
at the Sarah Bernhardt Theatre by the Ballet de Paris. At the
same time, the Elliniko Chorodrama danced two of his works,
*Erophili* (1956), with its Cretan story and melodies, and
*Block No. 40* (1957), in which he put together various
rhythms and motifs, ranging from the folk to the pop.

On November 8, 1958, a daughter, Margarita, was born to
Mikis and Myrto. Eager to share their new joy with their
families, and longing to see their homeland, they departed
for Athens the following month for a few weeks' vacation.
Mikis, who had been keeping up with political developments
in Greece, could detect certain hopeful signs. To be sure, the
country was still dominated by the Right, with the ubiquitous state and city police. But, in the May elections of that
year, a few liberal and left-wing votes were cast to parties
other than Karamanlis' National Radical Union, which had
succeeded Field Marshal Papagos in power on February 19,
1956. But the returns put Karamanlis in power for another
four years.

The most important period in Mikis' life and career was
now to come. In the fall of 1959, following a second sojourn
in Greece, he composed his *Antigone,* a one-act ballet with
eleven short episodes freely adapted from Sophocles' play.[10]
In this work, his most significant of this period, the composer finally resolved what conflict he had felt between the lifeless object, the mechanical device, on the one hand, and the
living human soul and spirit, on the other; between, that is,
abstract technology in playing with sounds and music as it
develops from the natural rhythm of the human body and
speech. Creatively, if not so far as theory is concerned, *An-*

[10] By this time the composer had written three works for the Ballet de Paris,
performed in 1958, and two more for the Elliniko Chorodrama, performed in
Athens. This was definitely his most productive period for the ballet.

*tigone* can be considered his experimental investigation into modern music and the ancient Greek mode. It was the culmination of—as well as a kind of valediction to—all his European training, and marked, too, the end of his musical studies in Paris. Aesthetically, he now stood between Greece and Europe, but his "revolution" was to begin in Greece, upon his return, with the *Epitaphios,* a cycle of eight songs by Yiannis Ritsos, in which the ancient and Byzantine *melos* is predominant. With this ballet, Mikis achieved his first recognition in the West.

*Antigone* was given its premiere at London's Covent Garden during the winter season of 1959 with the Royal Ballet. Hugo Rignold conducted the work, for which John Cranko designed the choreography and Rufino Tamayo, the Mexican painter, the scenery and costumes. The performance divided the critics. One critic, for example, wrote unfavourably of Cranko's choreography but favourably of the music: "The impression gained was that Mr. Cranko is more indebted to Theodorakis than to Sophocles. The vivid score has substance and even on a simple hearing makes its impress on the mind."[11] Another criticized what he considered "a serviceable but thickly orchestrated and episodic score derived from Stravinsky, Hindemith, and Greek folk-song."[12] And a third praised the work's harmonious unity:

> Here at last we have a complete ballet in the Diaghileff sense of the term in which the collaboration between choreographer, composer, and designer serves the story to perfection. There is clearly no intention to present a wordless version of Sophocles' tragedy. M. Theodorakis' score is a magnificent example of writing for narrative ballet. Every note advances the story and throughout there is the feeling of the inevitable tragic climax.[13]

*Antigone* was a clear example of Mikis' dilemma, that is, whether to remain a truly Greek composer or to become a

[11] H.S.R., "Antigone" (Royal Ballet), *Musical Opinion and Music Trade Review* 83:157, December, 1959.

[12] N. Goodwin, "Antigone," *Musical Courier* 160:8, December, 1959.

[13] A. L. Haskell, "Antigone—Royal Ballet," *London Musical Events* 14:19, December, 1959.

rootless international virtuoso like his friend Xenakis. "When I was writing my *Antigone*," he later said, "I used mathematical computations in the relationships of sounds to such an extent that I felt a lack in my knowledge of mathematics. Then I saw two roads opening ahead of me: I could either start my mathematics or attempt a radical return to the roots. The work, *Antigone,* itself offered the solution."[14]

In the beginning of the score, where, for seven minutes, the chorus accompanies the dead to their dwelling places, simple Byzantine motifs supply the background. This takes the place of the dirge that the chorus was to have pronounced. In most of the remaining fifty minutes of the ballet, Mikis made use of mathematical calculations to create the antithesis of the dramatic mood. This section, as the composer himself later confessed, represented the perfection of mathematical ratios, but it had no emotional impact on the audience. On the other hand, the chorus section "was smoothe as a Byzantine melody, supported by very simple harmonic lines springing from the Byzantine *isson*. And in this lies the success of the *Antigone*. In this part, my own true self was to be found. It was then that I realized my path was to return to the roots."[15]

From this time on, Mikis turned his back on the "artificialities" of electronic and other mechanical devices and proceeded to deepen his search into the nature of genuine melody, derived from the experience and needs of the human spirit. In this quest, although he always reached towards the ancient concepts as expressed in the tetrachord, he was particularly influenced by the subtlety of the Byzantine melody as a transmitter of the ancient song.

His creative urge drove him back to the reading of Yiannis Ritsos' poetry, which he had come across as a youth in Tripolis. One selection, in particular, caught his interest—"Epitaphios." A profoundly moving poem, it told of a mother's

---

[14] Mikis Theodorakis, "Return to the Roots," *E Genia mas,* January 15, 1966.
[15] *Loc. cit.* The term *isson* means the choral participation of cantors (*issokrates*) who support the song melody uninterruptedly as if it were an organ pedal.

heart-rending lament for her dead son, who constituted for her her sole joy and hope and whose untimely death, now leaves her life devoid of all meaning. How many such private scenes make up the story of modern strife-torn Greece! Mikis at once became obsessed with Ritsos' poem. Working feverishly he set the twenty songs from "Epitaphios" to music and sent seven of them, taped while he sang and accompanied himself on the piano, to Ritsos and Hadjidakis. Their enthusiasm encouraged him. He then added the eighth song, completing the whole *Epitaphios* cycle while in Greece in 1960.

Mikis now turned almost exclusively to modern Greek poetry for inspiration. Moved by the powerful works of George Seferis, he composed another song cycle, *Epiphania,* followed by the *Deserters,* the latter based on four poems by his brother Yiannis. Two more song cycles were written that year—*Politeia,* drawn from the poetry of Dimitris Christodoulou and Tassos Livaditis, and *Archipelagos,* a musical expression of five of his own poems as well as seven by Nikos Gatsos, Odysseas Elytis, Dimitris Christodoulou, and P. Kokkinopoulos.

Mikis' years in Paris were also quite productive from a literary point of view. He wrote a number of polemical pieces in which he laid the groundwork for the revolution in Greek music and poetry; and in one of his longest essays, published in *Epitheorisi Technis,*[16] he discussed musical trends in Europe. He explained the problems of the modern composer, who must contend with the vicious circles surrounding musical life and examined the performing and creative side of music, arguing that the public no longer cared what music was being performed but only who was performing it. He also decried the lack of theme and melody in much of modern music, saying that a musical work cannot be created according to a convenient set of rules and concepts, but must reflect, and indeed be one with, the atmosphere, the feelings and ideas, of its geographical and historical background.

In early 1959, Mikis, acting upon his conviction that an artist should not remain separated from his people, left

[16] Theodorakis, *op. cit.* (supra n. 1) 46-65.

Paris to return to Greece. With his ideas now crystallized and his mark made,[17] he was at length prepared to embark upon the revolutionary path that he had charted for himself years before and that led, in his words, "back to the roots," to what was fundamental and therefore sacred. To express the Greek ethos, he would have to go back to the very soil from which it sprang and there find both strength and inspiration.

[17] While in Paris, Mikis had gained international recognition for his works. He won the First Golden Award at the Moscow Music Festival, for example, under the composer, Dmitri Shostakovich, in 1957, and the American Copley Music Prize as the best European composer of the year, in 1959.

# The Theodorakis Musical Movement

# 4

# Musical Education

> Our music today is at a level of provincialism; go back to Greece, settle all your differences among all the musicians, and together work on Greek music.
> DIMITRI MITROPOULOS to Theodorakis

## MUSICAL STAGNATION AND THE "MANIFESTO OF MUSIC"

In 1959, the Athenian musical establishment was celebrating the fiftieth anniversary of the National School of Music. Mikis' contribution to the anniversary was an article he wrote for the magazine *Kritiki* entitled, "Greek Music—Year (circa) Zero."[1] The choice of date as much as the contents thoroughly angered the Athenian musical world. The title was intended to be provocative and the arguments more so.

[1] Mikis Theodorakis, "Greek Music—Year (circa) Zero," *Kritiki* 1:3 (1959) (infra n. 5, 85-92).

Mikis declared that, in spite of the wealth of native Greek musical tradition, the "old guard" had failed to create a style of any worth. Moreover, they had succeeded in killing any desire on the part of the people to elevate its musical appreciation. With the death of Economidis, in 1957, and Manolis Kalomiris, in 1962, the National School of Music, whose founders they had been, came to an end also. Mikis, attacking the establishment that fenced the school, wrote: "Their time has been up for a long while now, but, as they continue to hold the keys to the positions, they inevitably drive backwards every aspect of our musical life." The article was followed by an interview with the daily newspaper, *Ta Nea* (August 20, 1959), in which he explained his arguments for the larger reading public.

Mikis' attack on the stagnant musical life of Greece was immediately backed by the composers Argyris Kounadis, from Germany, and Yiannis Xenakis, from France. Those in control of Greece's musical life were, to be sure, angered by Mikis' "insults," but they were not shaken in the least; for they were secure in their position and had nothing to fear from a leftist upstart. To everyone's amazement, the first attacks did not come from the "old guard" but from the Left. The music critic of the newspaper *Avghi,* Vassilis Arkadinos, came to the establishment's defence in a series of polemical articles disagreeing with Mikis and his intentions. Mikis was furious with Arkadinos' diatribe and wrote a protesting letter to *Avghi,* in which he said: "I believe that your columnist's series of articles reveal that he—psychologically, intellectually, musically, and ideologically—belongs to exactly that world in regard to which, for good or ill, we young people have decided once and for all to explain ourselves. We hope, if possible, to eradicate it. . . . Our ambition is to create a renewing movement that will sever their roots. The forces are dead set against us, and the times are impossibly difficult."[2]

---

[2] Arkadinos' columns appeared in *Avghi* on September 22, 23, 24, 1959, and Mikis' on October 31. A second response of Arkadinos appeared on November 6, 1959.

The forces and the times Mikis referred to were hardly a novelty in the cultural and musical life of the Greek people, nor was the history of the National School of Music outside the trend of Greek society. Both relied on a past whose deep roots had perniciously grown and spread among the people without their awareness. It is, therefore, most necessary to present a very brief view of the state of musical affairs in Greece, so that one may get some impression of the powerful stream of obstacles and difficulties, both aesthetic and cultural, that Mikis and the youth of the Resistance generation had to face.

After the liberation from Turkish rule (1453–1821), several abortive efforts had been made by various rulers and personalities to develop an ethnic culture. In the realm of music, these efforts involved, above all, importing an Italian or German musical culture and style of composition. The difficulty that arose from the interdependence of culture and politics in the new nation—for both shared exactly the same birth and development—resulted in two opposing forces, the foreign versus the native. Thus the foreign, a product of the nineteenth-century romantic notions about classical Greece and the revival of the ancient Attic dialect through the *katharevousa,* could not let its idealism be disturbed by the reality of the poverty, internal feuding, and fierce individualism of the new nation. It was an importation, and hence an instrument of the foreign, imported palace. The palace, although of Bavarian origin, employed in its circles people with foreign backgrounds and intentions. In the sphere of musical culture, two trends prevailed—the German and the Italian.

From the beginning of their appearance, both trends instilled a sense of shame in the Greek for his own heritage—the religious and secular (folk and pop) traditions. Encountering no obstacles, both trends continued to coexist, but in a state of incessant rivalry. Each faction tried to establish orchestras and conservatories of its own and disparaged the work of the other. By and large, in all these efforts, only foreign musicians and conductors were involved, and the transplanted music would not take root. By the beginning of the twentieth century, the German school gave up the task, and the field was left to the Greeks of the Italian school. The burden of musical education was thus shouldered by the Athens Conservatory (1871), but it made no effort to relate to the needs of the people, especially the youth, in understanding their own heritage, and the vast majority of the Greek population, the people in the rural areas, remained completely untouched by the Conservatory's endeavours. It was with the creation of the state-supported Conservatory of Greece in Thessaloniki, in 1914, which expanded to various other cities, that the rural areas became somewhat involved in musical training. One of its founders, Manolis Kalomiris (whose book on solfeggio was Mikis' first introduction to notation), later broke away to establish the National Conservatory in 1926, which also opened branches in other cities. The significant difference was that these two institutions were subsidized by the state, while the Athens Conservatory relied completely on private support until 1942, when it, too, finally became a state-subsidized organization. Unlike the practice in the Western world, but totally in keeping with the traditional clientage system in Greece, the latter ultimately became a tool of family position and power politics, dependent as it was upon individuals who used it for their own personal aims at power. One's knowledge of music, or extent of musical training, was not as important as where one acquired it. The Athens Conservatory became the school for the élite.

The Conservatory of Greece was received with wide acclaim by the people, particularly because of its branches in areas other than Athens. The students and teachers who worked there retained their enthusiasm for music, and thus the institution created friends and patrons of its own. It could be called the first genuinely fruitful musical effort in Greece, even though its orientation was far from ethnic. Spurred by its success, the Cretan politician, Venizelos, encouraged Skouloudis to establish, in 1924, the "Society of Fine Arts" of Chania. The 1920's were full of abortive efforts, such as the creation of a symphony orchestra by the famed Mitropoulos when he returned to Greece, in 1926; it closed down after a short while due to lack of state interest and public apathy.

Interestingly enough, it was an American, Eva Palmer, who came out against the injustice done to the people by those in charge of musical affairs in Greece. Eva, after marrying the poet Angelos Sikelianos in 1906, devoted her whole life to learning everything she could in the field of Greek music. Unlike the majority of those Greeks who were studying music in the 1920's and 1930's, she concentrated all her energies on the ancient and Byzantine traditions. Her desire was "to develop Greek music that would spring from its own prehistoric roots."[3] To this end, she intended to found a music school that would concern itself primarily with Byzantine melos as a continuation of ancient Greek music. Her efforts, and those of her husband—who, disillusioned with the failure of the League of Nations to solve the crises of war, had sought to establish an intellectual and artistic league at Delphi—received virtually no support from the Greeks. Granted that, at the "navel of the world," the first Delphic Festival did take place in 1927, but this was largely through the financial support of her own family in the States and of close friends. The greatest tragedy, however, was her repudiation by the country to which she had dedicated her life. She was labelled a Communist for having supported the Resistance, and was denied a visa by the Royal Greek Consulate in New York, in 1951, when she wished to see her dying husband. A year after Sikelianos' death she was finally allowed to visit Greece, but she died a month after her arrival and was buried next to her husband.

No other efforts were made in the decades preceding World War II to change the existing system of musical culture and education in Greece; nor was there any moderniza-

---

[3] "The Greek Music and Eva," *Eos* (103-107, 1967) 270. This is an issue dedicated to Eva Palmer-Sikelianou, containing, *inter alia*, details on her contribution to Greek cultural life.

tion of methodology to keep up with the new trends in Europe. During the war, of course, all aspects of education were suspended. The vast majority of schools were taken over by the Germans and Italians, and classes were sporadic at best. Most of the rural branches of the Greek Conservatory were closed, and even the Athens Conservatory barely functioned. That it managed to stay open at all was due to the superhuman efforts of Economidis, Mikis' mentor. But its stranglehold on Greek musical life continued after the war. The same indifference to new ideas and techniques, the same archaic teaching methods faced the would-be music student of the 1950's as had prevailed years before. Those who attempted to bring about changes were met with typical bureaucratic antagonism.

For years, the apathy and resistance of state officials and professors of the Athens Conservatory had driven the most promising students of music abroad for study. Some never returned. Nikos Skalkottas was one of the early victims of the indifference of Athenian society. Having worked under Kurt Weill and Arnold Schoenberg, he returned to Greece, in 1933, to face a public that was totally unable to appreciate the new and original music he was composing. Until his death, in 1949, he refused to perform or publish any of his music. Were it not for London musical circles, who have been performing most of Skalkottas' works, he would still be unknown.

A final sad case is that of the world-renowned pianist Gina Bachauer. In 1958, Miss Bachauer attempted to bring some vitality into Greek musical education by proposing a series of summer seminars, to be held in Greece, for music students by well-known world artists. She secured the cooperation of the German soprano Lotte Lehman, the violinist Yehudi Menuhin, and the cellist Gaspar Cassado, among others. She herself volunteered to teach without charge, and obtained support to cover the expenses of the other artists from the Greek shipowner Karras.[4] She set up a programme of studies

4 See details in Mikis' interview in *op. cit.* (infra n. 5) 132-133.

for highly qualified students, proposed scholarships, and set aside a portion of the treasury for aid to poor musicians. Before making her request to the artists on a formal level, however, she had to secure the approval of the Greek Government and responsible members of the music world. Yet, instead of extending approval, or even a gesture of encouragement or praise, the bureaucrats responded, ostensibly, that her idea would annoy the unemployed and lowly paid Greek music teacher. The real reason, however, was their own inveterate resistance to change: "Why bother? Things are all right the way they are." Miss Bachauer's enthusiasm was destroyed, and she never again concerned herself with Greek musical matters.

Finally, there were the music critics, who helped foster their people's misguided approach to musical appreciation and training. Their columns reflected the artificial and romantic approach to art that had prevailed for over a century. The critics' mission consisted, above all, in titillating the taste of the half-learned elite with their "beautiful" *katharevousa* phraseology, presenting the artist as an ethereal and mystical creature. Hypocrisy, pretence, and hatred utterly dominated the field of artistic criticism. Mikis described the situation in a letter to Economidis thus: "You know better than I that criticism in Greece is written by three types of people: (1) those who have failed; (2) the semi-learned ignoramuses; and (3) the agents of the semi-learned and the failures."[5]

This state of affairs in the professional and purely artistic area of musical education and training affected only a small minority of the population. The rest, over eighty per cent, were living their own musical life and had their own local forms of entertainment. But they, too, depended on the groups in power for general education and culture. This dependence was intensified after World War II, especially with the establishment of the National Broadcasting Corporation (EIR), in 1945, as a state organization. For such an

[5] The letter has been included as an introduction to Mikis' book *Yia tin Elliniki Mousiki* (On Greek Music) Athens 1961, 13.

underdeveloped country as Greece, the radio as well as the press has always been the main avenue of communication with the people.[6]

The news media—dailies, weeklies, and all other periodicals—were controlled by the established political groups, whose main preoccupation was how they would maintain their position among the people. Even the "artistic" programmes of the radio were always a political issue. In the last decade or so, records and films were pushed into the market in large numbers, and these were of minimal artistic quality. Besides, it was only a minority in Athens who could afford these luxuries. The major means of entertainment still remained the radio broadcasts or whatever records could be bought cheaply. But these radio broadcasts were literally "brainwashing" the listeners with cheap Greek and foreign music. After the war, American songs predominated and filled the homes of those who possessed a radio—and possessing a radio meant that they had to register it with the National Broadcasting Corporation and pay taxes on it every three months. The amount depended on the decision of the EIR tax collectors. Refusal to pay the 300 drachmas (£4)—a sizeable amount for a Greek wage-earner—resulted in a summons from the police and revocation of the owner's licence. A second offence would be tried in court. Finally, the official festivals, especially the Athens Festival, inaugurated in the early 1950's to increase tourism, were intended only for foreign audiences and artists; for only between three and five per cent of Athenians went to a performance of a classical work or were interested in classical records.

Neither the official encouragement for tourists nor the bourgeoisie's fad for Western dance rhythms had much effect on Greece's eighty per cent rural population. They contrived to participate on festival days and social events in their

[6] From the year of its establishment up until the Papandreou administration (1963-65), EIR had 18 directors, five of whom were ex-army and navy officers, and all the rest, with the exception of one or two such as Sakis Peponis, a lawyer, appointed by Papandreou, were activists of the right-wing parties in power. Peponis was not only dismissed by the coup of April 21, 1967, but also imprisoned for a while.

traditional folk rhythms and melodies. Hence, the people in the villages and small towns would go only to local tavernas to find their own form of entertainment, while in Athens and the major cities the middle class danced only to European and American tunes. In port cities such as Piraeus, the rebetic music was the daily joy of the *Lumpenproletariat.* The people were thus divided musically, and the situation was made only worse by the rejection not only of art-music as a serious occupation by all but of music education in general. "It is an illusion to talk about responsible musical education of a people," said Mikis in an interview with the centrist weekly *Tachydromos,* "and refer only to the orchestras, the opera companies, and broadcasts. Musical education starts at the grammar-school benches, and even earlier with the folk songs that envelop us from the cradle and follow us to our death. We must select the songs carefully, create new and better ones, give the child conscientious teachers and instructors, play recordings of the world's musical masterpieces, explaining the works to him as simply as possible, and take him to special concerts or anywhere else to acquaint him with music."[7] Such being the needs and desires of the people the war generation began for the first time to examine and experiment seriously with the raw material of Greek music and its tradition, and present it to the people in the light of the fall and reconstruction of the old and new values of the European and hence Greek scene. Music, however, was only one of the myriad problems of general education and culture. The responsibility of fostering new, up-to-date attitudes toward progress in Greece lay with that noble and culture-hungry war generation. In the realm of music, the group of young musicians and composers—Mikis, Xenakis, Kounadis, Hadjidakis, Yiannis Christou, and others—were to be the vanguard of this revolution. Yet, despite their common bond of suffering, European training, upon returning to their homeland, the political situation, and the need to protect their own career by working within the established patterns, eventually forced them into submission. They quickly

7 In *op. cit.* (supra n. 5) 129.

learned that, because of the strong influence foreign opinion had on the Athenian snobs, the way to success was to court the European and later American market and to be well known to Western critics and journalists. Once accepted by the foreigners, the Greek social hierarchy would then also accept them, and their works would be played everywhere in the state theatres and the Athens Festival as well as on the radio. But, for those who would not join the establishment, there was no recourse but to fight in the left-wing press or perform in municipal theatres or athletic stadiums, as in Mikis' case.

Mikis' theories on musical education are almost inextricably bound up with his ideas of what Greek music really is. Nevertheless, his pragmatic theories on education crystallized before his aesthetic ideas, and it was these theories that culminated in the famous "Manifesto." In spite of the promising career that was opening in front of him in Europe, he was inwardly unsatisfied with the dodecaphonic trends in Western music. He felt an ever increasing urge to work with the traditional music of his own land, which he believed would be the raw material for a cultural renewal. Furthermore, he had never forgotten his own bitter experiences during the war years or that he was almost completely self-taught. "I must state," he said during the first months of his revolution in 1960, "that from the beginning I have not been as interested in my own personal creations as I have in the renaissance of Greek music and the musical culture of our people."[8]

Immediately after the birth of his son, Yiorgos, on May 5, 1960, in Paris, Mikis returned to Greece to pick up the challenge just as Gina Bachauer had left it. Collaborating with four other composers—Argyris Kounadis, Yiannis Xenakis, Yiannis Papaioannou, and Dimitris Chorafas—and the musicologist, Phivos Anoyiannakis, he drew up a plan for the reorganization of musical life in Greece. This plan, which shortly came to be known as the *Manifesto of Music,* was first published in Thessaloniki in the May-June, 1960, issue

8 Theodorakis, *op. cit.* (supra n. 5) 253.

of *Kritiki,* the same journal that had published several of his earlier articles.[9] It attacked the lack of systematized instruction in music at all levels, from grammar school through the university and conservatory, and the absence of a State Academy of Music. It proposed solutions for these problems as well as for existing inequities in sponsoring Greek artists and composers, both pop and classical, in concerts and on the radio. It emphasized, in this connection, particularly the need for autonomous symphonic orchestras. It stressed the need to reach the people at their own level in the provinces through public concerts and "pop seminars." The Athens Festival should be given a truly national character by presenting not only ancient Greek drama and foreign ballet, opera, and orchestral companies but Byzantine and modern Greek works as well. In the *Manifesto* re-evaluation of the pseudo-Byzantine music of the churches and a revival of the genuine Byzantine *melos* was recommended. Lastly, it underlined the necessity for compiling a representative collection of the wealth of native folk and pop music and dance, and the need for a responsible scholarly publishing firm.

The document produced quite a stir in the musical world, among critics and musicians alike, unfortunately not just for its novel ideas but even more because of the conspicuous absence from the list of Manos Hadjidakis. All wondered why he had not signed.

For four months, however, there was not a word from Hadjidakis. Finally, concern for his image, and public demand, forced him to make a statement, published in the magazine *Tachydromos* on November 26, 1960. "I have not signed the famous *Manifesto,*" he explained, "although I was asked repeatedly, because I do not believe in the importance of those who are involved in this movement, and therefore in the effectiveness of their proclamations, which are absolutely nothing else than the visions and desires of Mikis Theodorakis alone, the only able one in the group." Hadjidakis' remarks infuriated the other musicians, and the winter

---

[9] Cited in full in *op. cit.* (supra n. 5) 116-121. Because of the importance of the document, a complete English translation is included in Appendix I.

months of that year were filled with attacks and counter-attacks from all sides. Mikis felt the need to intervene and pacify the quarrelling artists; in a letter he sent from Paris, where he was working on the ballet *Honeymoon,* to *Tachydromos,* on December 17, he begged his fellow musicians to put aside their polemics and once more asked Hadjidakis to join the movement for the renewal of Greek music. But there was no response from Hadjidakis.

Years later, after he had moved to New York, Hadjidakis, when asked again about his reaction to the *Manifesto,* added a further reason for his refusal to participate—the political situation:

> Yes, I do recall the *Manifesto* and what followed. There were many who contributed to it, but Theodorakis stood alone. I did not sign the *Manifesto* at the time—I have given my answer about this—for I do not believe that the public can be educated by such means in the field of music, especially in Greece. Another far more important reason was that, at that time . . . we had reactionary governments in power. We would have lost our seriousness of purpose, for reactionary regimes never help such efforts in Greece. They never would consider such collective ideas and approach. That is why I did not sign.
>
> I believe that only individual attempts are fruitful and achieve anything definite. Of course, in that case, an artist must consider that he will have to suffer a great deal.[10]

He went on to comment on the later efforts of the two to try to establish orchestras in Athens and experiment with new ideas, and said that only in a free and democratic environment could artistic endeavours flourish normally.

The rest of Mikis' articles which appeared in newspapers or journals after the publication of the *Manifesto* either enlarged upon or defended its different points, and let the Hadjidakis issue pass. At the same time, he attacked the custom, so prevalent in Greece, of overpaying foreign artists in

[10] These reminiscences were part of Hadjidakis' remarks to the author in a discussion in New York, April 12, 1969. They were also an indirect reply to those who had criticized him for not coming out openly against the junta, and for not supporting his fellow-musician, Theodorakis, who was then imprisoned.

order to entice them to bring their companies to Greece, while underpaying the Greek artist from a low budget. This practice not only resulted in second rate orchestras but, even worse, created a feeling of shame in the Greek musician. "I remember that, six years ago, when I was leaving to go abroad, I was possessed . . . by a deep inferiority complex that derived from my occupation as a Greek musician, a Greek composer," Mikis said in another interview that July.[11] The musical profession was not fully recognized as a serious occupation by the state. Owing to the inefficient handling of the administration of musical institutions, the artist (even the most successful) had to hold two or three different jobs at once. For instance, half of those working at the State Symphonic Orchestra would also work at the State Ballet Company, and the other half in the National Broadcasting Orchestra, while others would have to go elsewhere to make ends meet. Thus, music, instead of being a proud, creative profession, was a degrading one. Mikis declared that every professional group should be able to support and employ its own artists on a permanent basis, so that they could concentrate all their talent and creativity on their home orchestra. But this radical change struck at the heart of the musical establishment.

It was time for the "open war" that he had advocated in the *Tachydromos* interview, against the entrenched interest groups. By avoiding taking sides with any existing group of older artists, young musicians could form a nucleus for the revival of musical life around them and stimulate artistic competition.

The war was on. Step by step, Mikis set out to realize the various propositions of the *Manifesto* on his own, since the authorities remained hostile. The battle would be waged in the next four years on every level—the verbal, with lectures, interviews, debates, and articles; the musical, with his own compositions and those of other young musicians, and by establishing the Little Symphonic Orchestra of Athens for classical compositions and the Theodorakis Ensemble for

11 *Ibid.*, 138.

pop music; and, eventually the political, with his leadership
of the Lambrakis Youth.

## REVOLUTION FROM WITHIN:
### THE EPITAPHIOS BATTLE

Mikis was not, however, content with words alone. It was
essential for him to give his feelings, his convictions, a living
proof, and for him that meant musical compositions and
their public presentation: sound and sight. After having
thrown down the gauntlet with his *Manifesto of Music* in
June, 1960, he "presented his arms," the song cycle *Epitaphios,* based on the poetry of Yiannis Ritsos, "the rock." It immediately caused a furore among the scholars and music
critics, more so, because large public gatherings and press
coverage only added arguments that lasted over a year. The
work was too revolutionary, because it brought together too
many opposing elements. In the first place, the poetry had
been written by the leftist Yiannis Ritsos, in memory of the
terrible May, 1936, massacre of a crowd of unarmed factory
workers that had gathered in the centre of Thessaloniki to
protest unfair wage controls. Thus, the combination of poet
and subject-matter constituted two strikes against Mikis in
the eyes of the authorities. A third was his choice of singer,
Grigoris Bithikotsis, the "hero" on Makronissos, who was
then working as a plumber by day, while playing the *bouzouki* in a taverna by night. A fourth objection was that no
serious composer should waste his talent with the *bouzouki,*
or debase good poetry by wedding it to such music. Mikis'
daring step to break down the demotic, fifteen-syllable meter
of Ritsos' poetry, and set it to the 7/8, or 4/8 of the rebetic
rhythms, angered the literary scholars and the musical aes-
thetes. Many of his concerts during the following year were
turned into riots, firstly, because large masses of people were
involved, and secondly, to protest the systematic sabotage
and intervention of the police. In order to understand the
phenomenon of official hostility, and the complex political,
cultural, and aesthetic attitudes it represented, a brief picture
of Greek musical tradition and society is essential.

Greece has indeed been a land of music, song, and dance through all the centuries of her existence. But, for the creative artist of the twentieth century, there remains the burning question: What, in modern times, constitutes a genuine Greek style of music? For Mikis, there was only one answer, one way to establish such a style—to go back to the roots and trace the melodies, rhythms, and instruments of Greek music, as preserved by the long tradition. The task was complicated because of the isolated and localized nature of Greek music, which, during the four hundred years of Turkish domination, had never come to represent the collective flowering of the national life. As Mikis wrote:

> In the same period when Italy was giving birth to Vivaldi and Rossini, Germany to Bach and Mozart, and France to her Couperins, our "composers" were "writing" their masterpieces: the dirges of Mani, the Cretan *rizitika,* the songs and dances of Roumeli, Epiros, and the islands. But as our "composers" were either shepherds or fishermen, it was not expected that their technique would go beyond the limits of unsophisticated inspiration. Thus the song fermented, hidden amidst the people, remaining forever unknown.[12]

The diagram on page 120 illustrates this "hidden," yet very living, music. It examines the traditional, the contemporary style of songs, and, in particular, what is called *laik,* or pop song which, since the beginning of the twentieth century, has assimilated all other traditions into its own distinctive style, to become the national music (song and dance), with the bouzouki as its medium.

The first of these sources for modern Greek music, the *Byzantine melos* (a melodic and tonal system clearly linked with ancient Greek modes), together with its method of notation, constitutes one of the most significant achievements in musical history. It expresses with amazing simplicity the complete tonal range of the human voice and its infinite rhythmical possibilities. The church fathers set Christian words to the traditional folk music, with the result that the

[12] *Loc. cit.* (supra n. 5) 86.

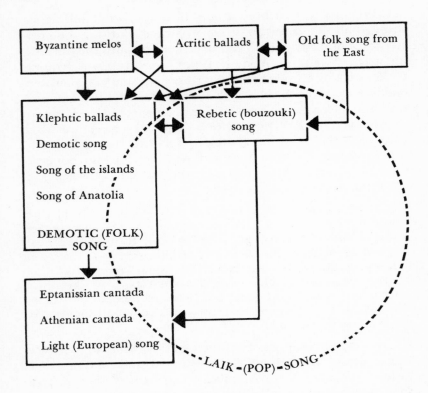

liturgy preserved from Byzantine times to the present contains elements of the secular tradition of those centuries now lost to us. The second of these "roots," the *Acritic ballads,* are epic songs which celebrated the deeds of the ninth century Byzantine hero, Digenis Acritas. A third source, old Eastern folksong, incorporating the rhythms and strains of Semitic, Arabic, Indian, and Turkish music, exerted a long-lasting influence on native Greek music, not so much because of the melody but because of the instruments and the voice.

Side by side with the church developments in music and the heroic ballads, folk music continued to exist. Towards the end of the eighteenth century one variety became extremely popular in all areas of subjugated Greece. This was the heroic tale, celebrating in recitative and refrain, the deeds, and manner of death, of the Klephts, the mountain chieftains who were the first to take up the struggle against the Turks for liberation. After the events of 1821 the *klephtic ballads* increased in popularity and became ingrained in the national consciousness as the song-symbol of resistance. During the course of the nineteenth century these klephtic ballads became part of the popular heritage which included the songs and dances native to mountains and other rural areas (*demotika tragoudia*), the music from the islands (*nissiotika*), as well as those from the Asia Minor territories of Pontos and Smyrna, all of which came to be known as demotic or folk songs and dances. Finally, what is known as *cantada* is nothing but an import from Italy, via the Ionian Islands, adopted with facility in the capital to become a city song. The light (or Western European) song was a late-comer, first appearing in the 1920's.

All of these "branches" of Greek music with the exception of the liturgical, were associated with instruments and various dances. There are at least fifty dances preserved from earlier centuries, and more than two dozen instruments. This fact clearly shows the continuity with ancient Greece where music, dance, and instrumental accompaniment were inseparable. The dancing, singing chorus of ancient tragedy was the embodiment of Greek citizenry. Such a collective participation in song and dance is most evident in modern Greek tradition in the demotic (folk) dances: the *kalamatianos,* a chain dance traditionally for women; the *tsamikos,* a chain dance for men; the *pyrrhic* or *serra,* a warrior's dance from Crete; the many varieties of dance rhythms from Epiros and Pontos. All of these dances have their peculiar instruments—the *clarino* (folk clarinet), the *lyra* (a miniature three-stringed violin), the *lauoto* (lute), the *santouri* (a trapezoid-shaped string instrument placed flat and struck with two cotton-covered, wooden mallets), the *daouli* (a large double-headed drum), not to mention the ubiquitous folk violin. One further type of folk song should not be overlooked because of its influence on Mikis' style, though it involves neither musical instruments nor dance: the *moirologia* or wailing dirges improvised by women mourners at funerals. Finally, there are the imported *cantada* and Western European rhythms, whose main instruments are the guitar and the accordion with other instruments added according to the preference of performance—dance or group singing.

The *rebetic*,[13] or bouzouki (song, dance, instrument) with which Mikis began his musical revolution, serves as the point of separation of the above traditions of folk music, Western and light song, and the *cantada,* both sociologically and aesthetically. The exact dates of the birth of the rebetic song and its blossoming have not yet been determined. The chief characteristics of the rebetic song are its melodic line and its rhythm patterns. The rebetic songs have as their subject-matter the life surrounding the jilted lover, the outcast, the downtrodden, the wronged, and, of course, the addicts of hashish and other opiates. Their vocabulary and intonation are drawn primarily from the life of the bouzouki-type man—the "antihero" of sorts in his poverty, unloved, and going from the life of the fisherman to that of the hashish smoker in life after death. Yet, the words of the rebetic songs, which are often puerile and repetitious, play a subordinate role, serving merely to embellish the melody and provide sound for the singing of the melody and accompaniment for the bouzouki. Moreover, just as in the case of the language used in American jazz, the *rebetes,* denizens of the city marketplace, developed their own symbolic, secretive language and coined words for things they wanted to communicate to each other without outsiders, and especially the authorities, understanding.

The chief instrument of the rebetic song has always been

13 Scholars differ as to the derivation of the term, some ascribing it to a Turkish term for irregular soldiers, and others to the Western word "rebel." It is most likely that the term *rebetic* (rebetica, the plural for the songs), comes from the Moorish name for an early three-gut-string lute, the *rebet* or *rebec,* and therefore things involved with the music and environment of the player of the rebet. Only recently has anything like adequate research begun on these songs, since they have been disregarded for so long by the upper-crust scholars and musicians.

the bouzouki,[14] and thus the same types of songs and dances were called either rebetic or bouzouki. The rebetic song developed in Greek seaports—Piraeus, Constantinople, Smyrna, Thessaloniki—and harbour cities in the Middle East, where commodities and cultural values were exchanged. This is probably the reason for the degree of similarity between the Moorish *rebec* or *rebet,* the Nubian *oud,* a larger version of the same, the Turkish *saz,* and the Greek *bouzouki.* The bouzouki instrument is a work of art, made of laminated strips of ebony wood with inlays of nacre or even ivory in the very beautiful models. It is made up of three or four sets of double strings, tuned D-A-D, strung from a fretted neck to a bridge on a half, pear-shaped wooden belly. The modern bouzouki has maintained its tradition of beauty, but it is strung with steel strings instead of gut, horsehair, or thread, as in its primitive version. In order to produce a sharp and penetrating sound, the bouzouki is plucked with a plectrum, even as the ancient *kithara* was.

Traditionally, the bouzouki is a solo instrument upon which the performer improvises in the *taqsim,* an Arabic word given to the solo performance or the long solo introduction to a song. The voice, or song, is more an accompaniment to the instrument than the other way around, although the roles of soloist and accompanist are so interchanged that the whole performance becomes a climactic expression of mood. Emotions seep through, not necessarily in the lyrics, but in the way they are uttered. An image, a phrase, a colour, is enough inspiration for a composition. The solo bouzouki-player came to be joined by a second or third, as well as by other instruments, such as the guitar and tambour, the oud, and, at the turn of the century, the accordion. Another addition, although exact analysis of the development of the "bouzouki orchestra" is impossible because of the lack of sufficient historic data, was the *baglamas,* a miniature bouzouki. The reason for its size is connected with its origin. Designed originally by inmates of prisons and hideouts during the Ottoman

[14] The derivation of the word, connoting its round back, is Turkish. In classical Greek, we find the term *trichordon* ("three-stringed").

occupation, it was built small so that it would be easy to hide and the sound would be subdued. It has a much higher range than the bouzouki and generally complements a phrase or passage the bouzouki has played. To see what a long and continuous tradition the bouzouki has had, one need only observe the many frescoes in the churches, and even the icons.

The dances that characterize the rebetic, or bouzouki, music are almost entirely solo performances, such as the *rebeticos* (not to be confused with the Turkish *zeibek*, a circular dance for men). Although the dancer has to follow a strict pattern of steps, he is nevertheless allowed to interpret it according to his own way and mood. The rhythmical pattern of the dance itself is always the uneven 9/8 (2+2+2+2+1). The second dance is the *chassapikos*, which, as legend has it, originated in the meat market of Constantinople. It is danced to a 4/8 (2+2) beat. Two or three participate, forming a straight line and placing their arms on each other's shoulders. The movements go from left to right, with small steps forward and backward but never in circles. Slow movements are essential, and they must be executed according to a strict set of rules. A third dance, the *tsifteteli* (from "fine chord") is for a man and a woman together. They never touch, but complete freedom of body movement is allowed, and gyrations here strongly suggest sexual desires. It was originally a woman's dance, the step-child of what is termed the "belly-dance," which originated in the Arab lands and Turkey, and first made its appearance in the harem. Today, in Greece, it is primarily practised by the gypsies. Another word for the same dance is *karsilamas*, describing the position the dancers take with their "bellies" one opposite the other. Finally, the *chassaposervikos* is a combination of Cretan steps and the chassapikos pattern with a fast beat.

A mixture of all these dances is the world-renowned "Zorba dance," or *syrtaki*, danced to the musical arrangements that Mikis wrote for the main character in the film *Zorba the Greek*. (The word *syrtaki* is a diminutive of syrtos). It starts with the slow steps of the chassapikos and gradually develops into a solo dance incorporating both the rebeticos and the chassaposervikos, following the mood and the ecstasy of the dancer as in the ancient *corybantic* dances.

This indivisible relationship between genuine song and dance is another factor that distinguished them from the borrowed Italian *cantades,* which are meant only to be listened to—reminiscent as they are of old-fashioned barbershop quartets—but which have nonetheless exerted a strong influence on the laik song. They themselves developed into pleasant songs for group entertainment.

After the Asia Minor Catastrophe in 1922, interest in the bouzouki milieu increased, as was natural because of the influx of refugees, fresh from their traditional environment of the ethnic Greek communities in Anatolia. Many of them had been in positions of comparative wealth, or at least secure, and now were faced with only abject poverty in the urban slums. They found their outlet in the bouzouki music, and it was from this time that *bouzoukia*—places featuring rebetic music—began to be frequented in great numbers. The rebetic songs, however, had been considered immoral since the closing decades of the nineteenth century. To respectable people bouzouki music was hashish-bearing, and to the Greek chauvinists it was considered Turkish, Oriental, and, hence, non-Greek. Small wonder, then, that, as soon as the Fascist dictatorship of Metaxas was imposed, the bouzoukia places, and the rebetic music itself, were banned by public decree.

But the bloody violence and the total destruction of all familiar patterns of life during World War II shattered forever the romantic illusions of the wealthy upper classes. Siblings were divided against each other and children against parents, some collaborating with the enemy to survive. People, wanting to escape the bitter experiences of daily civil strife, found refuge in things irrelevant to the political situation, and thus indulged in lamenting the tragedy in the bouzouki music. Moreover, owing to the mixture of nationalities and languages, and the movement of the population from their homes for survival, as a result of the war, the rebetic spirit suited their loneliness and assuaged their personal grief. The bouzouki became a part of the underground milieu, once more playing its role of "anti-hero," with its lyrics and music reflecting the desperate environment in which it lived. Some of the songs, however, satirized the German and Italian invaders, but most were songs of escape. Death, the great leveller, brought the sons of the rich to the shacks of the bouzouki musicians to escape their own agonies and to find some temporary pleasure in a world that was offering some solace in the midst of chaos. This is how Hadjidakis has described the situation:

> In the desperation of those years, only one voice had the heroic bravery to survive firmly and truly—the laik song, which the bourgeoisie scornfully called rebetic. The laik song, from its birth, had been cast by the wayside, illegal, was neither eminent nor loved at all by the bourgeoisie, but functioned in pride within the two most powerful themes of war and postwar reality, the mood for escape from the tormenting surroundings, and an unsatisfied eroticism. The one jewel came to be added to the other, unnoticeably, but intensely, so that it embraced our youth with its magical comfort.[15]

The most tormenting fact of all, however, was that the war, instead of uniting the Greek population politically and culturally against a common foe, had the opposite result. Moreover, the scars of the ensuing Civil War were more indelible than those of the war against the invaders. We may recall the conversation Mikis had with Hadjidakis when they first met in 1947, and the subsequent results of the Civil War. Hadjidakis had joined the establishment and was entertaining the Kolonaki aristocratic milieu. In spite of the interest that the wealthy class had shown for the bouzouki, the gap, both politically and culturally had become unbridgeable. Mikis' sufferings during the Civil War, already mentioned, serve only to highlight the gap which had steadily widened between the young musicians of the Resistance generation which had become closely acquainted with the laik music through their war experiences, and the older established "Na-

---

[15] Manos Hadjidakis to the author in a discussion in August, 1968, in New York.

tional School" of the Athens Conservatory. We may also recall the fact that Economidis who had founded the National
School in the first decade of the twentieth century was the
one still in charge of the Athens Conservatory when Mikis
enrolled there in 1943.

The dilemma between joining the establishment or striking out on a new path caused a separation of the ways in the
development of laik pop music. One group turned it into a
popularity contest, wooing the tourist market and the bourgeoisie; the other wooed the youth and the few intellectuals
by bringing it ever closer to the folk tradition. It is hardly
necessary to state in which camp Mikis took his stand. Significantly, Hadjidakis consistently took an ambivalent position, never coming out with any direct pronouncements but
always clearly oriented towards the aristocratic and foreign
approval. An example of this was a concert he put on at the
Moussouris Theatre in January of 1949 for the Kolonaki
crowd, personal admirers of his who came to watch the curiosity—the "rebetica." The immoral "Turkish" bouzouki, the
hero of the evening, was introduced to the cultured. For the
first time, this music was performed in a "civilized place," a
real theatre, not the joints and dens of the harbour. Giving
their "debut" were the veteran bouzouki performers, Markos
Vamvakaris and Vassilis Tsitsanis (both of whom are still
going strong), whom Hadjidakis, in his introductory remarks, heralded as the new Bachs of the laik song. Other
artists were not so fortunate to occupy their talent and interest in such attempts. Mikis himself was fighting to stay alive
in the concentration camp on Makronissos. In a later recol-
lection of the event, he wrote: "After 1946, the persecution
began—hiding and exiles to the islands. This could be one
of the answers to those who insist that Hadjidakis was the
first to lecture on the laik song. He spoke in 1949, and I
heard about it while in Makronissos. That does not mean
that the Greek people and we [the musicians] did not know
the laik song then. We were living it. Hadjidakis spoke to the
aristocracy. The people knew Tsitsanis, for example; he was
living by his music. He was in our daily life and struggles.

There was no need for the laik song to be introduced to us, nor to the people."[16]

These were the years of Mikis' first articles on the rebetic songs, most of which only the left-wing press would publish. Serious interpretations of the laik music were not considered by the right-wing establishment.[17] He was among the first composers to study the laik music, its history, content, and form, and to compile over one hundred songs—notation and words. In the rebetic songs, he saw a bridge between the modern *Lumpenproletariat* and the traditional rural demotic music. The new element that the rebetic songs were to apply was an emphasis on the melodic line. The lyrics, he admitted, were generally cheap and banal, repetitious to the point of absurdity. Nevertheless, they reflected the dignity, pride, and sensitivity of this rootless culture.

These were the years that a differentiation between the demotic, or folk, and the laik, or pop, music began to be drawn. The terms demotic and laik have a social connotation, in view of the fact that the first is derived from the "learned" *katharevousa* word for people, *demos* (an ancient Greek word meaning those males from the *demoi,* or districts, of Athens of voting age), and the second is derived from the demotic word for people, *laos* (also an ancient word, but one that had no connotation of citizenship). Demotic music refers to that of the countryside—mountain, valley, islands—whereas laik refers to the music of the cities and their districts, the working class, the *Lumpenproletariat,* the commercial, the middle class, and whatever has to do with tourism. Musically, the contrast between the two concepts can be best illustrated if one considers that the National School of Music accepted only the demotic and broader folk song, as well as church music, as truly Greek sources for its compositions, the state authorities and the ruling circles accepted the demotic song

[16] Theodorakis, interview: "The Climate That Gives Birth to the Genuine Songs—Theodorakis: Return to the Roots," *I Genia mas* (January 15, 1966).

[17] The left-wing music critic Vassilis Arkadinos had written serious essays on the interpretation of laik music, which far preceded any other attempts. Cf. "On the Rebetic Song," *Elefthera Grammata* 1-2 (1948), and "The Laik Song and the Light Music," *Elefthera Grammata* 2-8 (1949).

as their national property and product alone, and still others linked it to the *foustanella* (a remnant of the romantic days, symbol of the royalists, and a tourist attraction) as an expression of their chauvinistic desires.[18]

The young musicians were forced to strike out on their own, abandoning completely the existing musical establishment in order to produce a genuine Greek, yet contemporary, product. But, again, the group that favoured commercializing the bouzouki habitat gained the upper hand during the 1950's. This was the result partly of the economic prosperity that came to the country with American aid and the growth of tourism, and partly of the pushing of the laik song through records, the vaudeville, and, above all, the cinema. The film *Never on Sunday,* with Hadjidakis' music and Melina Mercouri as the star, did more to spread the commercial cult of the bouzouki inside and outside of Greece than all the articles and debates in newspapers and journals, or "concerts" like Hadjidakis'. Once the foreigners had adopted it, "cultured" Greeks could not remain far behind. This popularization of the *rebetica* inevitably led to a bastardized, "nightclub" product. Its original rhythms and melodies were simplified and commercialized so as to entertain the international jet-set. A vast quantity of ridiculous tunes, with trivial lyrics, were turned out having no relation whatever to the original use of the instrument and music as a genuine outlet of true feelings. The one good result of the *rebetica's* rocketing to stardom was that the state was forced to admit the existence of bouzouki music. Nonetheless, it kept a careful check on all the records, so that nothing which might have any "political" message to the people should be played on the radio. This censorship guaranteed the continuance of the empty, sentimental lyrics, but all the new recordings were good business for the tavernas; the bouzouki joints became

[18] Upon the enthronement of Otho, the costume was adopted as the official uniform of the Greek Royal Guard, the *tsoliades* (or evzones), and rapidly became associated with all that was false and romantic in the chauvinism of the elite and foreign elements, and became the accepted costume of the dancer of demotic songs.

quite respectable. Thus, the subculture was mixed with the high culture, to the former's disadvantage as genuine art. Like rock music, the bouzouki was coopted by the System or completely distorted. A radical revolution from within was the only way out from the downhill path. The stage was set for Mikis' dramatic battle.

Mikis' primary weapons were his newspaper articles, press interviews, and lectures he delivered on every occasion, but it was to the concerts that he devoted his greatest energies. He combined his music concerts with poetry reading at a night club, "Myrtia," in Kalamaki, a seaside suburb of Athens, that was decorated especially for the occasion by the cartoonist Bostadjoglou. Mikis himself conducted the bouzouki ensemble during most of the summer of 1960 night performances. In September, he toured Eleusis and then Herakleion, in Crete, in a miniature pop festival of the arts, taking with him the actresses Irene Papas and Aleka Katseli, as well as the poet Christodoulou and the singer Bithikotsis, two bouzoukia, a guitar, and a contrabass.

His chief concern, however, was with the performance of *Epitaphios*. The director of the radio orchestra, Spyromilios, had agreed to let Mikis use his ensemble along with his own bouzouki instrumentalist, Manolis Chiotis, and Bithikotsis in a premier performance. But Spyromilios reckoned without the hostility of the orchestra itself. At the first rehearsal, the musicians got up and left, refusing to play their symphonic instruments together with a nightclub singer and the bouzouki. The next day, Mikis attempted to smooth ruffled feathers and substituted a guitar for the bouzouki. The music was all wrong, however, and the rehearsal a failure. Finally, the composer protested to the director that there could not be any concert without the bouzouki, since the whole tone and message of the music was lost, and a guitar could not do what the bouzouki was supposed to do. Spyromilios conceded that Mikis had a point and warned the musicians that they either must play with the bouzouki or else would be fired. They gave in, and the rehearsals proceeded smoothly. But on the day of the performance another crisis occurred. When Bithikotsis, who was performing for the first time in his life in a formal concert hall, took the microphone, he was struck dumb and could not sing. Mikis, who was conducting with complete aplomb, grabbed the microphone and carried on the performance as soloist himself. At the end of the concert, Hadjidakis joined in and played one of the songs at the piano, since he had such an interest in Mikis' music. All in all, it proved quite an evening.

Hadjidakis' interest, however, was mostly shown in the music of *Epitaphios,* so that he decided to make his own arrangement and recording. He eliminated the bouzouki entirely, emphasizing, instead, the rebetic rhythms as interpreted by the strings and the saccharine voice of Nana Mouskouri. Hadjidakis' performance as recorded by his company, Fidelity, was intended to be a chamber piece; Mikis' intention, on the other hand, was to use the bouzouki as a solo protagonist, supported by the forceful, natural vibrancy of the voice of a man who had suffered, even as the mother in the poem had suffered. Mikis' recording with Columbia came out in September together with Hadjidakis'. Now the commercial hostilities were added to the obstacles: The advertisements in the newspapers by the Fidelity company fostered the animosity by stressing Hadjidakis and Mouskouri in large bold type and putting Theodorakis' name and that of Ritsos in tiny letters! It was a trivial matter, but it showed the feelings Mikis had to cope with.

The most dramatic presentation of the music, however, took place at a public performance at the Venizelos Hall in Athens and was organized by the Association of Cretan Students. It was more than just an evening of music. It took the form of an open debate between those who supported Hadjidakis and those who supported Mikis. The symbolic association with Venizelos (the Cretan politician who was a distant relation of Mikis), was enhanced by the presence of two parliamentary deputies from Crete, Brillakis and Vardinoyiannis, and the president of the Federation of All-Cretan Associations in Athens, Malagardis. The Student Executive Committee of Athens University also participated. The three speakers were the musicologist Anoyiannakis, Hadjidakis, and Mikis.[19] Anoyiannakis made the introductory remarks, giving biographical details about Mikis, his musical talent, and experience. Then, Hadjidakis took the platform and spoke of the differences in their styles of approach. Objecting to Mikis' purely laik interpretation, he argued that he wanted to give "more" with the interpretation of Nana Mouskouri.

Mikis acknowledged Hadjidakis' "exoteric" approach to the bouzouki music with his interpretation of the song cycle *Epitaphios*. He then explained that both the music and the bouzouki performance of the cycle carried on the tradition of the elegiac threnody found in the klephtic ballads, the songs of Epiros, the dirges of Mani, the songs and dances of the islands, and the Cretan *rizitika*. "The bouzouki, the instrument that performs the laik song, is for modern Greek music what the guitar has been for the Spanish flamenco, the balalaika for the Russian song, and the accordion for the Parisian waltz. The bouzouki is, to a large extent, the modern national pop instrument."[20] Thus, his interpretation was completely and totally laik. As to Hadjidakis' interpretation with Mouskouri, Mikis said: "Another *Epitaphios*—lyrical, nuptial; it is the epitaph of a sister to her brother and a lover to her lover, rather than a mother to her son. But, if the first *Epitaphios* is lyrical and nuptial, the second is of the market-places and the alley-ways, where the brave youth gasped and loved just before he got a bullet in his heart."[21]

The statements presented that night, outlining the problems of and the need for a serious examination of the laik music, prompted a series of broadcasts, interviews, lectures, and articles, in which all sorts of people in the musical world took part. The brilliant performance of the bouzouki artist, Manolis Chiotis, and the gifted voice of Bithikotsis were a challenge that the radio took up by playing on its broadcasts,

---

[19] An account of the events was serialized in *Avghi* (Oct. 6-8, 1960) in *op. cit.* (supra n. 5), 169-180.

[20] *Ibid.* (supra n. 5) 176.

[21] *Ibid.* (supra n. 5) 179-180.

first, the Mouskouri version and, then, the Bithikotsis version. The Kolonaki aristocratic crowd embraced the former; the proletarian neighbourhoods of Athens and Piraeus, the latter. At the same time, magazines and newspapers welcomed comments and conducted interviews to present the "Theodorakis camp" and the "Hadjidakis camp."

The popularity of the songs (the records of both Hadjidakis' and Mikis' original versions were sold out and second and third releases made) and the upheaval they created in all strata of Greek society were ample justification for the composer's convictions concerning the existing relationship between music and the public's demand. Here was visible proof that this was the music the people had been awaiting so long. In the first of three important articles that appeared in October, 1960, an interview he gave to the magazine of the peace movement in Greece, *Dromoi tis Eirinis*,[22] Mikis made the bold claim that the bouzouki was the only instrument which could be embraced by the majority of the Greek people. He also elaborated upon the art-laik songs by insisting upon respect for the rebetic tradition and discussing its potentialities for development into a more sophisticated art, the embodiment of a genuine Greek musical form. He illustrated his arguments by referring to Schubert, Schumann, and Brahms, who had also been inspired by common roots but arrived at different creations.

Rebutting the attacks from all sides that he used beautiful poetry to cleanse a low and degrading musical instrument, Mikis, unyielding as he was, insisted that the sailor, the taxi driver, the salesman not only could but wanted to sing and understand the poetry of Ritsos, if it were presented in their own musical language. Replying to the contention that there would be a danger of over-involvement with bad psychology if the rebetica, with their elements of weariness, escapism, and fatalism, were embraced by the people, Mikis said that the rebetica were an art, and as such expressed the genuine problems of the people.

[22] Interview in *Dromoi tis Eirinis* (October, 1960) in *op. cit.* (supra n. 5) 180-185.

I do not believe that there is optimistic or pessimistic art.
There is only Art, and non-Art. The first strengthens us, gives
us the joy of life, uniting us with the roots of man. The second
does not cease to undermine the foundations of our moral and
spiritual vigour. The real danger is the light song, which *makes
us forget*. The laik song *makes us remember*.[23]

As to the charge of failing to show respect to Ritsos because
of the choice of Bithikotsis as the performer, he declared that
it was unthinkable that there should be a class of people
"worthy to sing" and a class unworthy to do so. He insisted
that Bithikotsis' voice, and the way he trained him to sing,
would become the collective voice of Greece.

In connection with this ingrained prejudice about class division—why should not a chauffeur perform Ritsos, or a field-
hand?—he took up the question in a second article, published
the same month in *To Proto* (The First), a youth magazine
of the dual nature of the problem of laik music—the aesthetic
and the social. He maintained that it was false to assume that,
because of the class of the composer or performer, the people
would sink into the hashish atmosphere or other practices de-
spised by the aristocratic, cultured circles. "Our people, like
all peoples, when singing a tune, does not think of whether
the one who composed it is a Christian or an unbeliever,
black or white, clean or dirty, saint or murderer. Its only interest is to feel its innermost nerves and sinews vibrating, its
pains soothed, and its dreams turned into sounds."[24]

Throughout the rest of the fall and into December, although he was occupied with the production of the ballet
*Honeymoon*, performed by Ludmilla Tcherina at the Place
Clichy in Paris, his mind was tuned to what was going on
back home. He kept up a constant correspondence with the
press over the problem of Hadjidakis' not signing the *Manifesto* and the tremendous importance of *Epitaphios*. A man
who attracted Mikis' attention was Arkadinos, who attacked
his interpretation of the music for being purely laik and re-

[23] Included in *op. cit.* (supra n. 5) 185-188. Definitive comment made in this
article written from Paris defending his version of the *Epitaphios* against the
attacks of Arkadinos. It was published in *Epitheorisi Technis*, 73-74. [Italics
supplied.]
[24] *Ibid.*, 189-191.

betic and praised Hadjidakis for his "fine sensitivity" and faithfulness to the style of the poem. Arkadinos emphasized the excellent choice of Mouskouri as the performing artist, whose voice was a true expression of the grandeur of Ritsos' superb poem.

In response to Arkadinos' sharp criticism, the composer not only insisted on the importance of the role of Bithikotsis' voice in the performance, contending that it would create a striking success in Greek pop culture, but also gave a detailed account of how he came to compose the songs of the *Epitaphios* cycle.[25] Mikis showed how careful he had been to adjust the poetic syllable to the note and rhythm of each song-dance. He explained every detail of the metrical patterning of each rebetic song in order to indicate to the public the relation of laik and demotic dance rhythms. What closer correspondence between musical rhythm and metrics than the 7/8 of the *kalamatianos,* with its fifteen-syllable line of demotic poetry, so faithfully portrayed in Ritsos' "Epitaphios." This traditional meter, with its caesura after the eighth syllable and two principal accents on the sixth and eighth syllables, reflects the same divisions and accents in the rebetic rhythm. An example of the composer's style is given here in one song, in transliteration and word for word translation:

| | |
|---|---|
| Méra Mayioú mou míssepses, | A day in May you met your death, |
| Méra Mayioú se cháno | a day in May I lost you. |
| Ánoiksi, yié, p'agápayes | T'was spring, my son, which you |
| ki'anévenes epáno | so loved, |
| | and you were going up on the sun-roof. |
| | You kept telling me such beauty |
| Sto liakotó ke moúleyes | would be ours one day; |
| ta oréa tháne diká mas | but now your life has been put |
| Ma tóra esvístis ki'ésvise | out, |
| to féngos ki'e fotiá mas.[26] | and our light and fire have gone out as well. |

[25] Mikis Theodorakis, letter to *Epitheorisi Technis* in *op. cit.* (supra n. 5), 192-202.

[26] This is the first stanza of "Mera Mayiou" (the third song of the *Epitaphios* cycle).

He was fascinated, as a creative artist, with the juxtaposition of odd and even rhythm that is the major characteristic of most Greek rhythms, the 2+2+2+1 that is the *kalamatianos* rhythm and the 2+2+2+2+1 that is the rebetic.

The battle was joined by other music critics: Mikis' foes of both Right and Left and his supporters defending or attacking the bouzouki because of its association with brothels, hashish dens, and the like. Soon, the whole population was divided into two camps, and the poet Eleftheriou remarked, in a letter printed in *Anexartitos Typos* on December 29, 1960:

> A small civil war is raging these days in the musical sector of our intellectual life. . . . They call Theodorakis' *Epitaphios,* composed to the verses of our first-rate poet Yiannis Ritsos, a product of the brothels and an apotheosis of the bouzouki establishments. So they prolong endlessly one musicological difference between the interpretation of the famous threnody by Hadjidakis and Mouskouri and that of Theodorakis-Bithikotsis, until it becomes a fuse about to ignite national dissention.[27]

The sparks flew back and forth all that winter and into the spring, as Mikis expanded his musical activities in schools and colleges—and even the police force! On March 28, 1961, the Law Students Association, impressed with the seriousness of the movement and the significance for their own understanding of laik music, organized a debate to which they invited Mikis as well as the poets Livaditis and Christodoulou. The review of the evening in next day's *Avghi* summarized the questions and their answers.[28] In general, the questions concerned the history of music in Greece, particularly the effect of the War of Independence, and that genuine Greek music of the nineteenth century was mostly country music, since Greece was a nation of villages. Mikis explained that the laik song grew as the cities grew, and the big problem, therefore, was joining the laik with the demotic, since both were expressions of the people, to create an art work. The interest and involvement of creative poets such as Christodou-

[27] Letter in *Anexartitos Typos* December 29, 1960 in *ibid* 203-204.
[28] *Ibid.,* 235-238.

lou, Ritsos, Elytis, and Gatsos were needed, he said, and he appealed directly to the poets: "As I accept the differentiation between the laik and the artistic, you poets, also, must accept it, and, while maintaining your own personality, be inspired to create the genuine laik song." *Epitaphios* from then on became an almost daily issue on the university campus; even other schools, such as the school of Berzan and the American College for Girls, extended invitations to Mikis to lecture and perform in a kind of teach-in method, with the participation of both students and teachers. The musical demonstrations and the teach-ins, however, were not limited to schools alone—the working class people and even the police did not want to be left out. Thus, the Association of Greeks from Pontos and labour unions from Piraeus attended pop-musical seminars in hundreds, and the Officers' School of the Athens Police organized an evening for Mikis to perform and speak on the laik music.

While such surprising events continued throughout that season, Mikis proceeded with new musical creations. In the spring of 1961, he presented the recording of another song cycle, entitled *Deserters,* the poems of which had been written by his brother Yiannis. Mikis had written the music in October, 1960, while he was in Paris. In this song cycle, the composer himself is the vocal artist. The twelve songs, entitled *Archipelagos,* with lyrics by Mikis, his brother, Gatsos, Elytis, Kokkinopoulos, and Christodoulou, was performed as the second part of the revue *Hop! Hop!* in July, 1961. The bouzouki had now invaded the theatre. He had just delivered a lecture and was giving a musical demonstration at the Metropolitan Theatre, in Athens, when he was informed that a prize had been awarded to him at the Third Festival of Light Song, sponsored by the National Broadcasting Corporation for his song "Abduction" from the *Archipelagos* cycle. In the performance, his three "discoveries," Bithikotsis and Mary Linda, who had been the artist in a second version of *Epitaphios,* and Marinella, shared the honours, along with Manolis Chiotis as the solo bouzouki. Because of the prize, he was once again the subject of controversy, which was intensified as he turned to another poet, this one of conservative politics, George Seferis.[29]

Mikis' whole creative energy was directed towards proving that the most dynamic wealth of material for music as art lay in traditional Greek music, if this music were united with serious poetry of dramatic substance and realism. In turn, such poetry, previously unknown to the great majority of the people, if introduced by a musical language with which they were familiar, would be spoken by the lips of everyone and not just a tiny percentage from the poetry circles in Athens. It was the duty of the poets to write even better verse specifically geared to the song form. "It is not only the bad habits of the public which must be changed; our poets must overcome some of their weaknesses. The line which will be put to music must be in harmony with the melody, *direct, perceptible,* and *clear.* Writing verse for songs is something completely different from independent poetic creation," he wrote in an article for *Dromoi tis Eirinis* in July, 1961.

Thus, the musico-cultural revolution, set in motion by the *Manifesto of Music, Epitaphios,* and the subsequent song-cycles, established first and foremost the notion of the song-cycle as a serious art form. Secondly, the laik (rebetic) music, expressed by the pop (bouzouki) singer and the bouzouki instrument, became the accepted means of expressing difficult poetry. Thirdly, by pushing aside the foreignisms of Eastern and Western vocal intonations, a genuine "Greek voice" was established. Fourthly, the revolution created a direct communication with the larger segments of society, in the form of the pop concert which broke with the traditional type of formal performance and entertainment. The stage constituted no longer a barrier between the creator and interpreter, on the one hand, and the people, on the other. Each communicated with, and benefited from, the other.

[29] A third version of *Epitaphios,* choral this time, was released with Terpsichori Papastefanou conducting the Choir of Trikala. Three more cycles were released at the same time: *Politeia* (eight songs), the twelve songs he wrote for the film, *A Neighbourhood: The Dream,* and Seferis' four poems, *Epiphania.*

# 5

# The Evolution of Theory, 1960–70

A genuine and truthful composer is one who gives birth to genuine and true melodies, as has been the case with Monteverdi, Bach, Mozart, Beethoven, Stravinsky, Prokofiev, Weber, Shostakovich, Gershwin, Tsitsanis, Hadjidakis, and Dylan.
MIKIS THEODORAKIS, Oropos Prison, 1970

## THE EXPANSION OF THE MOVEMENT: CINEMA AND STAGE

During the 1960's, the most prominent and influential medium in Greece, as elsewhere, was the cinema, in which creative young artists were experimenting with considerable success and gaining a wide, enthusiastic following. Because of increasing public and professional interest, an annual film festival was finally inaugurated in Thessaloniki in the fall of

1959, under the direction of Paul Zannas, who ten years later was imprisoned for his anti-regime activities, and cinema, like all the other arts, was placed under the heavy censorship of the colonels.

Mikis, perceiving the didactic possibilities of cinema, soon came to regard it as perhaps the most effective means by which to reach the Greek people at large. His music, however, because of the composer's political commitment to the Left, was for the most part banned from the radio from the early days of his movement; only isolated songs were permitted to be played that had, from the authorities' point of view, less "harmful" material as their subject. But the cinema, being still a rather new art form, remained relatively free of direct government control. Moreover, it cost very little to produce a film in Greece. It was only natural, therefore, that Mikis, like other young Greek composers, should have turned to the cinema before venturing into the theatre, whose strictures and traditions afforded less opportunity for innovation. Moreover, the cinema, unlike the theatre, was accessible to the majority of the Greek people and constituted for them the only link with the outside world. In 1961, in an interview with the periodical *Dromoi tis Eirinis,* he pointed out how important it was to join the laik or pop song, with its power to move and inspire, with the new art form and thus create what he called "cinematographic opera."[1]

Indeed, he had begun working towards this end as far back as 1953, writing the score for various films which, although admittedly less than significant from the point of artistry or worldwide success, nevertheless achieved their purpose by helping to bring to the Greek public both his music and the neglected Greek tradition he sought to revive. Between 1960 and 1967, his most prolific years in this medium, he composed the score for twelve Greek films, the most notable of which was *The Tempest.* Produced in 1965, it played throughout Greece and had as its unifying theme the song

[1] Mikis Theodorakis, "From Pop Song to Pop Opera," *Dromoi tis Eirinis,* July, 1961.

Mikis Theodorakis in Mytiline
at the age of two.

Mikis on the mountains of Arcadia
with the members of his cenacle in 1943.

Mikis as a soldier in Alexandroupolis in 1950.

Mikis with
his father,
mother, and
brother in
Galatas,
Crete,
in 1954.

A scene from the *Greek Carnival*, choreographed by Rallou Manou and performed by the Elliniko Chorodrama in 1954.

Mikis in London, where his ballet *Antigone* was premiered in 1959, discussing the performance with John Granko, Beriosova, and Rufino Tamayo.

A scene from the filmed ballet *Honeymoon*, choreographed by Léonide Massine and danced by Ludmilla Tcherina of the Opéra de Paris in 1960.

"A Day in May,"
from the manuscript
score of the *Epitaphios*
cycle, based on Yiannis
Ritsos' poems in memory
of the May, 1936, massacre
of factory workers.

Mikis rehearsing the
*Epitaphios* in 1960.

Mikis being arrested by
police during demonstrations
protesting the shooting
of Lambrakis in 1963.

Mikis and Yiannis Ritsos
surrounded by students
near the hospital in
Thessaloniki where
Lambrakis died on
May 23, 1963.

Mikis and Manos Hadjidakis
at the premiere of their
musical revue *Enchanted
City* in July, 1963.

Mikis at the Marathon Peace March in 1964.

A Lambrakis Youth Centre that paramilitary
gangs defaced with swastikas in 1965.

"The Cells Breathe," from the manuscript score of
*Sun and Time*, the song cycle written while Mikis was
in a Security Police cell in September, 1967.

Mikis' wife Myrto and their children under house arrest
in Vrachati in 1968.

Mikis being welcomed at the U.N. by Secretary General U Thant in July, 1970, when he addressed the World Youth Assembly.

The politics of unity. Mikis at a rally in Düsseldorf, Germany, with the centrist deputy Mylonas and the rightist Voloudakis in May, 1971.

cycle *Little Cyclades* (Elytis' poetry set to music and sung by the actress and Mikis' singer Dora Giannakopoulou). In other films his already known song cycles, including *Epitaphios*, served as background music.

During the years he was writing the music for Greek films, he also directed his talent toward the world market, composing thirteen scores for English, American, and French films. One of these, *Honeymoon* (1960), explored the didactic potentialities of cinematography, while serving to release the ballet from the limits of stage performance. This was also true, to a certain extent, of his last attempt at ballet through cinema (a combination very much in vogue in the 1960's)—the 1964 French release *Les Amants de Teruel,* in which the music was danced by well-known stars of the ballet—Robert Helpmann, Moira Shearer, Ludmilla Tcherina, and Anthony Steele. The British producers, Powell-Pressburger, also got the important choreographer Léonide Massine to collaborate. The theme of the seventeenth-century Spanish epic poem *Los Amantes de Deruel* of Juan Yague de Salas was ideally suited to Mikis' inclinations and to classical ballet. The film was a great success, for it combined originality, artistic sublimity, and a dancing which looked like a moving sculpture, motioning to the dynamic melodies and rhythms of Mikis' score.

The film in which Mikis' music achieved its most triumphant expression, however, was *Zorba the Greek*, for here, at last, was a theme close to the composer's heart. For, indeed, the character of Zorba represented to Kazantzakis, the author of the novel from which the film was adapted, to Cacoyannis, the director, and to Mikis, the ideal man—the primitive, sensual, free individualist—the Greek male. Mikis was able in this plot to explore his talent and bring to the score all his convictions concerning the vitality of the Greek musical tradition. The liberating power of the bouzouki music and Zorba's dance at the close of the film, the *syrtaki,* became the property of the whole world. Millions who had not seen a Greek dance before acquired at least a visual image of "Greekness."

The film's incredible success created, however, a twofold problem for Mikis, as usually happens to such collaboration of the arts. First, he was given the opportunity of reaching huge numbers of people. Second, this same opportunity created a disadvantage for an orthodox composer to present, and be identified as composing, a salable item for public consumption. Along these lines, in some of his film music, Mikis tried his hand at combining Greek and Western pop music. A good example of this technique can be seen in the score for Jules Dassin's *Phaedra*. This film, released in 1963, is a modern adaptation of Euripides' classic, altered by having a foreign youth in love with the Greek matron, in order that the score might combine both foreign and Greek elements. The foreign, ranging from modern rock rhythms to Bach, reflected the background and the emotional outlet of the youth in love, whereas the Greek themes were used to convey the emotions and aspects of the Greek character. In *The Day the Fish Came Out*, the 1967 release by Cacoyannis, the foreign element took over almost completely, since it involved tourism in Greece. The bouzouki played some rock-and-roll rhythms, while gorgeous bikini-clad hippies and VIP's danced; and the score, an arrangement of Mikis' music by Cacoyannis while the composer was imprisoned, managed to project a certain quality of timelessness and spacelessness.

Mikis did not work personally with *The Day the Fish Came Out*, nor with his most recent triumph, *Z*, the dramatic reconstruction of the murder of the leftist deputy Grigoris Lambrakis. Nevertheless, the director, Costa-Gavras, skilfully worked in the score by putting together various melodies from the music written in 1962 for Brendan Behan's play *The Hostage* and which a year later were to be identified with the Lambrakis affair like "The Smiling Lad" and some new compositions which were smuggled out of Greece in two of which the composer sings and plays the piano. The score for *Z* helps to heighten the tension of the dramatic moments, although the music played a subordinate role. The choice of composer and songs was in keeping with the theme of the film, for there was fear that Mikis himself, in the hands of the colonels, was liable at any moment to share Lambrakis' fate.

In all these films, Greek and foreign, Mikis wrote music that was suited to the taste of the international public on the one hand, and on the other he followed the modern trends in pop composition. With only one film he showed his real aesthetic credo and his belief in the unity of the arts. That was with the score for Euripides' *Electra* (1962), directed by Cacoyannis and submitted to the Thessaloniki and Cannes film festivals. The score for *Electra* was Mikis' first attempt to unite the classical technique of drama with the modern technique of cinema, so as to identify thereby the ancient unities of *logos* (poetic word), *mousiki* (performed melody) and *orchesis* (rhythmical movement). The music was intended to evoke a visual image of the drama on the screen, as the listener was separated from the visual participation in the theatre. The score consisted not of melodic motifs simply to be remembered but of whole strophic melodies flowing behind the dramatic speech and tragic conflict of the heroes. It achieved a dramatic unity that reflected the harsh, dry, rough landscape that was an expansion of the ancient stage, and served as a counterpoint to action and emotion in the same way as in Prokofiev's cantata, *Alexander Nevsky*. *Electra* stands as a landmark in the mergence of music, film, and acting, and in his score Mikis reached a new height of lyricism, power, and passion. With his score for *The Trojan Women* (1971), Mikis follows faithfully the aim of the director Cacoyannis to produce a work as primitive as possible with speech and dramatic economy touching the very essence of human passion and drama. The score allows for a greater use of instruments—santouri, sitar, electric guitar, and basso with sounds that bring one's feelings closer to the primordial nature of drama.

In all twenty-three of Mikis' film scores, whether for films with themes of social protest, poverty, oppression, political statement, war resistance, love, or purely artistic expression, the predominant tone is that of the Greek outlook with universal dimension, reflecting the tragic disposition and yet strong masculine joy in the life of a free mind and body.

Nevertheless, the cinematic medium, due to the indirect involvement of the creator with a concrete audience, and hence no chance is given for a direct dialogue of the two, Mikis explored other artistic means for such communication through the theatre. He devoted his greatest efforts for the success of his movement to the theatre, which offers the opportunity for communication with a live audience.

Mikis, like all modern Greek composers, began his efforts in drama with the ancient classics. But writing music for the ancient tragedy and comedy is not an easy task, for, due to the uncertainty and unsettled nature of music—its style and tone—it is bound to cause arguments and be a subject for doubts. Mikis first expressed his musical theories with regard to ancient drama while still in Paris, in an essay entitled "Music in Ancient Greek Tragedy," and published by *Kritiki*, the cultural journal of Thessaloniki, in 1959. A year later, after experimenting with the tragedy *Phoenician Women* and discovering that there were still many problems about the music for the chorus that had not yet been solved, he published a second article, "The Problem of Music in Ancient Tragedy," in the leftist newspaper *Avghi*, on December 4, 1960. The purpose of the score, he opined, was to illuminate and set forth vividly the psychological aspects of the play, and transcend the historical moment to become eternal, that is, relevant to modern times. This could not be achieved, however, by imitating the dark and gloomy Gothic-Germanic expression, nor by following the lighter Latin expression of the French and Italian composers. The Greek composer who would write for classical drama must search for the musical language of his country, with all the influences, melodies, and rhythms inherent in the demotic (folk) and laik (pop) tradition. He must be careful, however, in using these rhythms and melodies, not to create temporal and regional associations.

The decade from 1960 to 1970 has been evolutionary in terms both of theory and of demonstration. Aware of the fact that since, in classical drama, the music was an integral part of the action of the characters as well as of the choral song and dance, the modern score, he established, must be equally connected, illuminating the dramatic action and demonstrating the human conflicts. The audience, nevertheless, must not become conscious of the role of the music, for otherwise the tension is broken. "It is no longer the 'moira' [fate] of tragedy that enfolds us, but motifs and irrelevant sounds."[2] Consciousness of the emotion in the union of speech and rhythm, and not the individual character, is to be stressed. Always, the composer's aim must be the search for the perfect harmony of *logos, mousiki,* and *orchesis*. Music must be absolutely one with the intensity of the tragic moment.

Mikis made the word the deed with his first score for Euripides' play, *Phoenician Women*. The play was presented at the Festival of Ancient Tragedy, at Epidaurus, in the summer of 1960. It was the first time the government of Karamanlis had accepted a score by Mikis to be performed in one of the "sacred places of the ancestors." But the composer was not satisfied with the results. He had followed the German concept of recitative for the choral parts, and the product seemed to him lifeless. In agreement with the manager of the National Theatre, and the director of the performance, Alexis Minotis, Mikis had the choral parts sung. But the result was not too effective then. In the essay written in December of that year, he explained his increasing awareness of the nature of the choral music, rejecting the idea of the *Sprechchor*. The words, the lyrics themselves, contained hidden music, and the composer must listen to and develop that sound and rhythm, he reasoned. He must also adjust his music to the spirit of each individual author, and to the specific spirit of the plot. Then, together with the director, he must follow the lyrics themselves, so that every small breath and movement be balanced and controlled.

With these ideas freshly in mind, Mikis composed the music to Sophocles' *Ajax* for the summer, 1961, festival at Epidaurus; his work was well received, and the play was later

[2] Mikis Theodorakis, "Music in Ancient Greek Tragedy," *Kritiki*, No. 2, 1959, 79.

performed again at Dodona in northwestern Greece. After *Ajax*, Mikis turned to Euripides' *Bacchae*, the most challenging of the ancient plays in rhythm, and melody, and especially the choral parts. Here, Mikis became convinced after studying the text, the chorus must not only sing but dance and be made to play musical instruments, as well. Hardly had he composed the choral parts, however, when the government, seeing Mikis' popularity increase among the people, suddenly refused to let him complete the score and, instead, assigned the work to Hadjidakis. But by now the chorus, in working with Mikis, had become enthusiastic about his ideas concerning the dance and instruments, and Hadjidakis necessarily went along.

A year later, after the election of the Papandreou government (1963), a breath of "fresh air" blew over the land, which affected all cultural life of the people. Mikis presented a new score for the Epidaurus festival. This was Euripides' *Trojan Women*, in which he incorporated all the aesthetics he had developed and reached a perfection in music for the ancient drama. His most progressive work, however, in the ancient theatre came in the last summer of freedom, 1966, when he cooperated with the actress, Anna Synodinou, and the director, Minos Volanakis, in the production of Aristophanes' *Lysistrata*. This was the same summer that ended with the first week of the Festival of Pop Music, in which he also presented all the new Greek composers. The outdoor theatre of Anna Synodinou on the hillside of Lykavittos, the central mountain of Athens, was turned to a contest of culture and politics. To perform the play in Synodinou's theatre was a gesture of independence on the part of the artists from the more hidebound National Theatre. Miss Synodinou herself, in 1965, had broken with Minotis, who had become something of a dictator, and established her own privately financed Lykavittos theatre. This gave artists freedom from state control, and they could compose and perform as they felt. *Lysistrata*, which was performed thirty times that summer, with its caustic sociopolitical satiric spirit, gave to Mikis the opportunity to take greater liberties with the score than he had taken with the drama scores. The orchestration was simple, light, and without the heavy instrumentalizations and harmonies of Hadjidakis, or any other Greek composer of scores for comedies. The melodies of Mikis' score were free, in consonance with the comic, satiric mood of the play. The score for *Lysistrata* was significant for its rhythmical control and economy in the use of instruments, and, as his first comedy, was a fantastic success, a result, at least in part, of Minos Volanakis' talent as a director.

In all his scores for ancient drama, Mikis achieved the unity of *logos, mousiki,* and *orchesis.* The wind and string instruments as well as the tympani—a most important feature of Mikis' style of composition—reinforce the music in a genuine return to the spirit of the classical stage. From what he had composed up to that point, it was clear that Mikis was attempting to bridge the gap between the traditional folk and pop melodies, on the one hand, and the classical composition, on the other, and to the ancient sound, by way of the human orientation. In composing for ancient drama, he knew that the music must speak to modern man. These endeavours strengthened his sense of purpose in utilizing pop motifs when he turned his attention to contemporary theatre, while at the same time making him aware of the importance of the public. For, in ancient drama, the people were the chorus, and the chorus was the mouthpiece of the state. Therefore, modern drama, to be successful, must also be the mouthpiece of the people. His most recent ideas concerning ancient drama, namely, that the actors as well as the chorus must sing and that the chorus has four functions—as dancer, musician, actor, and singer—Mikis has also drawn from his experience with modern "epic theatre," believing the one an outgrowth of the other.

Theatre, he believes, in line with Georg Büchner, Brecht, Weill, and García Lorca, has to be a living experience, evoking the participation of the audience, much as did the ancient drama of fifth-century Athens. In this sense, it would be "political," as was ancient Greek drama, which involved the total experience of the *polis* (the state and its citizens). The modern political theatre, furthermore, would, again like the ancient, be inseparable from music. Its function would be not mere entertainment but the ancient concept of *catharsis,* a cleansing of the emotions, by projecting on stage the experiences and problems of the people. These were to be the raw material of "myth." Such myth existed, ready and waiting, needing only the creator to tell it in the drama. The only difference between the ancient and the modern concepts of theatre is that, in the former, the overpowering force was thought to be fate, or the will of the divinities, whereas, in the latter, it is historical necessity. In his evaluation of his own creative endeavours between 1960 and 1970, made in Oropos Concentration Camp in 1970, he wrote: "Always having as my model ancient Greek tragedy, I conceived the work of this period as a canvas on which the figures and ideas of our era could be embroidered, and, more specifically, the events and ideas that distress the Greek people."[3]

In his endeavours with modern theatre, Mikis began first of all with the musical revue. This form was the outgrowth of several existing traditions of popular entertainment—"Karaghiozis," or puppet shadow theatre, with its laik, bouzouki introduction and interludes and its demotic songs; Eptanissian theatre, improvisation on an impromptu stage set up in the public square; and vaudeville, with its short comic sketches, songs, and dance. His first contribution along these lines came in 1961, when he submitted his song-cycle *Archipelagos* for the revue *Hop! Hop!,* a production that involved many contributors.

The following summer, he cooperated in the revue *Beautiful City,* the first political satire of any importance produced on the Greek stage in modern times. It reflected, in an Aristophanic spirit, the daily experiences and problems of Greece, and was deemed by one playwright, Anagnostaki, the best work of her time. The satire of Part One was written by

[3] *To Kallitechniko Mou Pistevo: 1 Domi kai to Noima Mias Prospathias* (My Artistic Credo: The Basis and Meaning of an Attempt). Notebook kept in Oropos Concentration Camp, February-April, 1970; left incomplete upon his release. Translated from the original manuscript. (Referred to hereafter as *Oropos Notebook*.)

"Bost" (the pen-name of Mentis Bostadjoglou, a famous car-toonist), and the Second Part was written by Mikis. He dra-matically contrasted the prevailing poverty of a large seg-ment of the Greek people with the sumptuous display of the royal wedding of Princess Sophia and Juan Carlos, which was the big news event of the year. Cacoyannis directed and coordinated the large number of participants—dancers, act-ors, and singers. Mikis himself was responsible for the entire score, and his newly formed musical ensemble was the orches-tra. Two of his chosen voices were the pop singers Stellios Kazantzidis and Marinella. The plot, or "myth," was formed from fourteen songs, so that the total emphasis was on the music and the dance, replacing the traditional prose.

Because of the tremendous success of this revue, Mikis and Hadjidakis, who had offered a competing revue, *A Street of Dreams*, at the Metropolitan Theatre, a few blocks from the Park Theatre where Mikis' "City" was showing in 1962, de-cided to collaborate on a revue in the summer of 1963,[4] *The Enchanting City*, staged by the cartoonist Minos Argyrakis. Once again, there was almost no speech at all. In Part One, which was Mikis' responsibility, the recent tragedy of the Lambrakis murder (May 22, 1963), as represented by the sor-rowing mother, was the dominant unifying musical and dra-matic theme. Hadjidakis, in his Part Two, preferred to ex-plain with a taped oration his ideas about the music he had included. These pieces were actually nothing but a repetition of his *Never On Sunday* themes.

These musical revues, however, were only one aspect of Mikis' interest in the theatre. Far more important was his grave concern over the failure of the generally accepted mod-ern theatre, which had reached a dead end with its barren-ness. He ascribed the failure to the inability of such a theatre to perform a social function, as classical drama had done. To Mikis, it was a universal failure of great proportions. There-fore, when he was approached by the producer Leonidas Tri-vizas and asked whether he would like to write the music for

[4] By this time, he had contributed four more works for the theatre. See Ap-pendix I.

the sixteen poems in Brendan Behan's play, *The Hostage,*
Mikis jumped at the chance, inspired by the idea as well as
the lyrics. The theme was both genuinely political and contemporary, for the parallels between the struggle of the Irish
against their British oppressors and that of the Greeks with
the British in their involvement in the Cyprus question were
easy to draw. The issue was making the headlines daily. The
play itself had already been translated into Greek by Vassilis
Rotas, a well-known playwright, so brilliantly and sensitively
that it could easily be assimilated into contemporary Greek
"mythology."[5] The tragic "myth" of struggle against oppression affected the audience all the more deeply because of the
disarming light tone of alternating speech and song. Although each of the sixteen songs Mikis wrote for the play was
a separate entity, together they constituted a whole suite. Occasionally a passage of recitative, either solo or accompanied
by instruments, broke into a song, but in general the suite
built in momentum from song to song until it reached the
final climax of "Easter," the triumphant march sung in unison by the mixed chorus. The work was orchestrated for bouzouki, tympani, harpsichord, and a mixed chorus, and there
were places where the music had overtones of Renaissance
and English folk music. So moving were these songs that two,
"Easter" and "Smiling Lad," were incorporated much later
into the film *Z* as its theme songs. The "Smiling Lad," was
an immediate hit with the youth who adopted it as a protest
song against Greece's growing military involvement with
NATO. Not only because of its laik instruments, and the
people's music and contemporary experience, but also because
of its anti-British and anti-American message, at a time
when Karamanlis was relying on both countries for his government's survival, the play was a remarkably daring feat.
Because of the tone of resistance, the "Smiling Lad" and
"The Window," were banned from the radio, and were not
given licence to be included in the recording of the album,

[5] "Mythology" and "myth" imply an abstraction from, and making universal,
contemporary events, and the creation of symbols from historical personages
and objects.

which destroyed the unity of the cycle. Nevertheless, Mikis, with characteristic stubbornness, made a recording singing all the songs himself, and the album circulated secretly. The songs were interpreted as song-symbols in the struggle for freedom, and the play had a powerful impact because of its union of two international "revolutionary" artists, Behan and Theodorakis.

The most original, indeed unique, example of epic theatre was Mikis' own work *To Tragoudi tou Nekrou Adelphou* (The Ballad of the Dead Brother). Here was the quintessence of epic theatre: book, lyrics, and music by the same writer, and a true folk tragedy based on the people's own experience —the Civil War. In the family of Papamercouriou, who had been killed by the Germans, the two brothers, Pavlos (Mikis' leftist friend of Civil War days, who had been tortured to death in 1948), and Andreas (a rightist), each following his own ideology, join opposite camps. The mother in vain tries to reconcile them. At the peak of the Civil War Andreas is killed in battle. Pavlos is betrayed by his girlfriend, Ismene, in order to save her father who fought with the rightists, and is killed. The central figure in this sanguinary battle is the mother. Mikis, faithful to the traditional folk song which has treated the mother's love as the main element of tragedy, has made it the focal point in the drama. "The mother in the laik songs is the most sacred, the sweetest, the most priceless theme of the melodist,"[6] Mikis has observed in his very first articles on the Greek traditional song. On the epic level, the two brothers represent the warring factions of Greece, leftists and rightists; the anguished mother is Greece, destroyed by their hatred. The work, in terms of both history and aesthetics, becomes autobiographical; it is Mikis' own story and credo.

This play differs from the *Hostage* in that it is not a translation but a genuine Greek product, sprung from the Greek soil, wet with Greek blood and tears. The drama is centred upon the family, the heart of the Greek nation. It is there, in

[6] From his 1949 articles on the "Modern Pop Song," *Simerini Epochi* No. 3, November 7, 1949.

Mikis' understanding, that "mythology" is born. He later said about the play, writing in prison in 1970: "Mythological figures are those who, either out of belief or illusion, are turned into bearers and also victims of historic becoming."[7] This indicates his belief that the theme, as well as the problem of civil strife, is not only Greek, but universal.

Mikis wrote the musical tragedy *The Ballad of the Dead Brother* in the winter of 1962. Its music was premiered on April 20, 1962, at the Rex Theatre as a dance suite, performed by Rallou Manou and her Elliniko Chorodrama in celebration of its tenth anniversary. It was performed by an orchestra including two bouzoukis, and two singers, Bithikotsis and Dora Giannakopoulou. Its important production, however, as epic theatre, did not take place till the fall of that year, with its opening on October 15. It was produced by the veteran director Pelos Katselis together with Manos Katrakis' Elliniko Laiko Theatro and a full bouzouki ensemble. The hue and cry that had arisen over the *Epitaphios* in 1960 was nothing compared to the shocked protests of both Left and Right factions this time.

First, there was the aesthetic shock. Mikis was presenting something utterly new to the Greek audience—total theatre—in which instruments and singers, dead and living (actors and audience) interacted. In the Prologue, the chorus *is* the orchestra. Upon its entrance after the first song, "April," which sets a false mood of festivity, it moves onto the stage symbolically bringing the audience with it to participate. This is done through the song "The Dream," which gives the essence of the drama. Thus the audience learns the story of the play although historically it has already participated in its "mythology."

> You had two sons, my mother,
>    two trees and two rivers
> Two Venetian castles
>    two springs of jasmine, two worries.

7 Theodorakis, *Oropos Notebook* 28.

One goes to the East
    and the other goes to the West,
And you, standing in the middle,
    speak and ask the Sun:

If you ever see Pavlos, call me,
    and if you see Andreas, tell me;
I raised them with the same anguish
    and with the same sob I bore them.

But they take to the mountains
    and they cross the rivers—
One is seeking to find the other,
    one to kill the other.

And there, on the highest mountain;
    there, on the highest peak,
One next to the other they sleep
    and share the same dream:

That they run to the mother's—
    oh, to the mother's death-bed—
They both together join hands
    to close their mother's eyes.

And they plunge their knives deep
    and firmly into the soil.
And from there the water sprang
    for you to drink and slake your thirst.

The kernel of the "myth," with its three main characters, is found in this song, stepping out of it, as it were, to move and clash on a new level to become a new, larger song, a ballad. The composer explains, in his *Oropos Notebook*, that the events and figures in life come and go, like a dream, but the pop singers and the instruments (representing the people) in the play remain like the mountain, timeless. The musical instruments and the singers symbolize the permanent axis around which all peoples and nations turn. They become "characters" on stage. In the unfolding of the play, the characters often address the pop singers, who have taken places on a small platform, like those in tavernas, asking for advice or assistance. The pop singer is the eye and soul, the voice and memory of the people and of history. The "chorus" itself, however, only observes. It does not take part but only "delivers justice" through the song.

In Part Two, the "Act," as Mikis titles it, there is no chorus participating, no musicians. In their place are masks and the instruments that are hung on the wall of the platform area. The music of the *santouri* and the *clarino*—the elemental folk instruments—are played from below, in front of the stage, now placed together with the bouzouki ensemble. The plot of the drama itself ends with Ismene singing the song "Betrayed Love." In the last two songs—the exodus—"In the Garden" and "Unite," the dead participate along with Charon, the ancient ferryman of the underworld, who has entered and addressed the audience and actors alike, boasting of his power. The final song, "Unite," the instrumental version of which also opens the drama, signals the denouement, thereby symbolizing the complete circle of life and death. All those who have been killed in the Civil War—rightists, leftists, policemen, revolutionaries—march forward towards the audience, as in the parabasis of ancient drama, holding hands. They are not what they were before death but what they have become through their sacrifice. Thus, a new, permanent unity is projected into the future as a result of the past. The "Sun" and "Joy" are symbols of this unity.

> United stone and stone
> United hand in hand
> The mountains and the valleys begin the song,
> Cities and harbours join in the dance:
> Today we marry the Sun,
> The Sun to the bride, the dearest, the Joy!

Oh, our Joy, our daughter—
Our valleys, seas, mountains,
Mothers, daughters, dead brothers, fathers,
One tree, with one root, one well, one spring:
Today we marry the Sun,
The Sun to the bride, the dearest, the Joy!

It was a mad attempt on Mikis' part to use such material for the subject of an artistic work. Yet, to him, it was the ideal example of contemporary myth. The drama lay in the overthrow of political and moral values. The evil one—the collaborator, the coward—was not punished, and the good one—the one who resisted and gave up his life—was not rewarded. The national resistance had been turned into civil strife when the relationship between Greek and foreigner had been replaced by that of Greek against Greek. That was the beginning of tragedy. In Mikis' use of the myth, it acquired even greater strength by employing the present tense instead of the past. He did not write "It was" but "It *is*"; for the striking thing about such drama was that the audience not only lived through but was still experiencing the "myth." And therefore he made the myth embrace the whole people, using "we" and not "I." This close relationship between stage and audience precluded the need for lofty critics or obscure interpretation. Through the people's myth and music, the drama was instantly comprehensible. The catharsis of the drama would be brought about by the unity of hearts in song.

It was this conception of myth, the contemporary tragedy (and, in this, Mikis was far ahead of his times), that brought down on him the wrath of all the political factions, from the extreme Right to the extreme Left. It was a second shock even greater than the aesthetic one, for he had created an art-work out of a taboo subject. Marxists and rightists alike objected—the former because the notion of holding hands with Fascists who wielded the gun against their fellow-citizens was unthinkable, the latter because the Civil War was an unmentionable crime perpetrated by Communists. The musico-cultural movement of Mikis, however, had reached its peak with this play.

Mikis tried his hand at other examples of epic theatre and also collaborated on several other musical revues. *The Seven Deadly Sins* was a combined effort of seven artists, who wrote satirical sketches to be accompanied by Mikis' music. Iacovos Campanellis' *The Angels' Quarter* portrayed the life of an Athenian proletarian neighbourhood. Once again, Mikis' music provided the thematic unity for the entire theatrical action. He also started work on several pop theatre productions that were never completed. Another, Brecht's *Roundheads and Pointedheads,* contained fourteen poems translated into Greek by Yiannis Ritsos. At the same time he began work on these, he was touring the provinces with *The Ballad of the Dead Brother,* in the fall of 1964, so that he wrote the music for only a few of the poems. The rest of the cycle was left in the form of sketches. He also was attracted to the project of a pop opera, based on Alexandros Papadiamantis' novel *The Murderess,* as well as Angelos Sikelianos' *Digenis Acritas.* The poet Nikos Gatsos, however, was still in the process of working up a libretto for the first, and there were difficulties with the inefficiently run State Opera, which was to put them on. Both works were never carried through. While in exile in the mountain village of Zatouna in 1969, the composer wrote a dramatic dream-satire on life in Greece under the junta, which he entitled *Exodus.* The work uses all media—sound, action, music, and dialogue—but so far has not been produced and exists only in original manuscript and my translation.

In the composer's own evaluation of the decade, in his *Oropos Notebook,* he clearly states that, just as creative poetry and traditional Greek melody, if welded together and expressed through song, would produce a genuine style of music, so modern opera and tragedy would flower only when based on the two fundamental elements of contemporary mythology and modern pop song. But, freedom and unity are still in the future for Greece, and it would seem that the song of the dead brother may again have to be reincarnated.

### POETRY AND MUSIC: ART SONG

> We must expect Europe's music to reflect
> the many different tensions that character-
> ize its political and spiritual life, for that
> is the only healthy way for it to exist.
>                           AARON COPLAND

The prime elements of Mikis' music have always been *melos* and *lexis*. The two are inseparable in his creative proc-ess and as essential to his music as the vocal chords and into-nation are to singing. Although he is more a musician-poet than a poet-musician, he has, from early childhood and whenever unable to find other poems, written his own and sung them, too. In this, he is only following the ancient prac-tice of uniting the poet, dramatist, and musician in one—a practice observed also in Byzantine and medieval times and best exemplified in the modern era by Wagner. In his works, therefore, the sister arts of poetry, music, and singing are brought together on equal terms. The great challenge, how-ever, is how to render proper justice to each.

Mikis, for all his works, has tapped the vast resources of the melodic tradition which was cultivated with the passage of time. From this tradition, he has taken the "conscious-ness," the impetus and the inspiring force, but not the "per-sonality"—the external form or dress—as composers like Had-jidakis and those of the National School have. Avoiding the superficial, Mikis concentrated on linking his melodic line with the underlying stream. Mikis described the phenomenon this way: "The melody is found in its organic unity with the human sensitivity, so that it reflects the vibrations of the specific emotional weight it contains."[8] The emotional weight needs a rhythmical outlet and a degree of harmonic reinforce-ment at first. Then it needs words to describe its content— the message. And this is how he has put it:

> In the beginning was the Word! This truth is applied faultlessly in all my works. Hence, *one has but to take into consideration the poetic text each time in order to interpret my music.* More-

[8] Theodorakis, *op. cit.* (supra n. 3) 63.

over, from the beginning I intentionally stated that I place my pride in serving faithfully (primarily) modern Greek poetry. And this to such a degree that, *when one listens to a song, one cannot imagine the music with another text, nor the poem with different music.*[9]

We have seen that the aesthetic revolution was declared with the song cycle *Epitaphios* in 1960. From then on to the end of the 1960's, Mikis continuously wrote songs that range from the unit-song (the short, 3- to 4-minute metrical composition) to three stages of song cycles that incorporated these songs, and chose voices particularly suitable to interpret each unit or cycle.

Some thirty or more songs exist as individual entities, unclassified in any specific group. These are drawn up from all the traditional trends but have as their chief exponent the bouzouki. The rest of his art songs may be divided into three categories, according to content (music and poetry) and form of performance. These categories serve to clarify the composer's gradual and methodical growth from the simple to the complex in the art of composition. Of the three planes, or categories, the first is the simplest. In this first category of song-cycles may be included the following works: *Archipelagos* (1960), *Politeia* (1961), *A Neighbourhood: The Dream* (1961), *The Angels' Quarter* (1962), *Beautiful City* (1962), *The Seven Deadly Sins* (1963), *Enchanting City* (1963), *Songs for Farantouri* (1964), *Politeia II* (1964), *The Island of Aphrodite* (1965), *Twelve Laik Songs* (1968), *For the Mother and the Friends (Ark. III)* (1968), and *Negro Ballads* (1970). The songs of these cycles, in their majority, share a common root, in that the melodic force in each was drawn from the rebetic tradition and climate; they were intended, first, to be danced, then sung and, of course, remembered. In all of them are evident the traditional rhythms that converged in and influenced the rebetic song. The lyrics of each song were written by a different poet and therefore lack the complexity and thematic coherence of the next stage in the development of

---

[9] Theodorakis, *ibid.*, 6. [Italics supplied.]

the art song. At this stage, Mikis was writing his "orthodox" rebetic dances, much in the manner of an untrained bouzouki melodist. The unit-song, which made up the first category, was easily accepted. The people adjusted themselves to the refined form of the new art, followed it, and were caught up in a "dialogue" with it. And so it was with every stage of development. Through gradual familiarization with each new form, they were ready to receive the more complex.

A second plane, or category, presents a more sophisticated approach in form and content. Although the songs that make up these cycles are still rebetic, or pop, dances, they are now broadened and elevated to a stage above the serialized unit-song of the first category. The focus is no longer on the dance but on the aesthetic training of the public. The melodic line is broadened with harmonic alternations, but the melody still plays the primary role, while the rhythm and harmony are subordinate. The orchestration is enlarged with the introduction of other musical instruments playing a secondary role.[10] The bouzouki is not the chief instrument, in the sense that the lyrics are now more emphasized. These lyrics comprise thematically coherent poetic texts written by one hand and sung by one vocalist, such as *Epitaphios* (1958-59), *Deserters* (1960), *Epiphania* (1961), and *Little Cyclades* (1964), all of which have been performed and recorded. The remaining cycles in this category, beginning with *Letters from Germany* (1966) up to and including *The Vows* (Ark. IV) (1969), were either heard once or still exist only in sheet form.

To be of value, the poetic text must represent the myths of the people—their contemporary problems and experiences in the light of historical causality. They can be either concrete, as with the *Epitaphios,* where Mikis used the demotic fifteen-syllable meters of Yiannis Ritsos' commemorative poetry, or abstract, as in the case of *Epiphania,* where he took four selections from the free verse of George Seferis. This same abstract type of myth can be seen in the seven songs of the

[10] One of the first major changes in the orchestration was Mikis' intentional removal of the accordion, an instrument he felt did not suit the spirit or tradition of Greek music.

*Little Cyclades.* This song cycle set to music seven poems of reflection and contentment, speaking of love and the daily beauties of life, the sea, and the sun, all written by Odysseas Elytis specifically to be sung. These along with *Letters from Germany,* describing the daily life of Greek and other workers in postwar Germany, and the *Six Maritime Moons,* proved that first-rate poets could write songs without losing their personal style and tone. It also showed that Mikis could work intimately with the poet, blending his own vibrant melodies with the music of the poetry. These cycles reinforced his theory of the inseparability of poetry and art song.

A special training and polishing of the voice has given a more elevated tone to the performance as well. The tightness of the dance rhythm is loosened as much as possible, but it is still there. The composer here explores all the musical traditions, mostly the Byzantine and demotic. The most important characteristic of the song cycle to be noticed at this stage, and even more so in the third category, the ballad, is the pervasive "climate" and mood for singing the songs in continuation. The listener is given an emotional outlet and is enveloped in the spirit of communal joy.

As in the second category, the poetic text for the ballad (third category) must be contemporary and meaningful to the broad masses. The myth or story can be concrete, as in *The Hostage* (1962), or *The Ballad of the Dead Brother* (1962), *The Ballad of Mauthausen* (1965), and *The Ballad of Romiossini* (1965),[11] all of which have been performed. Two more still exist only on tape and were smuggled out of Greece, as were all his works from 1967 on—*The Ballads of Antonio el Camborio* (1967) and *Sun and Time* (1967). The common element of all these ballads is that they were each written by one hand—Behan, Theodorakis, Campanellis, Ritsos, and García Lorca. They all narrate an event or historic situation. Thus, the poetic text serves as the unifying power. A characteristic of all the ballads is a uniformity of musical

---

[11] The word *romiossini* (from *romios,* which itself is of unclear etymology) was coined during the Turkish occupation to refer to the Greeks. It has subsequently come to mean "down-home" people, or "the story of the Greeks."

climate, with a nuance of sadness and plaintiveness that reflects the content of the lyrics. But each cycle differs from the
other, in that each presents its own musical texture and lyrical content. The music, however, has a universal element, in
that the myth-story of the "dead brother," whether Greek or
Irish, in the modern musical tragedy does not find its dramatic unity in the form of incidental music or in the mass
hysteria of Holy Roller clapping. Instead, the individuality
of the vocalist and the pulsating rhythm are the unifying
thread. This emphasizes the importance of the single voice
that performs the cycle. Occasionally, as in *The Hostage,*
where Mikis wanted to stress the internal musical continuity and unity, he sang all the songs of the cycle himself. The
result is a suite for voice and an ensemble of pop and symphonic instruments.

Since the events in the life of a people change, and new
myths, as a result, are continually born, the composer's duty
is to live, follow, and portray them with his art. Thus, *The
Ballad of Romiossini* came into being. It is the story of the
Greek people from the days of Digenis Acritas in the ninth
century to World War II—a tale of revolutionaries and guard-
ians of the rocky, waterless, and sun-drenched land of Greece
as seen by Ritsos. It is an epic theme in free verse, inspired
by the Resistance and Civil War years, 1940–49. Such epic
style—the challenge of the themes of courage, privation, bit-
terness and hope—required a strong musical score to incorporate the heroic quality of the poem and the history. The tradition Mikis drew upon for his haunting music was that of
the klephtic ballads—masculine, sad, and brave. Most significantly, he selected the singer of the *Epitaphios* cycle, by the
same poet, to "tell" the story and "warn" the people of the
imminent dictatorship. It was the pop (laik) singer who took
the role of the herald of the ancient tragedy. He was the one
to tell the people in precise, articulate, and vigorous tones to
maintain a vigil against the threat to life and liberty. The
"bell" that tolled was the bouzouki, for, in *Romiossini*, it is
more than a rebetic instrument. It is connected directly with
the "action" and the meaning of the words in a most simple

melodic line without harmonization or excessive orchestration. It is a monody in the ancient concept.

The low key of the music of the *Ballad of Romiossini,* recalling that of the klephtic ballads, is delivered by the singer in clear, sharp, penetrating syllables. In many lines, he reaches the lowest of chest registers. The orchestration is utterly simple, stark, limited to strings and drums, which back the bouzouki. Practically no other work by Mikis has been so widely circulated.[12] It has become the property of all Greeks, no matter what their political persuasion. The distinctive quality of the music reaches out and impresses the message upon the mind of the listener indelibly. "This land is theirs, this land is ours." It was the perfect unity of two musical traditions, the klephtic ballad, whose "consciousness" —melody—the composer has taken, and the pop form, characterized by the bouzouki and the pop singer.

After writing *Romiossini,* Mikis set out to compose another ballad, in which he wanted to pay tribute to the nameless victims of Nazi concentration camps. He turned to the poetry of Iacovos Campanellis, who had been interned at Mauthausen, Austria, and composed a cycle of four songs, with Byzantine elements, entitled *The Ballad of Mauthausen.* To project these songs, he selected a young girl, Maria Farantouri, whom he had discovered in high school, where she was singing patriotic songs on special occasions. It was a voice in a million, so suited to his interpretation and sensitivity that she became, from then on, his chief "herald." The combination of her warm, feminine voice and the tragic text, on the one hand, and the composer's passionate music, on the other, produced an elegy of universal dimensions, which could appeal to the world at large and not just to the Greek public. This universality also exists in the *Ballads of Antonio el Camborio,* where Mikis set to music selections from the *Gypsy Ballads* of García Lorca as they had been translated

---

12 Pieces from *Romiossini* and *Mauthausen* have become part of the repertories of Pete Seeger and Barbara Dane, as well as many other American and particularly European artists, who sing the lyrics both in Greek and in their native languages.

by Odysseas Elytis. The listener can detect the merging of Spanish themes and elements, such as the *paso doble,* with mellifluous Greek tunes. The music unfortunately has never been recorded, because the coming of the dictatorship in 1967 interrupted all Mikis' activities. It exists only on tape and in sheet form. It was premièred finally on June 30, 1970, at the Royal Albert Hall in London with the recently released composer himself at the podium, and the voice of Farantouri and the guitar of John Williams to deliver the message of Lorca.

The most unbelievable circumstances surrounded the composition of his last "ballad," *Sun and Time.* What happens when a composer has no instruments to work with? What happens when he has no poetic texts? What happens when the creative, sensitive soul, burning with life, is thrown into prison? *Sun and Time* was Mikis' answer. Caught between life and death, unable to sleep with fear that any moment the guards would come to torture or kill him, he scrawled his despair, his memories and hopes and anguish, on scraps of paper—thirty-three poems in all. He turned fifteen of them into songs: "Hello, Acropolis," the prisoner cried out, "The Cells Breathe," "When Time Stops," "Violet-Crowned Land, No Other Has Loved You as I." An incident, a thought, a sound, was subject for a poem. One day, a flower was tossed from a neighbouring cell, where two friends, Nikos and Yiorgos, were imprisoned. This small sign of humanity inspired the haunting song "The Cells Breathe."

> The cells breathe,
> The cells that are above,
> The cells that are below.
>
> The rain unites us;
> The sun is ashamed to appear.
> Niko, Yiorgo,
> I am held by a flower.[13]

13 Broadcast by the BBC in 1970.

Even in prison, he gave birth to melody, an abundance of melodies—Byzantine, demotic, laik, art—all original, pouring from the agony of his mind and body. As creations from that tormented period, perhaps it is most fitting that, as yet, they are unfinished, in the sense of a definitive orchestration, arrangement, and delivery. They exist only on tape, sung by the composer, and in his original manuscript.

The ultimate development of the union of poetry and song is the "song-river" genre, which makes a clean break with every other form of pop music. It is an elaboration and extension of the melodic line, wherein the musical phrase flows out into a broad, melodious, and forceful stream, breaking down every formal limitation of the short composition. Because the melody follows long, usually free-verse, poetic texts, a song-river is three or four times the length of the average unit-song. With such a long composition, the great danger is that the melody will be repetitious and monotonous. Yet, despite the sad mood and the dirge-like quality of the music, the melodic line is always original and enthralling. Hauntingly Byzantine, with bold, simple, naturalistic images, the song-river impresses upon the listener all the horror of daily existence under oppression and in the midst of disaster. *Our Sister Athina,* by George Photinos, tells of a girl taken to prison and shot. *The Survivor (Ark. VII),* by Takis Sinopoulos, speaks of the fate of one who survived the World War II years. Most agonizing of all is the cry of the mother, always the bearer of tragedy, in *The Exile's Mother (Ark. IX),*[14] by Kostas Kalantzis, when she hears her son has been condemned to life imprisonment by the colonels, as well as *The Three Brave Ones (Ark. XI),* drawn from a poem by Notis Pergialis.

What direction Mikis will take with this new genre, now that he is in a foreign land, cannot be determined. First, he must test it with the public, as he has with all his earlier song-cycles. But one thing is certain: contemporary, burning poetry will be the "stuff" of his song-river type of music, which, in his mind, serves as the link between the art-song and "metasymphonic" composition.

[14] Broadcast by Radio Moscow in 1970.

## POETRY AND MUSIC: METASYMPHONIC WORKS

As is quite clear from all of Mikis' statements and compositions, art music is for him the highest form of creativity. As such, however, it cannot—indeed, must not—be alienated from the broad mass of the people, as has been the case with most of the Western classical music of the nineteenth and twentieth centuries, particularly the symphony. No matter how much such works are modernized, electricized, they will always be foreign intellectually to the public at large. And herein lies the root of the crisis in art music. Such a division between the people's life and experience and the music presented to them has resulted in a standstill, especially for the symphonic work in the modern era. It was not, however, until very recently that the barrier between the cultivated few and the uncultured masses began to break down, pushed aside, either aesthetically or socially, by people from both groups who refuse to accept the differentiations any more. Consider the innumerable rock-festivals of the young over the world. This is their music, their way of giving voice to their myths. This is the germ, in Mikis' eyes, from which the symphonic work must grow. The social import is the basis for musical creation.

Ancient Greek music was the product of a sharing by all citizens. The poet who wrote the tragedies and composed the music always had the people around him in mind and expressed their cultural experience in the universal language of myth. Ancient drama was a total participation. For Mikis, the only salvation for modern art music was to return to the ancient concept of the oneness of poet, composer, and people. Thus evolved what he has termed "metasymphonic music."

It is new, in the sense that it is to surpass the limits and orthodox standards of a symphonic work and its performance. Mahler, for instance, attempted such unconventional methods in his later works, but his multitude of artist-participants in a symphonic performance was rather a reaction to similar attempts by Berlioz and Wagner. In that sense, and also because it had no socially or aesthetically radical innovations, it has not been accepted as revolutionary. Four components are essential to metasymphonic music: melody, derived from the various Greek traditions—Byzantine, demotic, pop; musical instruments that are genuine and traditional—the bouzouki, baglamas, santouri, lyra, clarino; the poetic text, which gives the "mythological" cohesion to the work, so that the people can creatively and directly identify with it; and the multitude of participating vocalists, with pop singer, cantor, reader, and mixed choir. All together create a new sound, a harmony that, in the best of ancient Greek tradition, is born out of contradiction.

Yet, Mikis' concept of metasymphonic music did not spring, like Athena, full-blown from his head. On the contrary, as he himself admits, his ideas on this new musical form have evolved only slowly, after considerable trial and experimentation. Thus, in his first efforts with the metasymphonic idea—his score for *Electra* in 1962—he did not use a poetic text incorporated with the music. Nevertheless, the music actually followed, served, and commented upon the dramatic text along the very lines he later set down as his aesthetic rule regarding poetry and music.

The score is unique, because its message—the myth, so to speak—is equally forceful, whether the music is performed in the concert hall, heard on a record, or serving as background for the pictorial image on the screen. With *Electra,* he experimented with the instruments. These instruments have a particular mission, even while being used in conjunction with the normal classic symphonic instruments. They evoke the participation of the people because they are known to them, while at the same time preventing them from being reminded of the Western musical experience. Thus, the qualitative difference between the "Greek sound" and Western musical art offers a possible separate service. The drama of the speech and action is entirely presented in the music—the agony, the passion, even the groans of despair and death-throes of the murdered mother Clytemnaestra. The primitive folk instruments give them voice. Even the baglamas, the tiny bouzouki, is used, to interject the strident, piercing cries of human terror. The power of man expressed in the ancient Cretan pyrrhic dance, and his agony, are voiced by the stringed instruments that Mikis uses to get as close to the tonal quality of the Cretan lyra as possible. The nasal, dirge-like sounds of the clarino or the brass instruments portray the death-throes, occasionally interrupted by the "wood drums" (pieces of wood still used by the monks on Mount Athos, struck to produce the effect of a primitive atmosphere). Thus, the native and "uncultivated" instrument expresses the primordial nature of modern man.

His most powerful masterpiece, in which the *logos* (the concept) became the *ergon* (the incarnate reality), was Odysseas Elytis' magnanimous poem *Axion Esti*.[15] Mikis had been brooding over this "symphony" for four years before he finally delivered it to the people in September, 1964. First, he had to be sure in his own mind of the nature of the aesthetic, and then he had to train the public with his other song-cycles and ballads to accept the instruments of the people and the pop singer in art music. The singular characteristic of the metasymphonic work, the poetic text, was incorporated with the ideas already developed in *Electra*. He lifted up on the wings of sound one of the most difficult and comprehensive creations of any modern Greek poet. In his own appraisal of the poem, he wrote:

> In my opinion, the *Axion Esti* of Elytis constitutes a monument of modern Greek art. Moreover, its vast depth of Hellenism brings it to the forefront of our people for its completion—both for its concrete historical and ethical stance and for its presentation. The dimensions, as well as the form of the poetic text, lend themselves to carrying out a modern musical form. The work covers the entire history of the Greek nation in all its periods from the Genesis of this "small world, the Great," to the prophetic vision of the horrors to be imposed on us by the present Dictatorship.[16]

[15] "Axion esti" (it is worthy) is a phrase from the liturgical drama of the carrying-out of Christ's body, a ritual in the Orthodox church that takes place in the pre-dawn hours of Holy Saturday.

[16] Theodorakis, *op. cit.* (supra n. 3) pp. 6-7.

He reinforced the historical continuity and poetic vision with almost every element of Greek musical tradition, as well as some Western techniques, thus creating a new climate, in which poetry and music are joined as integral parts of one synthetic whole.

Elytis' poem is, first of all, a hymn to the physical-natural world of the ancient Greeks, vitalized by the sun. It is the essence of the lyrical, and has been called a "liturgy of the senses,"[17] for it reflects in its tone, diction, and structure the traditional liturgy of the Greek Orthodox church. This liturgy is pagan, however, in its philosophical outlook, rather than Christian. It praises the things of this world—light, colour, man, consciousness of freedom. Elytis grasps all the effusion of colours and aromas of Greek nature, and especially its light, weaving them into a multifaceted image that goes beyond the simple picture. His pantheistic love of nature, however, is anything but romantic. A tragic sense is there in all its force. The poetry hovers around the symbolism of the number 3, again reminiscent of the liturgical sense. It has three divisions—Genesis, Passion, and Axion Esti (Gloria)—representing the story of Christ in allegory, the story of the Greek people in microcosm (hence biographical for both composer and poet), and, finally, in its universal implication, the story of mankind. The poet expresses the just and clear demands of his people, any people, for a better world, and determines to rid himself, and therefore the world, of the dark forces that deprive him of life and light. This is the people's dream, for the song of the poet is the song of the people. As Mikis has explained: "Specifically, with *Axion Esti*—the Bible of the Greek nation—the Word of the poet is the word of the people. His Memory is its memory. The people itself is the creator of the events that inspire the poet. The Passion is his own, and the Glory as well."[18]

[17] Edmund Keeley, "*Axion Esti*—The 'Genesis': A Commentary," with text translated by E. Keeley and G. Savvides, in *Poetry* (Greek Number) 105 1 (October, 1964), p. 16. Professor Keeley is currently completing a translation of *Axion Esti*, having done the Genesis and Gloria. He and Kimon Friar, of all the scholars and translators who have shown an interest in this poem, have truly understood the message of both the poetry and the music.

[18] Theodorakis, *op. cit.* (supra n. 3) 15.

The inspiration for the poet was the bloody experiences of World War II, and the civil strife that followed, even as this period had influenced so much of Mikis' creative thinking. In setting *Axion Esti* to music, however, Mikis used only about a fifth of the whole poem, choosing the fundamental analogies of each of the three sections. Within the external divisions, he conceived of three internal ones, the recitative, hymn, and folk-chorale, corresponding to the prose, free verse, and metrical rhymed poetry of the text. In this way, he overcame the obstacles other composers and critics had found in the piece because of its diverse elements of linguistic phrasing and metrical difficulties. The parts are sung by a narrator, a cantor, and a pop singer—the *koryphaios,* or chorus leader, of ancient tragedy. Supporting these singers are the chorus of mixed voices, the classic orchestral instruments, and the pop ensemble—two bouzoukis, a guitar, a piano, a bass violin, drums, and, above all, the santouri. On page 170 is a scheme of the architectural structure, with both its external and internal divisions of the hour-long work, with a brief description of each component, as Mikis has explained them in his *Oropos Notebook.*

In Part One, the composer commences with musical chaos, reflecting the European tradition that he had just abandoned, a chaos as short as possible, demonstrated by an ensemble of instruments as if in rehearsal, out of which is born the world, order (the Greek word *kosmos* means both), that is, a new musical world.[19] This is delivered by the cantor and the choir, accompanied by a santouri, and a counterpoint between orchestra and choir suggests the ancient Greek choral role and musical modes. This first part lasts only six minutes—the six days of the Creation.

Part Two contains the main features of this metasymphonic work, for he develops the three internal divisions of choral, hymn, and narrative to their perfection. The five chorals comprise the best loved of all Mikis' pop melodies:

19 "Elytis' birth in Crete, in 1912, is paralleled by the birth of freedom in the land around him, as we see Crete liberated from the Turkish occupation," wrote Keeley, *op. cit.*

| Form | Text | Interpretation |
|------|------|----------------|
| | PART ONE: GENESIS | |
| Instrumental | Introduction | Orchestra |
| Hymn | "Then He Spake" | Cantor, Choir, Orchestra |
| | PART TWO: PASSION | |
| Hymn | "Behold, Here I Am" | Cantor, Choir, Orchestra |
| Narration | "March to the Front" (Resistance to the Italians, 1940) | Reader |
| Choral | "A Single Swallow" | Singer, Choir, Pop Orchestra |
| Hymn | "My Foundations Upon the Mountains" | Cantor, Choir, Orchestra |
| Choral | "Where May I Find My Soul" | Singer, Choir, Pop Orchestra |
| Narration | "The Great Exodus" (March 25) (Occupation and Resistance) | Reader |
| Choral | "Sun of Justice" | Singer, Choir, Pop Orchestra |
| Instrumental | (From the Hymn: "Temples in Heaven's Shape") | Orchestra |
| Choral | "Blood of Love" | Singer, Choir, Pop Orchestra |
| Hymn | "Temples in Heaven's Shape" | Cantor, Choir, Orchestra |
| Narration | "Prophecy" (Civil War, Dictatorship) | Reader |
| Choral | "I Open My Mouth" | Singer, Choir, Pop Orchestra |
| Hymn | "To a Remote Land" (Diaspora) | Cantor, Choir, Orchestra |
| | PART THREE: AXION ESTI (GLORIA) | |
| Choral | "Axion Esti the Light" | Choir, Orchestra |
| Hymn | "The Winds" | Cantor, Orchestra |
| Choral | "Axion Esti the Wooden Table" | Choir, Orchestra |
| Hymn | "The Islands" | Cantor, Orchestra |
| Choral | "Axion Esti the Stone Parapet" | Choir, Orchestra |
| Recitative | "Hail" | Cantor, Choir, Orchestra |
| Choral | "Axion Esti the Soil" | Cantor, Orchestra |
| Choral | "Axion Esti the Soil" | Choir, Orchestra |
| Hymn | "The Maidens" | Cantor, Orchestra |
| Choral | "Axion Esti the Causeless Tear" | Choir, Orchestra |
| Choral | "Hail the Little World, the Great" | Choir, Orchestra |

"A Single Swallow," "Where May I Find My Soul?" "Sun of Justice," "Blood of Love," and "I Open My Mouth." These are such beautiful songs that they have been extracted from the whole work and interpreted by individual pop singers with guitar or bouzouki accompaniment. One of the most famous interpreters is Kostas Hadjis, the passionate gypsy pop singer, whom Mikis first introduced to the public in 1962. In the symphonic work itself, the bouzouki singer, or *koryphaios* (for which role Mikis chose Bithikotsis), leads, supported, as if it were in a pyramid, by the chorus and the bouzouki ensemble. There is also a dialogue between the *koryphaios* and the choir, in imitation of ancient tragedy, that does not happen in the traditional folk or pop music. This adds a greater dimension to the music and is in itself an innovation in pop art song. The five chorals contain rebetic and island rhythms, cantades, and modern pop musical phrases, indicating that the composer intended to bring all types of songs together and expand their internal melodic possibilities.[20]

The hymns form a unifying element throughout the work, for they alone are found in all three parts. They can be divided into two categories: those based on Byzantine and demotic music, such as "My Foundations Upon the Mountains" and "Temples in Heaven's Shape," and those with atonal passages based on his European musical experience, such as "Lo, Here I Am," and "To a Remote Land I March." In the first category, Byzantine and demotic elements coexist, as seen in the pedal point (*issokrates*), an octave below the cantor, and the instrumental accompaniment inspired by the dirges of Epiros. In the second category, the chorus uses recitative to emphasize the primary rhythmical scheme. The role of the hymns with the cantor and mixed supporting voices, combined with the pop and symphonic instruments, creates an overwhelming liturgical effect. Mikis himself considers the hymns the most complete step in the direction of metasymphonic music, and the ending of Part Two, with its

[20] Mikis continued with this expansion in his song-river experiments from 1967 to 1970.

dramatic and rhythmical *Sprechchor* leading to the remote land, exile, breaks imperceptibly into Part Three, with its most triumphant doxology, "Worthy It Is."

The role of the narrator is to bring the chorale "into time," the historical time of the Greek tragedy 1940–50. Here again, Mikis chose a person who had suffered in the events, he was to bring to life with his voice, the actor Manos Katrakis. His articulate and vibrant delivery, as he functions as both a reader in the church service and a messenger-prophet, connects the whole tragedy of the Italian and German invasion and its aftermath with the five chorales and the timeless hymns.

Part Three, *Axion Esti*, is indeed a swelling of the Gloria, with the Byzantine psalm resting upon the traditional, male, strong dance rhythm of the *tsamikos*. "A chain of instruments, drums, piano, santouri, build up from measure to measure that peculiar modern Greek dance rhythm. On this rhythmical-harmonic-orchestral foundation the purely neo-Byzantine melody for two voices, primo and secondo, is developed by the choir in accordance with the Epitaphios of Good Friday."[21] The 3/4 rhythm of the *tsamikos* connects the last part with the second part through the instrumental "Temples In Heaven's Shape," ever tightening the tempo into a more clearly defined rhythm that eventually embraces the whole metasymphonic work. The climax, "Hail" and "Now," brings the allegory to the present, and forever "the small world, the Great!" The triumph of the "Hail" is reminiscent of the salutations to the glories of the Byzantine conquerors and a tribute to the whole pride of the nation. The interpreters of this great Gloria are alternately the cantor and the choir, accompanied by the symphonic orchestra.

As has been mentioned already, one of the most significant characteristics of metasymphonic music is the use of pop and symphonic musical instruments side by side. These were not a heterogeneous compilation but harmonized together so as to keep the character of the "Greek sound." In *Axion Esti*,

21 Theodorakis, *op. cit.* (supra n. 62) 21.

practically both folk and pop instruments can be found—bouzouki, guitar, mandolin, lyra, lute, mandola, askavlos, baglamas, clarino, and santouri. This last had figured prominently also in *Electra*. Because it is more melic and broader in tone than the bouzouki, it is especially suited for inclusion in a symphony orchestra. Mikis himself believes that there is a great potential for the instrument in the development of modern Greek metasymphonic music.

One of the most amazing things about the score for *Axion Esti* was the way Mikis so completely understood what Elytis was trying to do with his poem. The poet himself acknowledged this on more than one occasion, thanking Mikis, for instance, in a short article in the review *Epitheorisi Technis* for helping him to see the poem in a broader light and offering it to the people to sing and understand when he, the poet, "had been cherishing it to himself like a baby in swaddling clothes."[22] He was particularly enthusiastic over the Gloria section.

In the last part, Theodorakis reached, in my humble opinion, closer to the spirit of the work than in any other section. He gave that mixed feeling of rejoicing and nostalgia which I myself demanded for Part Three, in that section where exists the attachment to all the special feelings that our land offers, like independent values, in the form of a liturgy.[23]

Elytis also showed his awareness of Mikis' movement and its success through *Axion Esti* when he wrote, in the same article:

Theodorakis managed, with *Axion Esti,* to elevate elements from the tradition and to adjust them to his own world without distorting their characteristics. He succeeded, also, in giving an original form to multifarious material by digesting it to a coherent whole and thus elevating the level of pop music from the simple "citation of melodies" to the "composition."[24]

[22] Odysseas Elytis, "Poetry and Music," *Epitheorisi Technis* 20 118 (October 1964) 338.
[23] *Ibid.*
[24] *Ibid.*

However much a landmark *Axion Esti* was in Mikis' musical creativity, it was intended only as a beginning. Unfortunately, the political turmoil of the 1960's, and his final imprisonment (1967–70), did not permit him to experiment as much as he would have liked. Nevertheless, he did try other examples of metasymphonic compositions. His problem while in exile or prison, of course, was finding suitable poetic texts. One that fell into his hands was a collection of poems by Seferis. Having already composed a song cycle using the Nobel-prize poet's free verse, Mikis decided to take one song from the 1961 cycle *Epiphania* and expand it along the lines of the metasymphonic form. He called the work *Epiphania Averoff* (1968) after the Athens prison. The essential instruments are the cello, guitar, piano, bass violin, and trombone. For the pop version, he added the electric bouzouki, the mandolin, and a viola. This work differs from the first *Epiphania* in that he composed music for the whole lengthy poem, not as in the first instance when he had taken a few stanzas from different sections to set to music for a song-cycle.

The heavy, sombre mood of the poet suited those prison and exile days. In Oropos in 1970, Mikis worked on another long, free-verse poem by Seferis, *Raven—In Memoriam E.A.P.* (inspired by the homonymous poem of Edgar Allen Poe). The music is a challenge to the artists, because it is left up to them to interpret the two tempi, the free 6/4 rhythm at the opening and the 3/4 of the *tsamikos*. Furthermore, the composer allows considerable free interpretation throughout the piece because of its great length and the intricate nature of the chromatic tones. On the score, Mikis has written the suggestion that, in addition to the male pop singer, the work could be performed by a mixed chorus, a pop orchestra, drums, or perhaps a flute or other wind instruments from the classical orchestra. Here again, the musical colouring is Byzantine and archaic but very mellifluous, so that it seems perfect for a chamber sonata. In Oropos, Mikis also sketched Seferis' *Mythistorema–XV.*

One of the most tragic of all Mikis' compositions to come

out of his prison years was the *State of Siege*. He set to music a moving poem written by a young girl who had been imprisoned in 1968 who called herself "Marina." The music brings to life the free-verse poem, intensifying the emotions, the visions behind prison walls, and the agony felt by the girl on hearing the screams of "those who have been and those who still are tortured." The work is intended for male and female soloists, a mixed chorus, and pop as well as symphonic instruments. It opens with a dirge-like melos and develops into a Byzantine line, reminiscent of the funeral hymns of the Greek Orthodox church, especially in Part Three. The music then moves into demotic melodies comprising at the end the modern Greek sound. The work was arranged and recorded by the composer Yiannis Markopoulos and Evdoros Dimitriou in London in 1969, rather inadequately it must be said, while the composer was still in exile.

During the period in Zatouna, Mikis continued to develop his concept of metasymphonic music. He worked with poems such as Manolis Anagnostakis' *I Speak* (numbered *Ark. VIII*), or lacking poetic texts, he wrote his own. From the first of these, in two parts, he created a powerful composition which can be considered either a suite or a cantata, for soloist and chorus, accompanied by pop and symphonic instruments. Two of his own poems, *Thourion* and *My Name is K.S.* (numbered *Ark. VI* and *Ark. X*) he set to music which evokes the demotic tradition and the harsh melodies of Crete. Both consist of two parts with the same arrangements. None of these have been performed publicly by the composer. He has, however, taped them, singing and playing the accompaniment on the piano.

The most sustained and demanding work of this three-year period, however, was inspired by the eloquent poetry of Angelos Sikelianos (1884–1951). In this visionary and committed poet, Mikis found a kindred spirit, as can be seen in the composer's choice of the *March of the Spirit (Ark. V)* with its primary themes of the composer: belief in the supremacy of man and his dignity, and resistance to oppression. It may be recalled that "March of the Spirit" had been

written in 1948.[25] This union of poet and musician has produced one of the most moving of all of Mikis' compositions.
It is unquestionably the most difficult and breathtaking work
next to *Axion Esti*. Once again, the composer has managed
to overcome the challenges of the aesthetic principles set
forth in the poem—the superb unity, the grand and declama-
tory speech, and the free-verse form. An even greater problem he had to meet was that of being faithful to the music
within the poetry itself, a music of heroic tone as intended by
the poet. Sikelianos always thought of music while writing
poetry, and used it as a vehicle in his own recitation. He was
very conscious of the importance of the sounds of the Greek
language, particularly the vowels and diphthongs, using them
to express admiration, woe, pathos, or joy. In a most amazing
way, Mikis has managed to capture the mood and the music
of the poem. The melody is perfectly bound to the meaning
of the words.

The music for *March of the Spirit,* in eight parts and
drawn from Byzantine and the klephtic ballads, has a militant and grand spirit of melody and rhythm. Nonetheless, it
is very Greek in terms of sound and faithful to the metasymphonic form. The work shows a true synthesis of musical
tradition and poetry, fulfilling the intentions of both poet
and composer. It is, indeed, a celebration of the salvation of
the creative and genuine meaning of humanism.

### THE COMPOSER AT THE PODIUM

From his early youth in Tripolis, and later at the Athens
Conservatory, in prisons and concentration camps, and during his years in Europe, Mikis has always demonstrated his
passion and ability to organize group performances, and lead
symphonic orchestras at the podium. Here again, the communal operation and the spirit of collective work manifested his
need for conductorship and his ability to organize and com-

---

[25] See full commentary and English translation of the text by George Giannaris, "The Oratorio of Mikis Theodorakis," *Greek Report* Nos. 14-15 March-
April, 1970, 21-23.

mand. His conducting technique springs from his enormous theoretical knowledge and reflects all his musical aesthetic of simplicity and openness. He follows the letter of the score, more specifically the path of the music's soul, and imbues it with his own personality.

In the early years of his musical revolution, he wrote an article on the art of the conductor for the magazine *Epitheorisi Technis*[26] in which he stated that the traditional mission of the conductor is primarily to re-erect the works which have been misinterpreted by the romantic liberties and excesses of the last century. The modern composer, for Mikis, ought to develop a "philosophical interpretation" that would necessarily lead to the philosophy of music. Such an outlook will bring the conductor closer to the essence of music, its melody, and will be viewed as an aesthetic, ethical, and scientific manifestation of the human intellect, taking, of course, into consideration the time the work was written and the trend. Thus, the modern conductor will avoid indulging and following the concepts of the "faultless" musical interpretation; he ought, rather, to approach and hence conduct a work through his intuition and instincts. Concurrently, this dependence on the senses must be accompanied by a thorough understanding and knowledge of every orchestral instrument. Mikis has suggested three elements with which a conductor can approach and interpret a work: a) Temperament (the sum total of nerve-ending reactions); b) Emotion (the ability to accept the emotional elements of the work); c) Movement (the creative ability to transform these two elements into concrete gestures). In conclusion, a conductor's ideas ought to be subjugated to the message of the music he is to interpret.

Needless to say, Mikis has been doing that with his own works, for it is there that he shows us how the theoretical can formulate the practical element of the art of the conductor. Following his plan for the musical awakening of the Greek people he was forced to start with the chamber pieces of European composers. But again the works were performed

[26] Mikis Theodorakis, "The Art of the Conductor," *Epitheorisi Technis*, No. 92 (August, 1962) 167-169.

by his Little Symphonic Orchestra of Athens which later was to become the Symphonic Orchestra of Piraeus up until the coming of the dictatorship. He has mainly concentrated in performing his own works. His tendency to organize, lead, and conduct took on a variety of aspects. The need, for instance, to conduct his song cycles and other pop compositions betrays him as the conductor of a symphonic orchestra, although his bouzouki ensemble is a miniature orchestra consisting of between five to ten pieces. He conducts as if he were leading a whole symphonic orchestra. Mikis has been criticized for his "unorthodox" movement of his body and legs. Usually his right leg is placed one step forward, and his body is dancing to the rhythm of the work he conducts. Most often, he uses his arms instead of the baton, while his facial expressions reflect only the emotional impact of the melody that he is bringing forth. Gyrations and other liberal bodily movements are never allowed; he maintains the dignity and reverence for the work by giving only the melodic rhythm each work contains, but above all he avoids heavy orchestrations and remains as faithful as possible to the distribution of melody each work contains. Certainly, his gigantic stature, imposing body, and huge, long arms render a grandeur and imperious image to any performance. He maintains the pattern, masculinity, gentility, lyricism, and respect for the position of his body as the conductor of either a bouzouki ensemble or a symphonic orchestra.

John Barry went to the rehearsal of the oratorio *March of the Spirit* on June 28, 1970, and wrote the following description for the *Sunday Times:*

On Friday evening, in the oppressively civic setting of Walthamstow Town Hall, he faced the orchestra, the London Symphony, for the first time to rehearse.

It was, for both, educational—not so much a rehearsal, more a meeting of musical cultures. The LSO: casual in summer clothes, none of the wild-eyed musicians of fiction, draughtsmen perhaps? Only the airline bags on the floor—the evidence of their fame.

Curious conducting style. No baton, though an occasional

wave of the red biro he was using to correct the score. A few more or less orthodox bars, his right heel tapping the under-lying tempo. Then his shoulders shake in strange counterpoint. Out flies his left arm. He does not so much conduct the orches-tra as urge it on. Very Greek.

After three and a half hours, they broke up. . . . The or-chestra chatted. "You know," said the leader, "the rhythms are those of ancient Greek dances, each one from a different part of the country." "Oh," said the viola player, enlightenment dawn-ing. "Why couldn't he say so?"[27]

Following the première of the oratorio, however, *The Manchester Guardian* wrote that Mikis conducted like an emperor, slightly tipsy with power, in the lead of his armies. And armies they were: Participating in the London première, for instance, were a full symphonic orchestra, a choir of a hundred men and women (the Ladies of the New Opera Choir and the Gwalia Male Choir), three pop soloists (Faran-touri, Kaloyiannis, and Theocharis), and the most revolu-tionary bouzouki sets and mandolins in the symphonic or-chestra.

As he began his tour of European capitals, he was to en-counter new problems. In a letter to me, dated June 8, 1971, he wrote: "I just got back from Scandinavia. In Stockholm, I conducted the Swedish Radio Orchestra (105 musicians) in my *Oedipus Tyrannus* and *Suite No. 1* for orchestra and piano. It was not only the composer but the whole orchestra that was put to the test. As conductor, I was obliged to ana-lyse the score, and found myself swearing at the composer very frequently for putting in obstacles that were at times insurmountable. Obviously, when I composed this work [*Suite No. 1*] it was destined as a trap for conductors, but I never realized that one day I, too, would be caught in my own trap. But all went well. We held three six-hour rehearsals, and I found the solution in that sacred word: dance! I told the musicians that what they saw wasn't notes but dances. I told them to dance, and dance they did!"

[27] John Barry, *The Sunday Times,* June 28, 1970.

# 6

# Reactions to the Movement

A messenger arrives from the Great Gorge
every morn
on his face shines the perspiring sun
he holds tightly under his armpit the
*romiossini*
just as a labourer holds his cap in church.
The time has come, he says. We must be
ready.
Every hour is ours henceforth.
"Vigilance" by YIANNIS RITSOS

## SOCIAL FORCES

In 1970, after an eventful decade, Mikis, imprisoned and
aware of the fatal suppression of his movement by the dictatorship, sat down to write his reflections on this turbulent
period. His words were the lament of a man bursting with
creative energy and ideas, handicapped by the necessity of
struggling against the times and the oppressive forces around
him. He stated that he conceived of all the products of his

movement, from the song cycles to the metasymphonic works, as "experimental" and "suggestive" for the formation of a theory and the actualization of social change. "Unfortunately, our life, so filled with events and action in the years 1959–69, did not allow me to delve into that direction as I should have, although I consider it critical, serious, and essential for the future of our music. . . . For, it is not only with his work but also with his stand that the living artist must tie himself to his people and his epoch, whatever and whichever the consequences for him and his own work."[1]

Greek society, polarized and swept by strong antagonistic currents on every level, was the atmosphere in which Mikis' theory and aesthetic were born and nurtured. They were, consequently, bound to be militant in outlook and application. By 1960, he had successfully launched his "battle" in the Athens area, the "laboratory," both in theory and in practice. His songs were popular with the youth and the majority of the population of the cities, and now, the much more difficult test, that of development and endurance, lay before him. If his movement were to have true social import, its meaning and impact had to spread beyond the urban centres —which were, admittedly, more receptive to progressive ideas—to the outlying provincial and rural areas, where the majority of the population lived. But, just as he had found opposition to the theoretical aspect of his movement, so was the case again as he tried to approach the countryside. The first and most formidable obstacle confronting him was the state machinery under the administration of Konstantinos Karamanlis, that is, the National Radical Union party, the authorities, and all those who had gained the upper hand after the war. He was also to find resistance among those who had lost, the dogmatic leftists, who persisted in acting out their complexes and frustrations at home and abroad.

[1] Theodorakis, *To Kallitechniko Mou Pistevo: I Domi kai to Noima Mias Prospathias* (My Artistic Credo: the Basis and Meaning of an Attempt). Notebook kept in Oropos Concentration camp, February-April 1970, left incomplete upon his release, translated from the original manuscript 10, 21. (Hereafter referred to as *Oropos Notebook.*)

The state authorities were taken aback by this young composer's rising popularity and made various attempts to "buy him off," such as giving him a prize for his song, "Abduction." But in vain. A vast majority of the population in the capital and the surrounding districts had already given Mikis their approval and backing in his campaign for the renewal of Greek music and culture. It was a majority that saw in his movement the fulfilment of their long-standing desires for change and a chance to take off the blinders the state had been making them wear for so long. In Mikis' music, they saw a reflection of their own daily lives and experiences. There was no stopping or even slowing him down now; his ever increasing strength became an affront and threat to the authorities. This fear was augmented as the October, 1961, elections drew near. Karamanlis was afraid of losing; he did not want a repetition of the discrepancy of 1958. The Right, to guarantee its success through Karamanlis' victory, used all its invisible resources and strength to sabotage Mikis' songs and musical activities. After a bold public denunciation of the musical establishment he made at a recital at the Metropolitan Theatre on July 14, the first open official attacks against Mikis began: in early August, the National Broadcasting Corporation (EIR) banned all his "political" songs. The challenge, however, did not stop there but encroached on other fields. When the film *A Neighbourhood: The Dream*, premièred in Athens on August 10, 1961, for instance, the police stormed the cinema and stopped its projection, forcing all, dignitaries and general audience alike, to leave the hall immediately, even taking a few to the police station. Then, a few weeks later, in the beginning of September, a popular protest forced the Ministry of Education to let the film be shown at the Venice Film Festival. The Greek consul, though, saw to it that it was never presented.[2] The film, with its subject-matter of the daily life of the workers and unemployed families in Piraeus, was not a great work cinematically. But the artistic value of the film was of little

---

[2] The film was shown in local cinemas in New York from September, 1964 onwards.

concern to the censors; they cared primarily because the score was composed by Mikis, and known leftists like the actors Katrakis and Alexandrakis were involved in the production. The Second Week of Greek Films Festival, September 18-24, 1961, held in Thessaloniki, with the intention of including Greek films in the national cultural festivals, promised a certain degree of impartiality. *A Neighbourhood: The Dream* was submitted, but the music received no mention at all, even though all the films were awarded.[3]

Infuriated by this, and determined to proceed with his programme, Mikis in September took his Bouzouki Ensemble (two bouzoukis, a pianist, drums, and a guitar), together with several critics and poets, on a musical tour of the major provincial cities—an unusual thing for Greece—paying his first tribute to his father's native island of Crete; then to Eleusis and on to all the major cities of the North to spread music and poetry—Kavalla, Drama, Larissa, and Karamanlis' native city, Serres, where he found small disturbances. In Trikalla, however, the police director informed Mikis of an order he had just received stating that the eight "Communist" songs of *Epitaphios* were to be removed from the programme. Mikis, however, ignored the order and performed the cycle in its entirety. But in Verria, the authorities carried out their threats: Army units were called in to destroy all the brochures and posters advertising the concert, and the owner of the hall where it was to take place was "asked" to refund the money for the tickets. A special order was issued to punish any soldier who went to the performance; they were to go, instead, to a rally organized by the local political headquarters of the Radical Union Party, where Karamanlis would speak. But artistic events were a rare happening for the troops stationed in Northern Greece, and, despite the army's efforts, many soldiers did go.

In Kozani, where the Third Battalion was stationed, Mikis' concert was besieged. In the middle of the performance, a lieutenant stopped it and ordered all soldiers present to

[3] Another film, Kapsalis' *Dangerous Mission*, dealing with the Resistance, along with Georgiadis' *Flute and Blood*, was barred from the Festival.

leave immediately, while gendarmes encircled the hall. En-
raged, Mikis seized the microphone: "At this moment," he
cried, "I am standing on Greek soil. I am not afraid of anybody!" Infiltrators thereupon shouted from the audience:
"Communist! Traitor! Get out of here!" as rocks and other
objects flew on stage. The performance ended abruptly.
When Mikis protested to the public prosecutor, who "did
not know what he was talking about," and asked him, on his
behalf, to inform the Ministry of the Interior, he was blatantly
ignored.

The gangs proved even more zealous in Naousa, where they
seized the ensemble's instruments and smashed them to bits
as though they were symbols of some diabolical heresy. Once
again, Mikis protested to the authorities, but in vain. Undaunted, he appealed to a local friend of his who enjoyed
considerable influence in the area and, through his interces-
sion, finally procured a licence from the municipal government to hold his concert. The evening of the group's performance, the open-air theatre was surrounded by a band of
policemen. The people, in order to get through the police
cordon, covered their faces. The undercurrent of terror was
almost tangible as they quickly filed past the hostile authorities. As the audience took their seats, all the lights suddenly
went out. In the dark behind the curtain, Mikis caught the
culprit—a policeman. Threats rang out from all directions
against the artists: "If you continue, you will all be killed!"
Only the two bouzoukis, who had borrowed their instruments,
appeared on stage together with Mikis; the others, including
the singer Bithikotsis, disappeared. The audience sat on the
edge of their seats. Others sat in a nearby park, listening from
a safe distance. Then, the signal was given. A large rock was
hurled on stage, and, all of a sudden, pandemonium broke
loose. Over the ensuing screams and uproar Mikis' voice
was heard, calm and controlled, prevailing over the din. "At
this moment," he said, "I am writing *The Ballad of the Dead
Brother*. It deals with the Civil War. At the end the enemies
become friends again. The issues that must unite us are
stronger than those which divide us. There are people here

who still want to sow hatred. I, for my part, want to put an end to this hatred." He sat down at the piano and began to play and sing some of the songs himself. The last ones included the "Gloria" (Unite), in which both sides represented in the performance as fighting in the Civil War united and sang together holding hands. One by one the scattered members of the Ensemble began to join with Mikis at the piano, despite the continuing barrage of rocks and harassment of police. At the end of the last piece, hundreds of spectators escorted Mikis and the artists to their hotel, and remained there to guard them.[4] Later, when Mikis called the Ministry of the Interior in Athens to protest, he was informed that it could not guarantee his safety during the remainder of the tour. Thus the "indignant citizens," that is, the rightist gangs, continued to threaten the remaining performances of the tour.

The majority of the provincial press described events as they occurred, generally taking Mikis' side. The conservative papers, however, particularly those which backed the Karamanlis regime, declared that the tour was a "Communist campaign" and an immoral act, spreading the vulgar bouzouki. Later, though, Mikis found his chance to expose the gendarmerie and their militant cohorts. This was at a concert organized by admirers of his music once the Ensemble had returned to Athens. As a direct reaction against the provincial provocations, the Athenian populace mobbed the concert. The result of this popular demonstration was that Mikis was invited to the office of the editor of the Athens daily *Ethnikos Kyrix* (National Herald), Paraschos, who made a proposition close to blackmail. After feigning regret over the previous unpleasant episodes, Paraschos reminded Mikis that in a few days elections would take place, and the Right would win control of the state machinery again. "It can be yours, too," he said, "but on one condition: that you do not speak out. You are a Communist; we know your ideas. Play your

---

4 This same scene occurs in the film *Z*, which depicts the murder of Lambrakis two and a half years later. In it the police clearly encourage and incite the gangs.

music but don't speak your ideas. Then you shall have access to the radio, the theatres, the State Orchestra—everything. We admire you and love your music, but we cannot let you speak out against us." It was the confirmation of Hadjidakis' prophecy in 1947 when he intimated to Mikis that he would have to join the establishment, or lose. Paraschos was clearly revealing the conspiracy involved in the forthcoming elections.

In early October, at a conference held during the performance of his ballet *Antigone* in London, Mikis had a chance to expose to the British press the harassments under which he worked—the "fascist state machinery," and the plot of the Right to rig the October elections. He was summarily commanded to come to the Greek ambassador's office where he was warned against defaming and exposing his country to the world. Mikis was unperturbed. Later, in Stuttgart, after *Antigone* went on tour, he continued to denounce the forthcoming electoral coup. It was at this time that he was informed by close friends that, if he returned to Greece, he would meet with certain death. At the theatre where the ballet was being performed he received an anonymous phone call from a journalist in Athens: "If you come back, you will be murdered. Traitor! Pig!" Nevertheless, Mikis departed for Athens shortly thereafter. He was welcomed at the airport by hundreds of his admirers of all ages, singing his songs. But this show of popular enthusiasm could not stem the nationwide smear campaign that was in progress, nor the atmosphere of fear which was slowly enveloping the whole country. Some hidden force was at work. The first manifestation of this was the banning of all Mikis' works from the radio immediately after Karamanlis' success at the polls. A few newspapers raised a faint voice of protest. No one listened. A month after the elections, the authorities banned a film, *Saturday Night,* directed by the youthful Papakyriakopoulos, because of its subject—the poor neighbourhoods—and the fact that the director had been inspired by a song of Mikis' with the same title.

Thus throughout September and October things went

from bad to worse. The hitherto unofficial, or semi-official, attacks on Mikis' movement had been legitimized by the official banning of his music from the radio. Frustration took over. Mikis departed for Paris in November. Having decided to make his home there, he bought a three-room flat on the fifth floor of a house right off Boulevard Montparnasse. However, he was not to be deserted, as he had thought. His admirers and friends, especially the students in Paris and Greece, rallied to his defence. Once again, Mikis and his music became the centre of controversy. The journal *Epitheorisi Technis* picked up the gauntlet and, challenging official reaction, began to publish a series of studies on modern Greek cultural issues, starting with Mikis' essays, articles, letters, and interviews written before July, 1961. These were compiled in the volume entitled *Yia tin Elliniki Mousiki* (On Greek Music), which came out in November, 1961, as part of the musico-cultural movement.

Amidst this crisis, and to the surprise of both leftists and rightists, bouzouki enthusiasts and opponents, Mikis, faithful to his credo, turned to another poet, who was better known in diplomatic circles than to the public at large—George Seferis. An album of four poems, entitled *Epiphania*, circulated in December, 1961. This song cycle encountered the same antagonism his previous *Epitaphios* had, but now from the Left. Here was Mikis, the target of right-wing oppression and attack, now composing four songs written by a man of conservative politics. Mikis said to me two years later: "Some fellow-leftists have criticized me for working with poets of other political leanings, but I work with the poet regardless of his politics. There are good leftists who produce bad art, and there are good artists who are not leftists." This, of course, was the irony; for, in spite of Mikis' artistic credo, the dogmatists were far more cynical in their notions of poetry and life and still very distrustful of high-minded ideals like his. Two years later Seferis won the Nobel Prize.

The details of all the turmoil reached Mikis in Paris; once again, he was faced with making a drastic decision. The lines now were much more clearly drawn than they had been when he had left Paris in 1959. Now, he would return to Greece as the victor in the aesthetic battle, deeply loved by a public ready to defend him and his works. But to settle in Greece at this time would clearly be a commitment to fight the sociopolitical battle that seemed to be even more crucial than the aesthetic in actually effecting a cultural renewal.

What especially beckoned Mikis' return, however, was the general cultural and educational movement that was enlarged greatly by the students and the public at large, with their demands for change and modernization in Greek life. Three years of continuous fighting between the students and the state, and primarily the police of Karamanlis' administration, had gone by. Mikis' movement was a part of their struggle. They collected signatures protesting the banning of his music and organized musical demonstrations in defence of his programme. Along these lines, the Society of Friends of Mikis Theodorakis' Music was created. Telegrams, letters, and messages reached him in Paris. His apartment on rue Notre Dame des Champs was filled daily with friends, all asking him to go back.

The social revolution had been born in the schools, because the Greek students were aware of the many defects in their education. No other area had been so greatly neglected and kept in such an anachronistic state as the educational system of modern Greece. The problem became particularly acute in the late 1950's, when Greece was accorded associate membership in the European Community. Owing to the lack of educated people, scientists, and skilled workers, the country was looked upon as fit only for touristic exploitation and military bases. It was the students of the universities, those of Athens and Thessaloniki, and of the technical schools who then began to mobilize themselves for a modernized educational system and state support—a demand that became a daily slogan—and the general cultural and political liberation of Greek society. It was amidst such critical moments that Andreas Papandreou, then chairman of the Department of Economics at Berkeley, and many other young people who were educated abroad came to Greece in early 1960. Mikis and Papandreou shared, more or less, the same frustrations in their attempts to modernize the country, each in his field of interest and specialization. Both were forced into politics when their own disciplines by themselves proved ineffectual. Papandreou, however, went to Greece like a *deus ex machina,* and, uninvolved with the youth and the students, failed to cope with their movement, a fact he realized much later.

The student movement they both found was well developed and on the go. It was aimed primarily at obtaining academic rights, reorganizing the educational system, and alleviating the general cultural crisis; but it had also linked itself with the rest of Greek youth, the labour unions, and the peasants in demanding better economic and working conditions as well as solutions to domestic and international political problems. One of the major complaints was the Queen's enormous expenses paid for by taxes brazenly imposed on the Greek people. In addition to the multimillion-dollar budget of what was called "the Queen's Fund," the people were now saddled with "contributions" to the dowry of Princess Sophia, who was about to marry the Crown Prince of Spain, Juan Carlos, and the state "offered" the gifts and expenditures involved in the royal gala. It was in April, 1962, that the "Wedding of the Century" was to take place. A horde of titled freeloaders descended upon Athens like summer tourists, occupying every hotel and using every available means of transportation, but, unlike tourists, their bills were paid by the Greek people, who had never invited them. To this bold challenge, the students presented their educational demand of "Fifteen Per Cent!" Until then, only seven per cent was allotted to education, while forty per cent went for military expenditures. Every single day, following the announcement of the wedding, students clashed with the police and the gendarmerie. The universities were virtually besieged: Infiltration into the classrooms and police intervention on campuses and in all student life were rampant.

This state of affairs proved to be a fertile soil for the actualization of Mikis' ideas of social and cultural modernization. He was therefore persuaded to return in early April, 1962. A few days after his arrival, the National Theatre suddenly dropped the commitment it had made to him months earlier for the music of Euripides' *Bacchae,* without informing him. Later, through the press, he found out that Hadjidakis had been contracted to write the score, although he himself had already completed several of the choral parts.

The mass rallies of April 5, protesting the expenses of the pending royal wedding, in which a hundred thousand demonstrators took part, found Mikis in the main streets of Athens. He was sitting with Melina Mercouri and Jules Dassin in a café across from the Syntagma Square, where the students were clashing with the police, and was discussing with them the projected score for the film *Phaedra* when, all of a sudden, a group of students spotted them and came over to the table. One of the leaders of the Student Executive Committee of Athens University asked Mikis to compose a song to use in their activities. Mikis refused politely, saying that it was difficult for him to write marches at this time. He, however, wanting not to disappoint the students, suggested that they take a folk song tune and supply the lyrics, as his generation had done during the Resistance. Seeing that Mikis couldn't promise them anything, the students left. Mikis obviously had hoped that his musical movement would stand on its own with the masses at large and not be directly associated with specific groups. But now he could not ignore the challenge. He left his friends at the café, the students' request lingering over his head. Images of his own student days, fifteen years earlier, flashed through his mind. He went back to the places where he himself had demonstrated during the Resistance and Civil War and his blood had been shed. The whole terrible era came back to him. He felt himself again among the dead in the morgue in 1946.

As the clashes continued all over Athens throughout the afternoon, hundreds were wounded and arrested. In the university campus area, a police battalion attacked the demonstrators, beating them mercilessly. Mikis was amidst the collisions of students and police when a girl was left unconscious by the beatings in front of him. He managed to pick her up, put her in a taxi, and take her to a hospital. Mikis was deeply troubled by his experiences that day. The events he had witnessed blended with his memories and the blurred, pervasive feeling of malaise, like so many times before, had to be expressed in music. He sat down and wrote a song for the fighting students. A few hours later he handed the students the song himself. Within a few days, it was being sung by thousands:

> Holding hands in hands
> hands in hands tightly
> hearts with hearts unite
> Greece, oh Greece for you
> Oh, look, your sons who march on
> your chosen sons!

The spring of 1962 provided Mikis with a vigorous political and artistic schedule in Greece and in Europe. He had finished the music for the films *Electra, Phaedra, Honeymoon,* and *Five Miles to Midnight* and for the musical drama *The Hostage,* together with a few choral parts for *Bacchae* as well as two songs for Edith Piaf; meanwhile his magnum opus, *Axion Esti,* was waiting to be heard. The continuous rehearsals and his new professional commitments exhausted him. It was a constant, uphill fight, made more difficult by the political situation in Greece. All this frenzied productivity, together with the emotional upheaval, was bound to take its toll. While rehearsing his *Beautiful City,* he spat blood. This was the first sign: His long-dormant tuberculosis had flared up again.

He fell critically ill with high fever and pleurisy and was immediately flown to Paris. Myrto, who had run to his side, tried desperately with her colleagues to cure him with streptomycin, but the drug didn't seem to work. Distressed by the severity of his case, she took him to London where with the help of Lady Amalia Fleming, wife of the discoverer of penicillin, he was seen by the noted lung specialist, Dr. Thomas Price. The doctor ordered him hospitalized. In the mean-

time, Mikis had been invited by the Union of Soviet Composers to conduct a series of performances at the World Assembly of Disarmament in Moscow, and when the news of
his illness arrived there, the Union offered all the facilities
including his stay at a sanatorium in the Caucasus. Dr. Price,
however, had strongly urged Mikis to cut out all his creative
engagements and curtail all other activities. The invitation
from Moscow was therefore turned down, and on July 17,
Mikis left for the warm, dry climate of Greece following his
doctor's advice.

He arrived in Athens incognito and was taken directly to
the Tsangaris sanatorium on Mt. Penteli. A few days later,
on July 23, a tribute to the composer was organized at the
Park Theatre by the Friends of Greek Music and the Union
of Working Students. The singers Bithikotsis, Lydia, Giannakopoulou, the guitarist Fabas, the choir of Friends of
Greek Music, the actor Rigopoulos and the actress Konstan-
tinou honoured Mikis by singing a few of his earlier songs.
The composer responded with a moving message from the
sanatorium.

After a two-month stay there, Mikis' health improved
greatly, and he was permitted to return gradually to his musical productivity. From now on, however, he would always
have to be under a doctor's care. Two major foreign film
companies offered him enormous sums for scores, as well as
a villa in Italy, where he could work and relax. But he refused the offers, both because of his poor health and because
his musical movement urgently required his presence in
Greece. His first project was a return to the *Beautiful City,*
the work he had been rehearsing when he first fell ill. In
August, the antagonistic musical campaign began between
Mikis and Hadjidakis on Alexandra Boulevard. The former
presented his musical revue, *Beautiful City,* at the Park
Theatre and the latter his *Street of Dreams* at the Metropolitan. Mikis' presentation was packed every night and tickets
were sold weeks in advance, in spite of the composer-conduc-
tor's absence.

The following month, Michael Cacoyannis submitted his

film *Electra* to the Third Week of the Greek Film Festival
(September 17-23, 1962). Of the seven films awarded prizes,
Kapnissis' score for the Greek-American John Kontes' film
*The Hands* was acclaimed the best music presented. This
was an obvious gesture to attract foreign producers and foreign money into Greece. *Electra* did, however, receive three
awards, but Mikis' score was completely ignored. It was one
more affront against Mikis. The seventeen-member panel of
judges included seven who had been appointed by the state
who, of course, had no relation to, or even knowledge of, the
Seventh Art, the cinema.

More fuel was added to the fire with the presentation of
the political play *The Hostage*. The songs spoke against the
British and the palace—burning issues in Greece as they were
in Ireland. The police did not allow the album to circulate
until a number of songs were removed from the cycle. Finally the decree banning the album was made public in 1963,
and thus the act of state was official and on paper, pointing
out all too clearly the regime's sensitivity to any criticism of
its foreign friends.

Mikis had long known that, in order to carry out his programme for the renewal of Greek music and the development
of the public's taste, he would need a symphony orchestra
to perform classical works and continue his public contacts.
In late autumn of 1962, he gathered thirty, mostly unemployed, fellow-musicians, some of whom he knew from his
days at the Athens Conservatory. With them he created the
Little Symphonic Orchestra of Athens.

The first winter season—November, 1962, to February,
1963—covered the classical period of European music through
modern movements and with an emphasis on the primary
works of Greek composers of all periods. The aim of the
concert series was to familiarize the public, and especially
the youth, with higher forms of music. On opening night,
November 10, Mikis introduced the orchestra's programme:
"Classical music has been locked by some insignificant aes-
thetes in a crystal jar. This will break with a cultural movement, a movement of ideas that our symphony orchestra aims

to create." The purpose of the evening, beyond that of musical entertainment and instruction, was to allow Greek composers and conductors to show works. In the list were included people like Hadjidakis, Kafandaris, Apostolidis, Hodjeas, among others. Mikis himself conducted that evening a *Concerto Grosso* by Handel and a Bach *Concerto for Violin*. He then addressed an appeal to the audience, which was composed of people from all walks of life. After explaining the aims of the orchestra and the movement, he asked the people to assist him in the achievement of those aims, since the state was indifferent to all he was trying to do. He then concluded by declaring that, if everything went well, the concert series would increase not only in the capital but in the provinces as well, for, "We shall not wait for the people to come to us here; we shall go find them."

A representative of the Taxi-drivers' Union got up from the audience and, standing a bit self-consciously among the "lovers of classical music," told how impressed he was by what he saw there that night. "The taxi-drivers," he said, "regard the radio as our best companion at work. What I heard and saw tonight pleased me, and I want to hear some more of that kind of music." He pledged his union's support for the orchestra, and was followed by representatives from the construction workers' union and other syndicalists and student leaders, all of whom promised their support as well. Many suggested that the orchestra should avoid a political colouring and stance, to which Mikis replied: "It is not of much interest to us here if we are leftists, centrists, or rightists. We shall look to find our common humanism in the pure spirit of music."

From the first night, the Little Symphonic Orchestra offered stiff competition to the "famous" State Orchestra. Most of the time, its concerts and general performances were packed, while the other's remained nearly empty. The State Orchestra performed once a week, while the Little Orchestra did so twice a week and always to a sell-out audience. For a number of years, until the orchestra was changed to the Symphonic Orchestra of Piraeus, in 1966, many Greek conductors took the podium and a great number of soloists participated. The main financial backer of MOA was the Association of Friends of Classical Music, but, since they could not provide adequate funds or the necessary general business management, the orchestra was forced to contract with Theodore Kritas, the Sol Hurok of Greece. Kritas engaged the Little Orchestra at his Park Theatre and had it collaborate with the Bolshoi Ballet, making it, of course, dependent on outside support. Its popularity, and Mikis' movement in general, were growing ever stronger. The orchestra was particularly lucky in that Christos Lambrakis, the publisher of Athens' two largest dailies, *To Vima* and *Ta Nea,* as well as *Tachydromos,* the most popular magazine after the electoral fraud, shifted his politics from Right to Centre and started to give MOA full news coverage and occasional free advertising.

Following the success he had in the presentation of *The Ballad of the Dead Brother* as a ballet suite the previous April, Mikis decided to perform it as he had originally intended—as an epic theatre piece. Thus it was that, on October 15, 1962, Manos Katrakis' Greek Pop Theatre premiered the play, as directed by the veteran of the Greek stage Pelos Katselis, and with Zozo Nikoloudi's choreography. It ran for several weeks, amidst an ever louder hue and cry. The theme was a virtually taboo subject, the Civil War. Only a few days before the premiere the Council of State, the highest judicial body in Greece, finally recognized the end of the Civil War. One day before the premiere Mikis circulated an "Open Letter" that was widely read. In it, he gave his conviction about the message of the play: "In such critical moments for our nation and our people, I believe that an active artist must undertake works and deeds which will *directly* help achieve the solution and find a way out from the crisis." The crisis he was referring to was the Civil War, which, although now officially recognized as ended, was still, in fact, animated. "I am ready," Mikis declared, "to extend my hand, to forget forever my past suffering and exiles, if we can all agree on a large scale programme which could secure the renaissance of our country." The call was made to deaf ears; the bloody Civil

War was still too fresh in the memory of the people, as was shown by the immediate reaction to the thesis of the play. Hostility from both sides increased alarmingly, especially from the Right, which responded with police action. For more than a year the album of the songs from the play was not allowed to be sold. But what was more shocking was that now the dogmatic Stalinist faction of the Left revealed its true nature. While the majority of the Athenian press of both Centre and Right commented on the play, the left-wing press ignored it completely, showing that it had no intention whatsoever of becoming involved with the play itself or with the movement towards unity which it advocated. Finally, at the insistence of the composer, *Avghi* ran a notice two weeks later on the production. It was critical on both ideological and artistic grounds. After admitting the composer's talent, the commentary concluded: "When the reconciliation of a people becomes the subject of a theatrical work, the causal forces ought to be developed and what the opposing forces represent ought to be defined through the dialectical synthesis of the events. This should be its dramatic meaning."[5] Meanwhile, rumours continued to reach the composer that he was accused as being "romantic" and that his play was considered as having "nationalistic" tendencies, and much more nonsense. He soon became annoyed with the entire situation and, a short while later, went to one of the performances and addressed the audience himself.

> I am not the leader of a party; I create art. Consequently, I can't define the content and the form of the unity of the people. As a man and as a Greek, however, who suffers for my country, I conceive this unity as being broad, very broad. Let all of us honest people unite, all of us who want the good of our country, who hunger and want schools and cultural centres. Let us all be united, so that our nation can march forward, and thus we wouldn't have to walk the streets in shame. For, I am, indeed, ashamed to walk the streets of Athens when I think that nine-tenths of our agrarian population is destitute. If we, all of us who think thus, unite, then our country will go ahead.

[5] "A Critical Comment . . ." *Avghi*, November 1, 1962.

Enmities, nevertheless, continued unabated. Now, the right-wing press, especially *Apogevmatini*, spread the news that Mikis had broken away from the Left. Mikis, now more than ever, was given the chance to clarify his position clearly. Going beyond the artistic problems, he said, in a speech at the Second Panhellenic Convention of the United Democratic Left held from December 8 to 15:

> I want to state to you that what possesses me is the anguish that time is slipping rapidly away and our people remain poor. The serious responsibility for the future of the Greek people lies with you—to discover a sure and steady road, so that finally this people can pass from the primitive life to renewal and development.

The apathy and sloth of the "progressive" forces irritated those of the Left who thought like Mikis, and while George Papandreou was delivering his orations about the "Unyielding Struggle," the country fared no better than it had at the end of the Civil War, twelve years earlier. The workers and the young continued their struggle for better salaries and working conditions and improved education on their own. The "underworld" extreme right-wing gangs that had been sabotaging Mikis' concerts were preparing and awaiting the moment to strike more violently. Thus, the year ended in the midst of prolific productivity and a slew of obstacles.

The new year was to witness two events which would be decisive in Mikis' political involvement. First, he found himself in the front lines of a social revolution inspired by a visit to Cuba; and, secondly, he found the enemy striking at his door with the assassination of Grigoris Lambrakis.

During the Cuban blockade by the United States in October, 1962, Mikis had joined in a protest with seventy-three other Greek artists and writers. A few months later, the Cuban Government invited him to participate in the celebration of the fourth anniversary of the Cuban Revolution. He left for Havana on New Year's Day, and stayed in Cuba one week, visiting and speaking with Premier Castro, youth groups, factory workers, and school children. The progress and the

strong desire for productivity he encountered in Cuba left a
tremendous impression on him. After Cuba he visited several European cities for a month. Invitations to conduct as
well as perform in Havana, Paris, and London were piled one
atop the other. There were requests that he work with the
dancer Yuri Nureyev and perform his ballet *Antigone* in
Prague. All invitations had to be turned down, for he now
more than ever was determined to settle in Greece. His stay
in Cuba caused a profound and serious reconsideration of all
his sociocultural theories and programmes. He was greatly
impressed, as he stated upon his arrival in Athens, by "the
progress on all levels of a poor people just like ours, but primarily the youth." It was the final confirmation for a continuous fight in Greece.

The dogmatic hard-liners, that is, the Stalinist faction
of the Left, who were in charge of the Left's programme for
cultural affairs at home,[6] could no longer be fought off by
verbal arguments and statements alone. It was imperative to
meet them head on in the social and political arena. Their
antagonism towards *The Ballad of the Dead Brother* and
Mikis' movement was intensified and took new dimensions.
The occasion for open confrontation arose with an invitation from the Bertrand Russell Peace Movement, a committee
that led the pacifist movement in Greece patterned after the
programme of the British philosopher Bertrand Russell.
Mikis appeared at the rally which was given on February 10,
1963, with the poet Yiannis Ritsos to again present and analyse
the *Epitaphios*, and to discuss the music and the cultural message of the work with the audience. It was inevitable that the
"silent war" that the dogmatists of the Left had declared against
*The Ballad of the Dead Brother*, as well as other ideological
conflicts illustrated by Mikis' impressions from Cuba, should
be brought up. Disturbances occurred at the rally; someone
rushed to the microphone and prevented Mikis from continu-

[6] It was not only the leadership of the Left, but all the Greek political
parties that had never considered the cultural crisis to be one of the country's
greatest ills. No party had ever presented a platform or programme of action,
or had even indicated an interest in the problem.

ing, reminding him that this was not the topic for which he had been invited. He was supposed to discuss the laik song. A quarrel ensued, as Mikis refused to surrender the microphone, maintaining that freedom of expression and discussion was the most serious problem for the artist. "Wherever youth was to be found, "he declared, "all issues should be discussed openly. The youth themselves feared no one." Everybody then became involved in the argument, and lost no time in choosing sides, so that the rally soon threatened to turn into a free-for-all. "I remember the days in Makronissos," Mikis went on, referring to the fact that the guerrilla war of 1946–49 was lost because of Stalin's and his Greek followers' abandonment of the Greek Left. "You might prefer the prewar years," he continued with vehemence, "when Stalin would go to a concert of Shostakovich and leave before the end because he didn't like it. Then the newspapers would label the work 'bourgeois,' 'counterrevolutionary,' 'influenced,' and similar blames." The meeting finally came to an acrimonious end, but the arguments continued in the press.

While the ideological clashes within the Left, with Mikis' movement at the forefront, continued, the extreme Right, for its part, was preparing to strike at the leaders of the youth movement, as represented in the person of Mikis' closest friend, Grigoris Lambrakis.

Outside of Greece, Mikis was for the third time honoured by world musical circles. He was awarded the First Prize, in the commemoration of the Finnish composer Jan Sibelius, for "all his previous musical works" by the International Institute of Music in London. The committee included the cellist Pablo Casals, and the composers Zoltan Kodaly, and Darius Milhaud.

### THE UNDERWORLD REVEALED

When *The Ballad of the Dead Brother* was performed in Athens, in October, 1962, it provoked a wide and bitter controversy; its stirring call for national reconciliation drew the wrath of both the extreme Right and the extreme Left. For, so profound and so pervasive was the hatred engendered by the Civil War that even now, twelve years after the end of the hostilities, the two factions could not bring themselves, as the composer asked, to forget and forgive. Only the young, weary of strife and conflict, and the undogmatic Left, willing to lay aside the past for the greater cause of national reconstruction, responded favourably to Mikis' work. In order to understand the nature of society in which Mikis had to work during the 1960's, one must acquire a closer view of the vast network of official and unofficial obstacles put in his path, and what actually perpetuated the hatred.

At the end of the Civil War, Greece was left with two legacies. The first was political and military and was held by the palace, the army, the police, and the state machinery of the Right, all of which were maintained with American capital and arms. The second, inextricably bound to the first, was the sociocultural dictatorship imposed upon the population by the Right; the past and tradition were perverted and used for reactionary purposes. The Right wanting to keep its power by any means, predicated upon the "national attitude" (loyalty) myth by which anything modern or extraneous, be it a reflection, thought, or scientific achievement, was labeled dangerous, foreign, and, usually, Communistic.

> The specific feature of the Greek cultural system was that criticism and dissent were forcibly reduced to total silence by the class in power; all fundamental political and social alternatives were banished. If anti-communism as a political outlook was the common denominator of the "free world," in Greece it permeated every aspect of social and cultural life.[7]

Inherent in this cultural system was the morality of the village, coupled with the long-outdated Greek concepts of values like church (institution), family (morality), country (chauvinism) , and, above all, a "purist" (*katharevousa*) language—all parts of the device and means of those who ever tried to rule the land up to and including the present "Christian Greeks." This anachronistic and suffocating political and cultural structure, steeped in right-wing indoctrination and totally

[7] C. Tsoucalas, *The Greek Tragedy,* London 1969, 114-15.

devoid of anything resembling a "youth culture," was safe-guarded and enforced by agents and armed para-state organizations.

In 1952, the year Mikis finished his military service and began his musical career, the fate of Greece was determined by a series of events that set the pattern for all its future national life. On January 1, a new constitution was ratified, and, on February 18, Greece, under the liberal administration of General Nicholas Plastiras, became a NATO member. Plastiras' government, however, was short-lived, for within a year, it was replaced by the Greek Rally Party of Field Marshal Alexandros Papagos. Papagos came to power on November 16, 1952, after having resigned from active duty, through the not-too-subtle machinations of the United States Ambassador, John Peurifoy, who sought "stability" over the land. Papagos was to maintain control of the country until 1956, during which time he "stabilized" the Right and laid the groundwork for all future political and hence sociocultural developments in Greece. It was a familiar theme played over and over again in Greek history, with variations only in the personalities involved. The army, helped by a foreign power, seized control of the country. The developments in Greece were but a reflection of the international temperament of that bitter cold war period; the rightist government set out to deter and crush the "internal" enemy.

The force relied upon to do this was the police, both city and state. In Greece, unlike any other European country, except, of course, Spain and Portugal, the special task of the police has always been political, that is, to guard and protect not the citizen but the state, which means, in fact, the government in power. The citizen is regarded as a potential violator of the state's laws, as one who may at any moment take up arms against the government. The policeman's role, therefore, is that of a miniature ruler, always on guard against his potentially "insurgent" subject-enemies. Moreover, in order to justify his job and salary, he must constantly maintain an enemy camp, on the one hand, and look for friend-collaborators, on the other. Greece was rife with such collaborators after the Civil War. They were chosen from the lower and middle-class "failures" of the Metaxas regime who had never found their own milieu, as well as later rightist fanatics and those who had collaborated with the Germans. All these undercover elements operated primarily in the cities, due to the steady urbanization and modernization of the country after 1952. In the rural areas the parastate units and the National Security Battalions of armed civilians prevailed. These were supplied with guns and ammunition, and trained in military and police duties by army officers. The Security Battalions were, and still are, known for their terrorism and effective oppression of the peasantry.[8] Thus the secret parastate forces and agents, the police, and the military, were a formidable power to be reckoned with throughout the developments in Greece after the Second World War, and even to April 21, 1967.

The new Constitution of 1952 provided for the right of free association. Immediately upon its ratification, clandestine groups began to organize terrorist activities, particularly in Athens. Four months later, a group, subsequently registered as a legal body, was organized under the name Anti-Communist Crusade of Greece.[9] Its members were motivated by anti-communism, and inspired by the immortal Greek principles of "country, religion, and family." Its official symbol was a skull and crossbones. Open violence marked the beginning of its activities, with the tacit approval of the police. The magazine *Dromoi tis Eirinis* (March 16, 1966) cites a document in which is shown how the group operated with

[8] Enormous sums, never listed in the ordinary budgets and free from any kind of control, were credited to the security services, which, according to one estimate, had by 1963 over 60,000 persons on their payroll. Cf. Tsoucalas, *op. cit.* (supra n. 7) 148.

[9] A detailed account of these terrorist groups is given in the magazine *Dromoi tis Eirinis* June 6, 1963. It lists the names and addresses of the 20 participants at the first meeting, as well as its location. One of these, the lawyer N. Magginas, had the organization legalized. Most of the following information has been taken from *Dromoi tis Eirinis* (March 19, 1966) and *Tachydromos* (9 July 1964), and the investigations of the journalists, I. Voultepsis, *Avghi* (March 19, 1966), Betsos in *Athinaiki* Yiorgos Romaios, as well as many other journals and personal testimony.

officers and a leader, Panayiotis Kyriakos, an ex-Colonel, who was the liaison between the Security Police of Palaion Phaliron and the group. The communiqué is signed by the group's chief, Papadongonas, who had served in the Security Battalions in the Peloponnese, and openly collaborated with the Germans until their defeat in 1944. This neo-Nazi organization shortly established headquarters in all the major cities—Athens, Piraeus, Thessaloniki, Kavalla, Ioannina, Chania, Herakleion, Corinth, Kalamata, Patras, Chalkida, Tripolis, Nauplion, Argos, Aegion, and Larissa—while branches were created in smaller towns.

From 1952 to 1963, thirty-three associations like the Anti-Communist Crusade of Greece were formed under the leadership of right-wing extremists and ex-army officers. Nine out of the thirty-three were legally recognized. Most of their leaders had been found guilty of collaboration with the enemy and condemned for high treason in the late 1940's and early 1950's, but their sentences were never carried out. Others were common convicts, thieves, smugglers. And it was these underworld elements who were employed to "safeguard" the country, Orthodoxy, and the family, as if the Karamanlis rightist administration were not sufficient. In 1959, several of these organizations came out in the open. On August 4, the Corps of Hope-Bearing Youth and the National Youth Organization marched to place a wreath at the Monument of the Unknown Soldier in Syntagma Square on the twenty-third anniversary of the Metaxas dictatorship. Uniformed and marching in military formation, they stood and gave the Fascist salute at the ceremony. The two groups were well organized. Their members were trained in the use of arms and all military procedures at special training centres in Ioannina and Tripolis, and their special identity cards, issued by the police, enabled them to travel anywhere free. On December 13, 1959, when President Eisenhower visited Greece, the police asked the assistance of these same gangs to help maintain order.

The Neo-Nazi Organization of Athens, "NOA," whose official symbol was the swastika, operated clandestinely from

1958 on. It was the most secretive of all the organizations. In 1959, they struck, painting swastikas on the building of the Israeli Society of Athens. On subsequent dates, they threatened the lives of Frizis, the leader of the Jewish community in the Greek capital, and Osmo, the president of the Israeli Association. Threatening letters were sent to the actor Dimitris Myrat and to the director Karolos Koun, both of Jewish extraction, and to Smaroula Yiouli, an actress who often performed in antiwar and anti-Nazi plays. NOA also burned down the Orpheus Theatre in Corfu for presenting anti-war works, and expanded their threats and menacing activities in other directions.

One of the most shocking facts to emerge from the later investigations into these parastate gangs was the involvement of an American employed in a minor clerical post at the U.S. Embassy in Athens. *Dromoi tis Eirinis* produced documentation showing that, in December, 1960, he was a leader of a Ku Klux Klan branch in Texas and the direct liaison between NOA and other neo-Nazi groups in Europe. NOA possessed the KKK bulletin in translation, along with the person's Texas address. He had toured Europe before setting up extreme right-wing organizations in West Germany, in collaboration with Siegfried Schogelmann, an ex-SS officer who had been in charge of the murders in Czechoslovakia during the war. In December, 1960, he visited Athens for the first time. There followed a subsequent reactivization and reinforcement of all the neo-Nazi and neo-Fascist groups, particularly "EKOF," the National-Social Students' Organization, which concentrated on the youth and the university campuses.

As the elections of October 29, 1961, drew near, the American and an international band of neo-Nazis, including Schogelmann, went to Athens incognito. This time he centralized all the existing organizations under one headquarters, placing his greatest trust in NOA, however, since it had been his original link with Greece. In fact, he even recruited for his own home organization, enlisting members in the KKK and distributing red identification cards with the member's name in English and the word GRECIA for international use. Similar centres had been set up in Portugal, Spain, Germany, France, and Turkey; the red ID cards served as a bond among all the groups.

In anticipation of the elections, a top strategy meeting of another kind took place in Athens, with "key personalities from the Armed Forces, the gendarmerie, and the police, as well as General Natsinas, a key member of the junta of IDEA and the director of Karamanlis' KYP (Central Intelligence Service), and Lieutenant Colonel George Papadopoulos, Natsinas' assistant and liaison with the American CIA."[10] It was at this meeting that Operation Pericles, the military plan devised to subvert the elections, was drawn up. Those charged with executing the plan were the gendarmerie and the Security Battalions, who carried out a terrorist campaign to intimidate the people in the countryside. Soldiers dressed in civilian clothes and the paramilitary gangs worked at night, carrying out acts of violence against the citizens who belonged to the Left or the democratic Centre. As election day drew closer, the acts of violence and vandalism turned into a virtual orgy. The elections themselves were rigged, "and they amounted to an electoral coup. The army, the police, the gendarmerie had been used on a grand scale to forge the results. There had been violence in the countryside, where citizens had been forced either to abstain or to vote for Karamanlis, and fraud in the city, where the registers had been falsified on an unprecedented scale."[11] A part of this plan was to sabotage Mikis' tour of the countryside in September of 1961. After the elections, the people were infuriated by the officially con-

---

[10] Andreas Papandreou, *Democracy at Gunpoint: The Greek Front* (New York, 1970), 143.

IDEA (Sacred Bond of Greek Army Officers), formed in the army in the Middle East during the Occupation, was a powerful conspiratorial organization whose primary aim was the restoration of the Greek throne. George Papadopoulos, a junior officer at the time, joined Major Kourkoulakos' Security Battalion in 1944, and later worked in the Athens area. (See *Le Monde Diplomatique*, May, 1969.) Thus, in December, 1945, he was among the Greek and British officers hiding in the Palaiologou house across the street from Mikis'. In 1967, Colonel Papadopoulos became dictator and appointed Kourkoulakos director of the Agricultural Bank of Greece.

[11] *Ibid.*, 110. See also 221-225.

doned fraud and violence and by the intervention of the secret gangs. George Papandreou initiated his "unyielding struggle" among the people throughout the country. Incensed as it was, the populace adopted this struggle, and it fast became a widespread sociopolitical movement. Mass mobilization, with the youth in the vanguard, began all over Greece. The issues ranged from education and economics to anti-militarism, and the fight went on for two years. The extreme rightists, the army, and the palace had won by force and arrogantly let the people scream. They left the job of squelching the popular movement to the underworld and the police.

By the end of 1962, the Left had attracted a large segment of the youth with its platform of peace, disarmament, and the removal of American military bases in Greece. A leading figure in the peace movement was the leftist deputy Grigoris Lambrakis, who had just won a seat as an independent from Piraeus in the October, 1961, elections. He was a professor of medicine at the University of Athens, as well as a champion long-distance runner, and had become quite popular among the Greek youth in Athens and Thessaloniki and known abroad.

On February 2, 1963, the League of Fighters and Victims of the National Resistance of Northern Greece was formed with a certain Xenophon Yiosmas as its head.[12] On February 20, Yiosmas enlisted some combatant members in his organization, two of whom were Spyros Gotzamanis and Emanuel Emanouelidis. They were given official ID cards by the VII Police Precinct of Thessaloniki and were permitted to use them for any purpose they pleased. Both new members were shortly to play a very important role.

A month later, in March, Lambrakis was invited to represent the Greek peace movement at the Aldermaston Peace

---

[12] Yiosmas had worked with the collaborationist group Panhellenic Resistance Organization and in October, 1944, served in the quisling government formed by the Germans. He was found guilty of collaboration by the Joint Chiefs of Staff, Bureau of Information, Office II, No. of Protocol 21/2/10/9 of April 4, 1946. He was never punished. Instead he moved to Athens in 1957 and worked with four other Fascist gangs whose activities were centred at 43 Menandrou Street.

March staged by Bertrand Russell. While in London, he had an encounter with Queen Frederika. Perhaps Lambrakis did not choose the right moment to interrupt her. She was on her way to a reception in her honour at Buckingham Palace. She was all excited, anticipating ceremonies as grand as those held the previous year in Athens for her daughter's wedding. Lambrakis made the request that she intercede on behalf of a group of citizens whose relatives had been in prison since the war, among whom was the British wife of a Communist union leader, Tonis Ambatielos. The Queen refused to see Lambrakis, although he was a deputy in the Greek Parliament, whereupon there followed a demonstration against her.

Upon his return to Greece, Lambrakis and other leaders in the peace movement organized the First Marathon Peace March of April 21, 1963, in Athens.[13] The police and the Karamanlis administration tightened security and ordered to undermine the march—and the whole movement, if they could—as effectively as possible. For this, they relied chiefly on the para-state gangs, one of which was Yiosmas' group, which had been brought down from Thessaloniki. The march was banned, and 2,000 participants were arrested and detained at the Goudi military centre of Athens. The attacks were so violent that only one man, Lambrakis, was able to complete the march; at the end of the long trek, however, even he was arrested, in spite of his immunity. Mikis was among the thousands detained and mistreated, as were the poets Ritsos and Tefkros Anthias. The university professor Yiannis Imvriotis and hundreds of other intellectuals, artists, writers, young people, and workers were rounded up. The people and the press were outraged, and slowly began the shocking revelation of the role of the para-state network.

Three weeks later, on May 10, the various extremist gangs of the Right met at Piraeus to plan and coordinate their activities for that month, which, as subsequent events showed, was a busy one, indeed. Besides appearing dutifully as "volunteers" during the much heralded visits of President de Gaulle

[13] On March 31, Siegfried Schogelmann had left Athens for Frankfurt for consultation on the matter.

to Athens and Thessaloniki, they were secretly conspiring to assassinate Lambrakis, whose views were becoming dangerously popular. Lambrakis was well aware of what was going on. Ever since his return from London, he had been receiving anonymous telephone calls and letters, all threatening his life. Some of them contained Nazi slogans, such as "Heil Hitler," "Heil Eichmann," and "Heil SS," and were decorated with swastikas. On May 21, he was invited to speak at a peace rally in Thessaloniki. His friends, who met him at the airport, warned him of the threatening phone calls they had received. But he remained undaunted and insisted upon appearing at the gathering. It was only a matter of hours before the conspirators, Spyros Gotzamanis and Emanuel Emanouelidis, struck. In a prearranged "accident," while the police stood by and did nothing (the chief of police, according to plan, was conveniently at a performance of the Bolshoi Ballet), Lambrakis was hit by an iron bar as a motorcycle car careened wildly through the crowd and headed right for him. Felled by the blow, he was taken to the Ahepa Hospital of the University of Thessaloniki in a coma.[14]

Within hours of the attack, Mikis arrived in Thessaloniki. Immediately upon landing, however, he was arrested by the police, and only after vehement protests from various quarters was he released to visit his dying friend. Around the hospital, hundreds of students gathered, singing selections from Mikis' *Epitaphios*. Mikis asked the university to allow him to address the students. At first, the deans refused, but, after increased pressure from the student clubs, and afraid of further demonstrations, they gave him permission. It turned out to be a rally for outsiders, because the police brought in instigators and members of para-state gangs while forbidding the students to participate in any manner. Mikis, although

[14] I have deliberately avoided going into detail concerning the death of Lambrakis. The story has become well known through the film *Z*, based on Vassilis Vassilikos' novel of the same name. Vassilikos has given fictitious names, such as Yvango and Vango to Gotzamanis and Emanouelidis, and to the others. A photo of Emanouelidis taken with the royal family when he was on a welcoming committee at the time of their visit to Thessaloniki in 1960 was widely circulated in the Greek press.

trapped, did not hesitate to attack the police state and the university authorities who did not protest the infiltration of outsiders who were not students. The neo-Fascist gangs who had been instrumental in Lambrakis' murder just three days previously rushed in now to attack Mikis. His life was barely saved by a few bold students who ran to protect him, and rushed him out of danger. Only by a hairbreadth did the gangs miss their second target.[15]

Lambrakis' body was transported by train to Athens. In every city that the train traversed, people gathered at every opportunity to present flowers and pay silent tribute. It seemed that the whole of Greece went into mourning; in Athens, over half a million attended the funeral, solemnly carrying signs that declared "Lambrakis Lives!" and "Every Youth a Lambrakis!" Yet, these were no mere slogans, scrawled in haste and meant to be forgotten as the emotion of the moment ebbed and the tragedy receded into the past, where many similar tragedies lay buried. For, around them, there soon formed what by all accounts was the most dynamic and significant youth movement ever to appear in Greece—the Lambrakis Youth. Its leadership fell to Mikis.

[15] The composer dedicated a few words to Lambrakis after this incident, which were published in *Dromoi tis Eirinis* 66, June 12, 1963. An article also appeared in *Athinaiki*, June 16, 1963. These articles have been translated into Italian and included in *Conquistare la Libertà* (Rome, 1968), a collection edited by Aldo de Jaco.

# 7

# Youth and Politics

A man's native soil is to him as the root is
to the tree. If he is not wanted there, his
work is doomed, his song dies. . . . A
man must be himself. Only thus can he
carry his cause to victory. And I shall
carry mine to victory.

This people whom you and your like have
lulled to sleep shall be awakened. You
have softened and debased the good metal
of their souls. I declare war on you and
everything you stand for.

From IBSEN's *Father Brand*

## THE LAMBRAKIS YOUTH MOVEMENT AND THE PARLIAMENTARIAN

The Lambrakis assassination prompted the partial investigation and revelation of the secretive, institutionalized conspiratorial and underworld forces that had been plaguing the
whole sociocultural life of Greece. It became clear that the en-

gineers of the planned murder were highly placed in the police and the army, and that this incident was but one step
in the direction of today's open dictatorship. Several other
assassinations were either prevented or exposed by the liberal
and democratic people of the Centre, Left, and Right, and,
above all, by the youth. The second major effect of the murder was the impact it made on the postwar generation, which
was just awakening to the myriad problems of Greek society.
They reflected the budding feelings and trends of world
youth, as well as their own new awareness, and prepared to
revolt against the monolithic structure established by the
rightists as well as their elders. Greek culture in all its aspects
—music, art, literature, social life, and general youth activities
—had always been oriented towards the conservative older
generation.

In the 1960's, the young, impatient with their elders' failures, decided to try to solve their problems and those of the
country in general on their own. Together with the workers,
the unemployed, and the illiterate, they began to steel themselves for the fight against the most immediate obstacle, after
the school authorities and the labour unions—the police. Along
with national and international problems—the cold war, a possible third World War, Vietnam—the youth concentrated on
its desire to live according to its own principles and create a
life and culture that would fulfil its own needs. Thus, after
1960, they abandoned their existing groups, which had been
little more than messenger boys to the various politicians or
agents of the establishment, and banded together irrespective
of political, economic, or cultural persuasion. There was a
fresh breeze, a feeling of hope, of new possibilities in the air,
and hence a confrontation between the generations began and
was bound to lead to political clashes.

The initiative began in the liberal and left-wing camps, to
which the majority of the youth belonged. It was a majority
deprived of higher education, enjoyment, but, above all, jobs.
In the spring of 1963, the progressive youth movements, together with the pacifists and "Russellists," as they came to be
called, began to blossom. The students who held their Fourth

National Convention, the most important force for the improvement of education and culture, were even forced to face violence from the police.

On June 4, barely two weeks after Lambrakis' assassination, a group of intellectuals, students, writers, and unionists met to agree on the formation of a constitutional youth movement. Their aims were to carry on the ideals of Greek life, athletics, and a broad sociocultural youth programme. The group included four actors, two theatre directors, four student leaders, one unionist, several writers, and Mikis, who was one of the first to sign up and was eventually elected president. In its first communiqué, drafted that same day, the movement took the name Democratic Youth Movement Grigoris Lambrakis. It stated that it was not a political party, nor affiliated with any party, and called upon the youth as well as the political leaders and intellectuals to support it. Thus was formed a body to resist effectively the crime syndicate of the Fascist organizations, a resistance that struck at the heart of Greek society. Just at this critical juncture, the Lambrakis murder was felt in another quarter. Rumours, pressures, and implications of involvement by the military, as a result of the preliminary investigations of the affair, led to Karamanlis' resignation,[1] the end of his regime, and the decision to set new elections on November 3, 1963. Although most of the newspapers, including *The New York Times,* reported the assassination as an "accident," it became impossible to conceal the true nature of the crime from the public. Of course, the official excuse for Karamanlis' resignation was given out as a quarrel between him and the palace over a trip to London. The story behind his sudden descent from power, and subsequent departure from the country, is a mystery that only the former prime minister himself can unravel; but he has continued to remain silent over the whole affair. The palace immediately

---

[1] A few days before he resigned, Karamanlis burst out publicly with the famous retort, "Who, in hell, rules this country?" Six years later, in the fall of 1969, when the country was under the open control of the parastate clans, Karamanlis made a public appearance in which he called upon the army officers to revolt against the colonels.

appointed its favourite man, Panayiotis Pipinelis, to the vacant post. Four years later, on April 21, 1967, he was made foreign minister by the military junta.

The summer following Karamanlis' resignation was a time of feverish political activity. The Lambrakis Democratic Youth grew steadily as young people of all political parties joined its ranks. On July 23, the movement opened its first hall in the centre of Athens in an atmosphere that was potentially explosive because of the police and their civilian aides who had surrounded the area to keep order. Hundreds of youth had filled the hall beyond capacity and were overflowing into the street. Mikis, who had to struggle through police lines and push his way past obscenities and threats, arrived a little late. When he finally made his way to the speaker's stand in the hall, he took the microphone and boomed out: "Receive the message of Lambrakis. The fight for democracy is unyielding, even to the point of ultimate sacrifice. . . . We have been presented with a triple duty on which we must act immediately. First duty: Organize a Lambrakis group in every neighbourhood, city, and village. Second duty: Organize a Lambrakis group in every neighbourhood, city, and village. Third duty: Organize a Lambrakis group in every neighbourhood, city, and village." Loudspeakers carried Mikis' voice to the crowds outside; and, within a few hours, his message had been delivered to every corner of Greece.

The movement appealed to the young people's need for education, cultural activities, athletics, and progress in general. From the capital, Mikis supervised the organization of youth clubs and the erection of halls in various parts of the country. He also assumed responsibility for the movement's journal, *Ta Tetradia tis Demokratias* (*The Notebooks of Democracy*). In the first issue, he wrote a lengthy piece, entitled "Democracy or Fascism," that set forth the programme of the Lambrakis Democratic Youth. The programme went further than just incorporating the crucial issues the students had been fighting for up to now; as set forth in Mikis' article, it stressed national independence and reconstruction based upon Greece's own resources—her young men and women—

and proposed to fight emigration and poverty by calling for the creation of new jobs and greater government efforts to improve living standards. It emphasized innate human dignity and mutual respect between the state and the citizen, and enjoined youth to fight for peace at home and abroad. It also called for world disarmament and settlement of the conflicts in Cyprus, Vietnam, and elsewhere.

As was to be expected, the programme upset all the politicians from the Left to the Right. The movement included members from the youth organization of both ERE and the Centre Union, and this desertion to an independent group infuriated both parties. Youth centres were established in suburban areas. Roads were built by the youngsters with the assistance of the local population. Books were collected to start libraries. Choirs and small ensembles were formed, as well as amateur theatrical groups for play and poetry readings. People in working-class districts and in villages became involved with the youth in social activities.

In spite of his responsibilities and the pressures of his duties as head of the Democratic Lambrakis Youth, Mikis found time to work on his music. He collaborated with Hadjidakis on *Enchanting City,* a musical revue, and divided his time between the revue and MOA (the Little Symphonic Orchestra), which continued to give concerts to ever growing numbers. But the main thrust of his energy was directed toward the organization and expansion of the Lambrakis Youth. He was constantly addressing large and small gatherings to promote the cause. On September 2, he spoke to a crowd of more than 7,000 people in the soccer field of Kokkinia in Piraeus. And a few days later, in an address to another crowd in Piraeus, he announced, for the first time, the symbol of the movement. Raising his long arms high in the air, as if conducting a symphony, he traced a gigantic "Z," saying, "Let the slogan *Zei* (He lives) become a symbol . . . of the life of our movement." In a matter of hours, the letter "Z" appeared on walls, billboards, and windows throughout Athens and Piraeus.

Political events were moving at top speed. At the end of September, the caretaker government of Pipinelis, appointed by the palace, toppled, owing to the intense pressures from George Papandreou as well as other parties. Elections were scheduled for November 3. On October 7, a few days after the fall of the government, Mikis was invited to address a large gathering of intellectuals, artists, and writers at the Hadji-christou Theatre in Athens, sponsored by such cultural institutions as the Union of Greek Writers, the Human Rights Association, and others. The purpose of the meeting was to safeguard democracy and the intellectual freedom that had been shaken by the May crisis of the Lambrakis assassination. In his speech, Mikis strongly attacked Fascism as an ever-present danger to cultural development in Greece and called upon intellectuals and artists to resist censorship of theatrical works, musical compositions, and poems. As a spokesman for the Democratic Lambrakis Youth, he attacked the National Radical Union, in particular, and urged young and old alike to organize and vote in the forthcoming elections for a democratic Greece, a modernized way of life, and peace.

In an extensive interview with the newspaper *Avghi* (October 27), he announced that he would vote for the United Democratic Left (EDA),[2] because it was the party of the common citizen, the simple working man, the party of true national interests. "I believe that a decision to support the Centre Union and desert the United Democratic Left could lead to real political tragedy." This last pronouncement was a response to those deputies and supporters of EDA who were openly divided over whether to withdraw their support and give it to the Centre Union party of Papandreou, thereby assuring the defeat of Karamanlis' National Radical Union. Mikis was whole-heartedly against such a defection from the United Democratic Left, and, wherever he campaigned, he urged the voters to support EDA.

Papandreou won the elections, but only by a narrow margin. The state machinery, therefore, remained unchanged, and its *agents provocateurs* presented a continuous challenge to the Papandreou government. This, and the Centre Union's small plurality, made a workable government well-nigh impossible,

2 The United Democratic Left (EDA) was inaugurated as a party in 1951.

so Papandreou resigned and called for new elections. They were set for February 16, 1964.

At this time, the United Democratic Left, in an attempt to extend its influence, decided to include more candidates from among the youth and from the world of arts and letters. Mikis was asked to run under the party's banner, and he chose Piraeus and the nearby islands, in which to do so—the district that Lambrakis had represented. He soon established rapport with the voters, mostly workers and refugees from Asia Minor.

But Mikis' campaign in a "safe" district was not without its difficulties. For one thing, he encountered opposition from his own party, which took exception to his constant and emotional references to the Civil War and to the growing schism within the Left between the pro-Moscow faction that wanted to keep the hatreds of that conflict alive and the more moderate members who, like himself, advocated reconciliation. But, more importantly, the Right, which now seriously feared that a firm coalition of Left and Centre parties would result in an overwhelming victory for Papandreou, began a smear campaign to discredit that old liberal; and Mikis was summoned to testify at the XXII Security Station of Nea Smyrne, his home district, allegedly about "private matters," but actually about the Lambrakis Youth Movement. His interrogators strongly "advised" him to abandon the movement and stick to his music. Mikis protested the summons and interrogation to the government and the press. The Lambrakis Youth staged massive demonstrations in his support, and Papandreou was forced to state publicly that the incident would be investigated. But the rightists gangs were too entrenched. The police officer who had questioned Mikis was exonerated. Not long afterwards, on December 15, Mikis received an anonymous letter threatening his family and warning that he would meet the same fate as Lambrakis. The letter was signed with the initials KKK and a swastika. Mikis knew that he was the second target of the gangs, and that, having stepped into Lambrakis' shoes, he would be carried deeper and deeper into danger.

As for his creative activities, the government issued a decree banning his song cycle *The Hostage*. Mikis, not in the least dismayed by these obstacles, began the new year by launching a long-range cultural movement.

In the middle of January, Mikis, the writer Iacovos Campanellis, the painter Minos Argyrakis, the cartoonist Mentis Bostadjoglou, the actress Marietta Rialdi, the playwright Yerrasimos Stavrou, and the composers Stavros Xarchakos and Theodoros Digelos created the Piraiko Laiko Theatro (Pop Theatre of Piraeus) in Kokkinia, where they explained and performed plays, read poetry, and performed music. Each event was introduced by a performing artist and followed by a discussion period with the audience. In this "first cycle" of activity, which lasted until the elections, when others succeeded them in the programme, Mikis' Bouzouki Ensemble performed some of his works and those of others, and the Little Symphonic Orchestra of Athens (MOA) played classical works. He and Stellios Kafandaris alternated in conducting the orchestra in works by Vivaldi, Handel, and Tchaikovsky.

Meanwhile, he continued to appear at pre-election rallies. At Klauthmonos Square in central Athens, for instance, a throng of over 200,000 gathered, scarcely a week before the elections. Mikis continued to believe that, through the United Democratic Left, the people's party, the goals would be most securely achieved, and he rejected the persistent notion that the UDL should deliver its votes to the Centre Union. This, he felt, would only result in a splintered and ineffectual party. The UDL, however, decided upon a tactical manoeuvre. It withdrew from the race in certain rural districts, leaving the votes there to strengthen the Centre Union against the National Radical Union (ERE), now under Kanellopoulos, and concentrated on the cities, thus gaining only twelve per cent of the votes.

Mikis himself won more votes than any UDL candidate, but his success created jealousy on the part of other deputies. Some expressed doubts about his abilities as a deputy, saying that he was a musician or representative of youth more than a politician. Others criticized him for wanting the party to stand alone, lest it be absorbed by the Centre Union. But what antagonized the greatest number of people in the establishment was that Mikis, with his parliamentary immunity, and two movements—the musico-cultural and the sociopolitical—had become twice as powerful.

The February elections of 1964 resulted in the fifty-three per cent majority Papandreou was after. The Centre Union party was at last in power. For the first time in history, people were permitted to commemorate the Resistance, and freedom of thought and creativity was at last encouraged.

Under Papandreou, UDL could express its demands in terms of the party slogans—Peace, Democracy, Unity. It openly backed the programme of the Committee for Disarmament, which organized the Marathon Peace Marches protesting Greece's affiliation with NATO and calling for lower military expenditures. It called for a general amnesty for all political prisoners and the return of refugees from the East European countries. Furthermore, UDL backed Papandreou's policies for economic independence, cooperation with members of the Eastern bloc, less American influence in the country's affairs, and his drive for educational renewal. As further proof that it accepted Papandreou's proposal to forget the past, it sent a delegation composed of Mikis, Stamatis Mercouris, Melina's father, and other deputies to the funeral of King Paul on March 6, 1964. It was the first time UDL had participated in a royal affair.

But, if UDL presented a unified front on the national level, it was split over the issue of polycentrism in the international Socialist bloc. One faction wanted to follow the policy of the exiled Greek Communist Party, while another sought independence from it. In the latter faction were Mikis and a group of deputies who wanted UDL to be a form of "democratic defence," open to all who would adopt the ideals set forth by the National Liberation Front (EAM) during the Resistance.

The schism in the party widened not only because of the issue of the youth movement from 1963 on, but also because of Mikis' cultural programme as manifested in the controversy over the *Ballad of the Dead Brother* in 1962, and above all because of the insoluble situation in Cyprus. The Cyprus problem was hardly a new one. From the time the British left in 1955, it had been the chief policy question for Greece, regardless of what party was in power. In 1964, just after the February elections, violence erupted on the island once more. Its Constitution established by the Zurich Agreement in 1959 during the Karamanlis regime was proving unworkable. The United States pressed for the intervention of NATO to solve the crisis. Papandreou and the President of Cyprus, Archbishop Makarios, were adamantly opposed to this line of action, and advocated instead a settlement under the auspices of the United Nations. At stake was the decision whether to have *enosis* (union with Greece), which the Turkish minority did not want, or the island's division into separate and autonomous Greek and Turkish cantons, which the Greek Cypriots did not want, or finally, independence, which the Russians supported and the Americans opposed. The choice among these three alternatives was complicated by the strong emotional ties that existed between Cypriot and mainland Greeks, and by the existence of two Greek "authorities" on the island, both demanding total allegiance. One was Archbishop Makarios and the other was George Grivas, leader of the "X" rightist gangs during World War II, and now in charge of the Greek soldiers sent to defend the island against a threatened Turkish invasion. Since all Greeks, by and large, supported *enosis,* the United Democratic Left itself became divided between those Moscow-oriented members who, by definition, had to uphold Russian intervention in support of Turkey and the independence of the island, and those members who put national Greek issues above a vague international ideology and subservience to Moscow.

In 1964, Mikis made several trips to Cyprus to discuss the EDA position with Makarios. He found Makarios adamant in his demand that NATO stay out and that Cypriots be allowed to make their own decisions under the auspices of the United Nations. Immediately after his return to Athens, Mikis left for a quick tour of the major European cities with a corps of EDA deputies to gain support for the self-determination of the island.

In the spring and summer of that year, Athens went wild with celebrations. For the first time the Resistance became an open topic and there were mass commemorations of its most important events and home-coming celebrations for political prisoners. The climax of the celebrations was the Second Marathon Peace March of May 21. For the first time, the 800,-000 demonstrators were unmolested by the police and paramilitary groups.

In view of this new liberal atmosphere, the Right and the military felt challenged. In spite of Papandreou's victory at the polls, they were still in control of the most vital areas of national life. On July 7, Kostas Maniadakis, a well-known Security Minister under Metaxas, summoned the leaders of four groups—the League of Fighters and Victims of the National Resistance of Northern Greece, the Neo-Nazi Organization of Athens, the National Social Students' Organization, and the National Social Expedition—to his office. The following day more than two hundred men entered the Parliament building and clashed with the deputies. The leader, Renos Apostolidis, and twenty-three others were arrested, but the official police policy was "hands off." As a result of this policy, Papandreou's chief of police was forced to dismiss some of the officers, such as Vassilios Lambrou, who were directly responsible for the incident.[2]

The July 7 violence in Parliament had far-reaching repercussions. During the debates that month, many deputies revealed the results of their own investigations of neo-Fascist gangs and their clandestine activities. An investigation conducted by the Centre Union's weekly magazine *Tachydromos,* which came out two days after the event, stated unequivocally that there were at least 50,000 members of such organizations officially listed; that the state machinery was in their hands; that the police were in full collaboration; and that military officers were in close contact with them. The Royal Gendarmerie, or state police, of provincial Greece was implicated.

[2] Apostolidis was appointed head of the "literary" activities of the 1967 junta, while Lambrou has become infamous for his tortures as chief of the Security Police.

Impossible as it may seem, Mikis, between his travels and his speeches, completed the score for *Zorba the Greek,* the film that catapulted him to international fame. Cacoyannis had invited him to compose the score; and even managed to work it over on location with the company, on his way to Cyprus.

Mikis visited Cyprus again only a few days after the August 7 bombardment by the Turks, which had destroyed several villages, among them Polis, where he inspected the damage and talked with the homeless and wounded. Ten days later, he represented the Lambrakis Democratic Youth at a five-day International Youth Festival Conference on the island. In a speech there, he attacked the United States, NATO, Papandreou's soft stand on the crisis, and his slowness in deterring the parastate gangs. The new "liberal" Greek government, he declared, was not as liberal as it professed. He mentioned the sudden removal of his work *Axion Esti* from the Athens Festival, ostensibly because the "low reputation" of the bouzouki music and its interpreters made it unsuitable for such an artistic event. The real reason, he said, was to attack him (Mikis) and to render his work, as well as his movement in general, ineffective, for the pop singer and the bouzouki constituted the very symbols of both his art and his closeness to the common people. In a similar last-minute decision, *The House of Atreus,* inspired by the ancients and written by playwright Vassilis Katsanos, was also withdrawn from the programme with the excuse that it contained phrases insulting to the royal family and that the story itself was disturbing to the public.

Since *Axion Esti* could not be performed at the Herodus Atticus Theatre, Mikis arranged to have it presented at the Rex Theatre, instead, which was not included in the festival. The première on October 18 and all subsequent performances were mobbed. After this success, Mikis and his Bouzouki Ensemble began touring the provinces with the *Epitaphios* and his other works. They toured thirteen cities and were received everywhere with wild enthusiasm. But despite Papandreou's pledges for a democratic life, nothing had changed in the provinces since the Karamanlis days. The paramilitary groups, working hand-in-hand with the state police, sabotaged as many of these performances as they could.

In all these deliberate provocations, Mikis always remained calm. He was always quick to think up alternatives if the police interfered to break up a meeting, or if he was refused a hall for his concerts. But it had become quite clear, with the increasing number of such incidents and the frequent arrests of members of his movement, that the Lambrakis Democratic Youth would have to become officially affiliated with a political party if it were to have the right of constitutional protection. Mikis originally had wanted to keep the movement above party politics, so that all Greek youths would feel free to participate, and not aligned to any political party with its archaic clientage structure and dependence on foreign powers, but banded together for the larger cause, the future of the country. The dream was shattered; in Greece, power politics and cultural progress cannot be separated.

## THE ACME OF THE THREE DUTIES

In addition to alarming the parastate clans and the police, the unexpected growth and achievements of the Lambrakis Democratic Youth had become, in the year and three months of its existence, an extremely sore point among the parties of the Right and Centre Union. Their irritation increased when, on September 17, 1964, the movement merged with the small youth branch of EDA, with which it shared similar ideologies. The new group, now officially under the aegis of the United Democratic Left Party, took the name Lambrakis Youth Movement (DNL), and hammered out their constitution and bylaws (September 12–17).

Mikis, of course, played a crucial role in all these decisions. In a speech he delivered at the Diana Theatre in Athens, where the conference was held on September 14, he said: "The Lambrakis Youth—a ripe fruit on the tree of our vanguard movement, rooted in the hearts of the thousands of National Resistance fighters—raises the flag of the country, the flag that writes EAM-EPON-ELAS, that writes Veldemiris-Kerpeniotis, that writes 'one hundred fourteen' and 'fifteen per cent,' that writes LAMBRAKIS."[3] This speech brought a scathing retort from the Prime Minister that "the Left exploits Lambrakis dead and Theodorakis alive." Mikis replied by reminding Papandreou that it was because of Lambrakis' murder that he was able to win the elections of 1963–64.

Mikis was playing a daring game in challenging Papandreou to live up to his campaign promises of real democracy and freedom of political belief. But taking the opposite tack, or perhaps to counterbalance his restrictions on the Lambrakis Youth Movement, Papandreou permitted an anniversary celebration of one of the most memorable events of the Resistance: the first united Resistance attack against the Germans at Gorgopotamos. On November 29, the date of the celebration, there was a powerful explosion just as the ceremonies were ending. Thirteen were killed and seventy-five wounded in what an official communiqué described as an accident, caused by the explosion of an old World War II torpedo.

Mikis and another deputy, Leonidas Kyrkos, who investigated the site of the explosion late that night, declared in a statement to the press that their findings proved conclusively that what had taken place was an attempt at mass murder. The cry of conspiracy was echoed in Parliament as well, where a series of stormy sessions ensued; but there was no official investigation. Instead, the police arrested several of the participants, charging them with "assaulting the authorities."

Slowly, the affair was closed and attacks against liberalism and the Lambrakis Youth continued. In view of this situation, Mikis, who began devoting more and more time to the Lambrakis Youth, toured youth centres in ten cities and thirty villages of western Greece to observe their activities. At the same time, the Centre Union Party created its own youth group; and, in March, 1965, at the age of 76, Papandreou organized *his* youth movement, the Greek Democratic Youth

[3] Veldemiris and Kerpeniotis were two youths of the left (NEDA) killed during the Operation Pericles organized electoral coup of 1961. "114" was an article of the 1952 Constitution guaranteeing the right of every citizen to protect the Constitution. It had become a symbol in the youth movement from 1960 on. "15%" was what the students demanded be allocated from the national budget for aid to education.

(EDIN), which, despite its political influence, never achieved anything culturally. On March 11, Papandreou signed a decree making teachers personally responsible for the actions of their students. Later, thirty-five members of the Lambrakis Youth movement were expelled from high school for "having welcomed Theodorakis, the Communist composer, deputy, and leader of the movement." The students responded with a mass protest rally in Athens, on April 2, at which Mikis was attacked and clubbed by four policemen who had invaded the Athens University campus and the surrounding area.

Mikis reacted by throwing all the support he could muster behind the Third Marathon Peace March on May 23, which turned out to be the largest peace march ever staged in Greece. Furious, the palace criticized Papandreou for having allowed it in the first place and for not ordering the police to break it up. At the same time, there were rumours of secret plans for a takeover by officers and groups in the armed forces, among whom was a certain Colonel George Papadopoulos.

Then a ray of truth concerning the Lambrakis assassination appeared. For two years, investigation of the affair had been conducted in a very desultory manner, at best. The slightest evidence that seemed to implicate the palace or the state police was invariably suppressed, and witnesses were intimidated or put out of the way. Moreover, the Cyprus question was now receiving enormous coverage, and people had gradually lost interest in the case of a deputy who had been dead for two years, and whose place had been taken by Mikis Theodorakis, who was now constantly in the news. Unexpectedly, a young officer of the state police, Lieutenant Kapelonis, who had been arrested as one of those involved in the plot to get rid of Lambrakis, decided to speak out: That June, he disclosed that the demonstration against Lambrakis on May 22, 1963, during which he was assassinated, had been carefully planned and staged by Yiosmas' group and the State Security Police of Thessaloniki. This group, in turn, had acted under orders from higher up. He declared that he was constantly being visited by fellow prisoners and other high-ranking officers charged for the same offence, who repeatedly asked him to maintain a "conspiracy of silence."

After the disclosure of such shocking evidence, interest in the case was rekindled. The lawyers pushed the investigation as far as they could. General Mitsou, commander-in-chief of the state police in northern Greece, was found to have had complete knowledge of the plan. The investigation was proceeding to the point where higher officers and the palace were about to be implicated. Then, Constantine Kollias,[4] a Supreme Court judge, stepped in and ruled further investigation by the judge, Sartzetakis, pointless. The trial has dragged on inconclusively from then to the present. At the same time, a new frame-up was developing, the famous "Aspida" case, by which the paramilitary state tried to charge Andreas Papandreou, their third target, with high treason. Pushed, undermined, and sabotaged from all sides, George Papandreou was finally forced out of power by the King on July 15, 1965.

The July 15 coup marked the beginning of the end of democracy in Greece. The issue was not so much the verbal confrontations and clashes between political parties—for, after the King set up his puppet regimes, the parties were nothing but names—but between a police state now officially revived and the rest of the Greek population. A struggle was going on between the palace and the military as to which would have the final say, a struggle intensified by the American groups behind the Johnson Administration and the American Embassy, and those backing the Pentagon with its intelligence agency, the CIA. This strife within the high-ranking circles was reflected on the local scene in the reaction of the people and the press, who were trying to guess what was actually going on. Seventy days of continuous demonstrations followed, in which not just the youth but workers and farmers participated.[5]

---

4 This same Kollias became Prime Minister after the colonels' coup, April 21, 1967.

5 A number of authors have written about the crisis of these days. The most important are Papandreou, *op. cit.*, and Meynaud, *Rapport sur l'Abolition de la democratie en Grèce* (Montreal, 1970)—a private publication, and the "Anonymous," *Vérité sur la Grèce* (Lausanne, 1970). The anonymous author lives in Athens.

The Lambrakis Youth were in the forefront of the protests and street fights. They were joined by the Greek Democratic Youth of the Centre Union and the labour unions. The first victim of the confrontation from the ranks of the Lambrakis Youth was Sotiris Petroulas, a student, who was killed by the police. Mikis delivered a funeral oration at his grave and wrote the song "Sotiris Petroulas," which became the new theme song of the Youth.

In the next development, the King summoned all the political parties—except the United Democratic Left—to meet on September 1 and offer their opinions on the situation. The King asked Papandreou why he did not dissolve the Lambrakis Youth. Papandreou answered that it was a legal organization, since it functioned under the auspices of a constitutional party, the UDL (EDA). Furthermore, and with an ironic twist, he reminded the King that, since he had been ousted from office by the palace in July, he no longer had the authority to do so. Five days later, the parastate gangs began a series of terrorist acts against the Lambrakis Youth and anyone else with liberal tendencies. At Mylochori, in Kilkis in the North, a Lambrakis Youth hall was blown up with TNT. The police found excuses to arrest and interrogate "any suspect," especially members of the Lambrakis Youth, but none who might actually have done it. A decree prohibiting Greeks from singing Resistance songs was reactivated, and eight youngsters were arrested for singing such songs and the "revolutionary-Communist" tunes of Mikis.

During this period, Mikis went to Europe to ask for the support of fellow artists. Eighteen writers, artists, and theatre people in Paris, including Jean-Luc Godard, Jean-Paul Sartre, Louis Aragon, and Pablo Neruda, issued an appeal for the release of the recently imprisoned Resistance fighters and for the protection of human rights violated in Greece. Mikis had a long discussion with Sartre, who spoke specifically of Greece and France:

After thirty years of continuous struggle against Fascism and dictatorship, the Greek people have understood—and, in Au-

gust, 1965, have made us understand clearly—that there is no
such thing anywhere in the West as a simple national confrontation between democratic movements and local oligarchies.
Rather, these oligarchies would have been wiped out quickly
and easily had they not been supported by American imperial-
ism. . . . For this reason, your struggle is ours as well. For you,
as well as for us, the aims are one and inseparable: Democracy,
national self-sufficiency, and autochthonous culture.[6]

In this interview, Sartre praised the work and aims of the Lambrakis Youth and, in particular, the sociocultural movement
of Mikis, comparing it with that of Bela Bartok in Hungary.

Mikis, inspired by European support for what he was
doing in Greece, returned with new ideas and plans to reinforce a youthful "fighting culture," as events were taking a
belligerent course. The two royal governments of Novas and
Tsirimokos were succeeded by that of Stephanopoulos (September, 1965, to December, 1966), also a Centrist. Tensions
mounted; youth demonstrations against the palace and the police became more and more extreme, but the young could do
little against overpowering numbers of militarists equipped
with guns, hand-grenades, and tear gas. Putting aside ideological differences, they began to unite against a common
foe; Maoists and Trotskyites, as they called each other,
began to claim the attention of the radical elements of the
Lambrakis Youth Movement, whose membership had grown
with the influx of Centre and even right-wing youth.

Mikis was asked to meet representatives of the Political
Bureau of the Kolliyiannis Greek Communist Party in exile.
Tensions had risen between the United Democratic Left and
the Communists inside Greece; the main cause was the youth
movement, which the Greek Communist Party wanted to
control from abroad. Mikis strongly objected to this and the
way the political crisis had been handled by the GCP and its
followers in Greece. He stated that he wanted to withdraw
from the imbroglio and be left alone to work with the youth

---

[6] Complete text of interview has been published in Mikis Theodorakis,
*The Manifesto of the Lambrakis Youth,* Athens, 1966, pp. 75-78.

and his cultural movement; and, in a series of interparty memoranda to the United Democrat Left, he criticized the Left's complete lack of support of his "fighting cultural movement."

If the schism in the Left was not enough, trouble was also brewing in the palace. The King became a political activist. In his 1966 New Year Address to the Greeks, he said: "Communism is a miasma born outside Greece, inspired and directed from abroad. Its ethic is lying and treachery. It contaminates and turns into an unforgivable enemy of the fatherland anyone who comes into contact with it, be he an individual or a group, every good Greek who does not see the danger." The message, which separated the Greeks into "good" and "evil," provoked violent criticism from all sides except, of course, the extreme Right, the "good" Greeks. The inevitable clash occurred on January 6, during the celebrations of the Epiphany. Traditionally, the rulers, the church, and the people celebrate this Orthodox holy day together. But, this time, there were two groups. One was with the King and the members of his government, attended by no more than three hundred persons gathered along the shore near the Royal Yacht Club in Tourkolimano. The other group was with Papandreou, Mikis, and all the youth groups gathered on the bluff of the hill overlooking the harbour. Their numbers were in the hundreds of thousands. When the archbishop began to intone the hymn "Glory to the King," the huge crowd on the hill shouted with one voice, "Down with the Address," and started to move toward the group around the monarch. The King's ministers took to their heels. The police charged on the crowd, clubbing everyone in their path, but hundreds of people broke through the barrier and ran toward the fleeing officials, yelling "One hundred fourteen!" "Democracy!" "Elections!" Mikis, in the front lines as always, was rushed by a group of policemen crying, "Bulgarian!" "Communist!" They hit him and threw him to the ground, but a group of friends hastily picked up the "Bulgarian" and carried him home, bleeding. It was after this incident that Mikis sat down and composed his tribute to

Greek courage, *The Ballad of Romiossini* of Yiannis Ritsos.

As a result of the demonstration and violence, all Mikis' works were banned from the national radio, as well as those of a few others. The whole land, including musicians and eight literary associations, rose up in protest. The composer Christos Leontis, who was in charge of the national radio programme, resigned and would not allow his works to be broadcast, either. Mikis, Hadjidakis, and Xarchakos withdrew their works from any public hearing, performances in clubs, and other social gatherings, and stated that they would cease printing records in Greece. The strike of the composers was followed by similar activities of singers and artists as well as by a vast majority of Greek intellectuals.

A part of the organized protest against the government's policies was a series of tributes to Mikis by various groups, including the Lambrakis Youth. One such tribute was given by the Educational Association of Eleusis, celebrating the publication of Iacovos Campanellis' novel *Mauthausen,* from which Mikis had selected lyrical passages to set to music under the title *The Ballad of Mauthausen.* Mikis conducted the work at Eleusis and Campanellis read excerpts from the novel—his memoirs from the Mauthausen Nazi concentration camp. But Mikis, embittered by all the recent events, took his artists to Brussels to perform and analyse before a foreign and tranquil audience his *Axion Esti,* on January 18. When he returned to Athens, a few days later, he found the situation even more restive. By now, the right-wing newspaper publishers, including Eleni Vlachou and Savvas Konstantopoulos, who had called Mikis "the music director of the Soviet police," had joined the campaign against censorship. Mikis then staged his own protest by presenting his new work. *The Ballad of Romiossini,* with the singer Bithikotsis at the Lambrakis Youth centre in Kessariani in Athens. Hadjidakis, for his part, wrote a strong *coup de plume* in *Messimvrini,* in which, for the first time, he revealed that, years back, three of his songs had never been circulated. He went on to ask: "How can we neglect and not support the greatest musical reality in our country, Mikis? How can we forget that sixty per cent of the songs sung today are by Theodorakis?"[7] European radio and television stations communicated what was happening in Greece to all the world by broadcasting interviews with the composers on strike. The London *Times* and *Le Figaro* also criticized the censorship.

Needless to say, the crisis also infuriated the students. Demonstrations took place in the major cities, but the bloodiest of all was that staged by the students of the University of Thessaloniki on February 2, in protest against the banning. The state police violated university regulations and entered the campus, vandalizing the halls and beating the students, thus managing to paralyse any further demonstrations.

In such a charged atmosphere, the royal couple attended the opening of the spring season of Hadjidakis' Peiramatiki Orchestra on March 17. At the end of the performance, the King got up to leave, and, according to custom, the entire audience was supposed to stand up and applaud until he was gone. In the front, however, one member of the audience did not get up: it was Mikis. This immediately caused some annoyance among the ladies seated nearby. One said: "A certain gentleman must be tired from a long march" (Peace March). At the insistence of those all around him, Mikis finally gave in. (When he got up, the applause was reinforced by many more who had not applauded before.)

Mikis, Hadjidakis, and Xarchakos continued their strike and sued the National Broadcasting Company. At the trial, held on March 29, the composers were told that the Prime Minister had promised to meet their demands, but that he could not do much about the radio. There were promises, but no guarantee that censorship would end. On March 30, when Mikis went to the Columbia Record Company's studios, he was told that the Prime Minister's Office had forbidden them to record his work *Romiossini*, since it had not been approved by the censorship committee. He was also informed that the original tape had been destroyed. Mikis then recorded the work in Amsterdam. On April 3, the work was presented at the Diana

[7] Manos Hadjidakis, "Why the Censorship Must be Abolished," *Mssimvrini*, February 1, 1966.

Theatre in Athens at an evening organized by the Cretan Students' Association to protest the presence of missile bases in Greece.

Two days later, Mikis and his ensemble were invited by the University of Birmingham to tour England. The tour included appearances in British universities and various art and social associations in London. The Association of Cyprian Students sponsored a series of concerts and declared Archbishop Makarios, President of Cyprus, and Mikis their honorary chairmen. The orchestra went on to Frankfurt, Cologne, Düsseldorf, Hanover, Hamburg, Aachen, Nuremberg, Mannheim, Stuttgart, and Berlin. Each concert was preceded by a talk on the nature of Greek pop music and the struggle for a musical renaissance in Greece and by documentary films of the youth movement and the political crisis since 1965. Later, Mikis spent a few days in Moscow alone.

Upon his return from Europe, Mikis, together with Hadjidakis, was invited by the priest and scholar George Pyrounakis, of Eleusis, to compose, or rather synchronize, the Greek liturgy, which had not been touched since the fourth century, when it was composed by Ioannis Chrysostomos. There have been attempts to rework the music, but they were unsuccessful. The latest was made by Sakellaridis, who introduced European harmonics and orchestrations that have destroyed the nature and taste of the original Byzantine music. Father Pyrounakis saw in the collaboration of the two composers, and primarily Mikis, just the persons to do it. The Archdiocese of Athens became infuriated at such blasphemy and issued orders to all churches and cantors to be careful not to be influenced by "bouzoukologists" like Theodorakis and Hadjidakis and allow the bringing that "sinful and barbaric" music into the churches. The attempt was thus squashed.

Then, an interesting development began unfolding relative to the Lambrakis Youth Movement. Colonel George Papadopoulos was put in charge of "psychological operations," "propaganda," and "political indoctrination within and without the army." In such a post, Papadopoulos acted immediately and, together with Kostopoulos and General Spandidakis, who became Deputy Prime Minister and Minister of National Defence in 1967, circulated a decree that called upon all loyalist officers to take an "active stand" in all military and civilian matters. The decree specifically singled out the Lambrakis Youth Movement, and was instantly effective in the Fourth Marathon Peace March in May. The march was turned into a wolf-and-lamb struggle between the participants, the police, and their plainclothes henchmen. A few weeks later, the farmers in Northern Greece arose in mass demonstrations, using tractors and other farm equipment. The police responded with bullets. There were hundreds of arrests. At least 150 were wounded. Those arrested were not tried until 1968, a year after Papadopoulos took over.

Meanwhile, the Bureau of Arts of Piraeus organized a summer programme of pop music. They decided to sponsor both the modern and older schools of bouzouki musicians. On the bill were Mikis, Hadjidakis, Leontis, Loizos, Xarchakos, Architectonidis, and Glezos, representing the modern school; and, from the latter, were Tsitsanis, Vamvakaris, Papaioannou, and Kaldaras. Performances were given not only in the Athens-Piraeus area, but in the major towns of Greece, including Kavalla, Thessaloniki, Volos, Larissa, Mytiline, Agrinion, and Herakleion. That summer of 1966 marked the greatest, and the last, Greek festival of pop and art music. The whole land was involved, either in participating or in sabotaging it. Twenty-four concerts were to be given that summer and more than a dozen were organized for a European tour to begin in the fall. The places where the concerts were to take place were outdoor centres, such as playgrounds, soccer fields, and other social and popular centres. The concerts started on July 4 and concluded on September 4. Two months of heated activities for Mikis and his artists, two months of the greatest glory that bouzouki music has ever experienced were those two months when the national pop music resounded all over the land. In addition, it was a victorious battle against the Fascist intervention of the state in Mikis' work. Twenty thousand attended the concerts at the soccer stadium in Nea Philadelphia on July 4. Mikis' Ensemble and the Choir of Trikalla of Terpsichori Papastephanou presented all the works of Mikis as interpreted by Eleni Roda, Maria Farantouri, Grigoris Bithikotsis, Yiannis Poulopoulos, and Mitropanos.

The enthusiasm of the audience and its participation in the singing caused the concert to last for more than four hours, finally ending at midnight. It was the first plebiscite of the Greeks on pop music. A similar event took place at the "Near East" Stadium in Kessariani, followed by the concert at the athletic stadium in Neapolis of Kokkinia. The events, especially the first one in Nea Philadelphia, were televised and videotaped by French, German, and Italian companies and radio stations for broadcast in their own countries. A great number of Greek intellectuals and writers participated, including Yiannis Ritsos, who spoke a few words about his "Romiossini." It is important to remember that one of the reasons for the success of the concerts was that they were organized outside the jurisdiction of the Athens Festival.

The crypto-Fascist gangs went into action. They pressured the various directors of athletic stadiums and associations not to allow performances. When they did not comply, trouble was guaranteed. For example, on the night of July 11, near the stadium at Kessariani, the night before Mikis was to give a concert there, residents saw ten people wearing Ku Klux Klan–type hoods painting threatening slogans all over the walls, such as: "Death to Theodorakis!" "Mikis to Goudi prison!"[8] They hastily called the police, who arrived on the scene and arrested them all in the very act of painting the slogans.[9] As a result of this menacing action, so many directors were about to cancel concerts that Mikis went to see the Prime Minister in person. Stephanopoulos conceded that he had "no objection to the concerts taking place"—that is, he had no choice.

[8] Goudi is a military training camp known for the imprisonment and execution of six generals who were held responsible for the Asia Minor Catastrophe of 1922. In 1963, 2,000 participants in the First Marathon Peace March, one of whom was Mikis, were held there for a short while.

[9] *Avghi,* July 12, 1966.

To counterbalance Mikis' activities, the Bureau of Arts of Athens announced a contest between various Greek choral groups, sponsored by "Max Productions," an American firm that would give a prize and organize a tour of the United States for the winner. Mikis and his Ensemble departed for the concert in Kavalla under the auspices of the Bureau of Arts of Piraeus. Kavalla was under the full control of the gendarmerie and the TEA: Mikis was headed straight for the tiger's lair. Naturally, the concert was sabotaged and cancelled. At the same time, the Bureau of Arts of Athens was sponsoring a series of concerts by the Children's Chorus of Paris in Kavalla. A strong protest was registered by the Panhellenic Musical Association, but nothing came of it.[10] In Larissa, the Lambrakis Youth formed a fence all around a public square where the concert was held, while the whole city was bombarded by leaflets dropped from army aeroplanes asking the people "not to attend the concerts of the 'Slavo-Communist' convoy." The last stop was Volos, where, near the concert, a local band played military anthems at the same time to create a distraction. Upon his return to Athens for other appearances in the suburbs of Peristeri and Nea Smyrne, he was told that he could not use the athletic stadium because "musical presentations do not suit places of athletics."

The reactionary groups were relentless in their attacks. On August 5, Mikis was conducting Shubert's *Unfinished Symphony* with the Town Orchestra of Piraeus when a group of motorcyclists started driving around and around the open-air theatre of Passalimani, revving it up to drown out the sound of the music. The police did nothing to disperse the gang. Many people got up and left, either afraid of a showdown or unable to stand the noise. The performance almost folded. Another disgraceful act against Mikis and against the interests of the Greek people was committed by the Minister of Foreign Affairs—not in Greece this time but abroad. Mikis had been chosen to represent Greece in the First Festival of World Folk Music in Argentina. All the major coun-

10 Text published in *Ta Nea,* July 21, 1966.

tries were asked to participate. The invitation had been extended through the Greek minister. Then, one day, Mikis received a telegram from the president of the festival saying that he was to be replaced by someone else, since he had not replied in time. This was news to Mikis: The Greek minister had never informed him of the invitation. It was a clear example of how the hatred of petty officials and militarists could reach the point of sacrificing the integrity of a whole nation. Meanwhile, as Mikis was touring in Crete with his orchestra, the mayor of Herakleion summoned to his office the prefect of the area on August 19 to explain his reasons for attending a concert organized by the students in honour of Mikis and his orchestra. The concert had been conducted by the composer and Christos Leontis before a highly emotional Cretan audience.

Mikis spent the rest of August feverishly preparing for the musical event which was to prove the most triumphant in his life, as well as the most important for Greek pop music—the First Week of Pop Music. This took place from August 29 to September 5 at the outdoor theatre of Lykavittos constructed on the east slope of the highest and most central hill of Athens. The Festival was honoured by the members of the Stephanopoulos government, diplomats, editors and owners of the press, as well as literary men. The most talented, vital, and original composers performed their works. For the first time in history, the bouzouki was publicly honoured as a pop-art instrument.[11] The old masters were there: Tsitsanis, Papaioannou, Vamvakaris, Kaldaras, Mitsakis. The younger composers, most of whom were born at the end of the 1930's or the beginning of the 1940's, were represented by Leontis, Loizos, Markopoulos, Architectonidis, Glezos, Xarchakos, and Hadjidakis.

Each composer conducted Mikis' orchestra in his own work. For seven days in a row, thirteen composers and one

---

[11] The only music festivals even vaguely as artistically important elsewhere in the world have been the Pop Song Festival on the Isle of Wight, or the Woodstock Festival, both of which took place in the summer of 1969.

hundred singers performed over 160 compositions. Mikis paid a brief tribute to each poet who had written the words for the songs at the beginning of each performance. Among those so honoured were: Seferis, Gatsos, Christodoulou, Yiannis Theodorakis, Pergialis, Rotas, Thalasinos, Varnalis, Ladis, Elytis, Livaditis, Bostadjoglou, Ritsos, and Campanellis. There had never been such a dramatic glorification of music and poetry in the history of Greek music. Over 30,000 people attended. In fact, the theatre was so overcrowded that twice a whole section of seats collapsed, and enthusiastic fans scrambled to find a seat on the rocky hillside above the theatre or perched precariously in the trees. Yet, in spite of the mobs, there was not a single policeman around, or any other member of the paramilitary. The theatre, being privately owned and financed by Anna Synodinou, was beyond the control of the authorities, and the Stephanopoulos administration had given its tacit consent to the Festival of Pop Music.

The final day, Sunday, had a character all its own. Mikis wanted to celebrate peace and the unity of all Greeks—Right, Left, and Centre—and tourists. To him, the bouzouki was the symbol of the power of music to create human harmony. The final evening of the festival closed with his song from *The Ballad of the Dead Brother,* "The Gloria." A major dream of Mikis through all his life and artistic career finally came true.[12] Yet, he was always seeking further improvement; he never rested on his laurels. So, at this performance, he announced: "Now I am contemplating a Second Week of Pop Music. And why not a Week of Greek Poetry and Greek Theatre as well?"

Meanwhile, papers of the Left, Centre, and Right carried daily articles on the festival and interviews with the participating artists and composers. The theatre received tremendous publicity, at the same time, not only because of the fes-

[12] When Mikis was temporarily released for the first time by the junta, I was with Melina Mercouri when she called him directly at a secret number on February 2, 1968. His first words, in a choked and tremulous voice, were, "Remember the days on Lykavittos? Will they ever come again?"

tival, but because Synodinou's company was also performing Aristophanes' *Lysistrata* with Mikis' score as well as other classical dramas. Only during the week of the music festival were the classical plays suspended. Thus, the whole summer from July 30 to September 25 was one great cultural festival of music and drama. Lykavittos had been "conquered" by Mikis without a police permit. He had received a licence of approval directly from the ministry. The whole of Greece rejoiced at the events taking place high on a mountain overlooking Athens and the sea.

Despite the unexpected "musical orgy" on Lykavittos and the mobbed audience participation, Mikis' secret and anonymous enemies were not checked. They attempted a continuous and extensive propaganda campaign against him by distributing leaflets throughout Athens, making threatening phone calls to people, and other similar desperate efforts. One newspaper, in particular, *Acropolis,* attacked the festival on moral grounds, calling it a "First Week of Vulgar Music by the Leader of the Lambrakis Youth," in two consecutive articles.[13] The newspaper blamed the government for allowing such a "disgraceful" thing to happen on Lykavittos. In particular, the journal attacked the cycle of songs *Letters from Germany,* written by the young poet Phondas Ladis about the daily life of the Greek workers in Germany.

To offset the spectacular success of the Lykavittos festival, the mayor of Athens, George Plytas, organized a week of musical events that he called First Week of Greek Composers from September 5 to 11, at a public square in Athens. Participating there were the City Philharmonic Orchestra of Athens, the Band of the Military Police, the Orchestra of the Greek Royal Air Force, the Orchestra of the Greek Royal Navy, the Band of the City Police and the Band of the Greek Royal Gendarmerie. The works of seventeen (fifteen unknown) Greek composers were "executed."

On October 4, the Lambrakis trial began in Thessaloniki and, on November 14, a "parallel" trial, that of the Aspida fraud, opened. Mikis, who testified on November 29 at the first

13 *Akropolis,* September 3-4, 1966.

trial, exposed and accused the circles around the palace and Queen Frederika herself as the chief instigators of the Lambrakis assassination. This was one of the five charges brought against him when the dictatorship was imposed in 1967.

Tireless and still as enthusiastic, Mikis continued his musical as well as the sociocultural activities throughout the fall and winter of 1966. The Bureau of the Arts of Piraeus, acting on behalf of the Musical Society of Piraeus, organized a large-scale artistic programme covering not only Piraeus and other Greek cities but also cities in Europe and the Soviet Union. With his Ensemble, Mikis gave a series of pop concerts to always packed audiences in Piraeus and various cities in the Peloponnese. At the same time, a group of musicians founded their own band, the Little Pop Orchestra, patterned on Mikis' Ensemble. The musical life of Piraeus was then invigorated with young creative talents, which resulted in a spirit of competition with the capital. Piraeus became from now on the centre where Mikis concentrated all his power. After all, it was this city that elected him to Parliament. The pop concerts, however, were not the only means of communication with the public of Piraeus. The Little Symphonic Orchestra of Athens was changed to the Symphonic Orchestra of Piraeus, which performed classical compositions. The season opened with the national day, October 28, and, on the thirtieth, the classical works of six composers, including Mikis, were performed. The fall and winter of 1966 were the seasons for a large European tour of Mikis' Ensemble, which included seven cities in the Soviet Union and a dozen more in Germany and England, where he met with striking success and left a great impression, for already the "syrtaki" dance, inspired by the Zorba theme, had become known throughout the world.

By the end of the year, the plan to make Piraeus the heart of his movement had come to a conclusion. Through the favourable response of the mayor of the city, who was in agreement with the cultural programme of the United Democratic Left, he received a loan of 1 million drachmas ($33,000) to organize a larger symphonic orchestra as well as a large choral ensemble, and to establish a pop conservatory and an institute of Greek music. In order to carry on such a heavy programme, Mikis resigned from the presidency of the Lambrakis Youth and was appointed as the head of the cultural programme of the United Democratic Left.

Thus, the year which had begun with the "miasma speech" of the King and had seen so many acts of violence against Mikis and his movement, finished on a note of achievement and hope. The value and success of his ideals as witnessed in the spectacular support of the Lykavittos Festival, the sponsorship of these two orchestras by the Bureau of the Arts of Piraeus and the Musical Society of Piraeus, was unquestioned. It was the culmination of six years of musical creativity and action, during which he had given over 200 concerts —178 of them pop and 25 classical. The bright hope of a cultural centre in Piraeus was about to take real shape. Only the darkening political clouds did not disappear, but, instead, thickened and lowered ever more ominously. On December 20, the Stephanopoulos government fell. Once more, the King, stalling for time, set up another puppet regime, a so-called caretaker government until things were quiet enough to hold elections. At its head was the Governor General of the National Bank of Greece, Paraskevopoulos. The dangers that Mikis faced, however, remained the same under any government so long as the paramilitary state remained in existence.

To begin with, the Minister to the Prime Minister, Nianias, announced over the radio that absolutely all of Mikis' works would be banned, even the popular "Zorba." The ostensible reason was that the radio must be nonpartisan in its music, and Mikis was a deputy of the United Democratic Left and the leader of the Lambrakis Youth.

Committees of Friends of the Music of Mikis Theodorakis were formed in a number of cities to protect and perform the works of the composer. Beginning with February 14, there were five continuous productions of *Axion Esti* at the Public Theatre of Piraeus, under the auspices of the College of Agriculture. Mikis continued to ignore the bigots and militarists, as he had always done, devoting his energies to the task of musical education. He started a series of musical seminars at the Town Theatre of Piraeus under the auspices of the Musical Society of Piraeus. These offered the public both live performances of music and analytical, historical commentary of the works. In addition to these musical seminars, the Town Orchestra of Piraeus organized a two-month programme of performances of classical works, with guest conductors and artists. At the end of the two-month programme, on March 22 and 29, Mikis' *Concerto for Piano* was premièred, with Aliki Vatikioti as the soloist.

The cultural output during these "dying days" was the most prolific in Greek history. The political tension in the air, the ferment over promised elections, the smear campaign of the right-wing establishment, served only to intensify the cultural yearnings and involvement of the young people. The *boîtes* in Plaka, beneath the Acropolis, where poetry readings and the music of new artists were presented, were always crowded. Girls could go there unescorted and not seem out of place, even in Greek society, for the emphasis was on the poem or the song, or the skill of the guitarist and the vocalist. For such places as these, the youth had been starved. They were a far cry from the noisy tourist joints that existed side by side with the sole interest of profit-making.

Mikis, as head of the cultural programme of the Left, extended the activities of the Lambrakis Youth by inaugurating a two-month crash campaign directed towards (1) Political Literature in Greece; (2) Youth and Politics; (3) Self-Independence, Political Parties, and NATO; (4) The Past and Our Political Ethics; (5) Educational Reform; (6) The Greek Political Song; (7) The Modern Political Theatre in Greece; and (8) The Art of the Political Caricatures in Greece (accompanied by exhibitions). The most striking feature of the programme was the first, "Political Literature in Greece." The most important writers of the younger generation participated in that panel discussion: Vassilikos, Kotzias, and Tsirkas, as well as the commentators Sotiriou, Koumantareas, Ioannidou, and the publisher of *Themelio,* Despotidis. The debate was very stimulating, for the writers themselves proved to know modern aesthetics and world literature quite well. It turned out to be a unique seminar in comparative literature.

In the suburban areas and provincial towns, it was more difficult to carry on this programme, for those who participated were easy to isolate and at the mercy of the terrorists of the secret gangs. For example, the assembly hall in the village of Mylochori, in Kilkis, was blown up twice. Each time the LYM rebuilt it themselves.

The palace's desperate attempt at forming a caretaker government under Paraskevopoulos failed, and, in March, he was replaced by the leader of ERE, Panayiotis Kanellopoulos. On March 16, the Aspida trial ended and twelve officers were imprisoned, to be released in 1968, while Andreas Papandreou was not convicted. The same week, terrorist activities by the underworld began; three bombs exploded in the centre of Athens in order to create chaos and thus give the police a fresh excuse to make dozens of arrests of the Lambrakis Youth.

The "Fascist beast" watched eagerly and, with teeth sharpened, awaited the propitious moment to strike. Mikis, in two speeches—one delivered at the final plenum of the Executive Committee of EDA, toward the end of March, 1967, and the other, fatefully, in his father's island of Crete, just four weeks before the April 21 coup—warned his compatriots of the forthcoming danger. Mikis ended his speech in Chania with the slogans: Progress, General Amnesty, Unity of All Greeks, Democratic Resistance. All the Cretans were urged to strive toward these goals.

At the Executive Committee of EDA, Mikis insisted on the role of the cultural movement, especially among the youth, and expressed the thought that, if any change were to take place in the country, it would first have to come through cultural activities on an educational and social basis, with the mobilization of large segments of the Greek population. Concurrently, Mikis and all the organizers of the Fifth Marathon Peace March (scheduled for April 17), accepted its banning by the government, for, they reasoned, they would show their strength in the upcoming elections.

With these plans in mind—and exhausted from recording the song-cycle *The Hostage* with Maria Farantouri for Columbia and rehearsing seven songs by García Lorca, the *Ballads of Antonio el Camborio,* freely adapted into Greek by Odysseas Elytis—he went to sleep on that fateful night of April 20.

# 8

## The Coming of the Barbarians

> I see before me the abyss towards which we
> are being led by the oppression which has
> spread over the land.
>
> GEORGE SEFERIS, March, 1969

### LIFE AND ACTIVITIES UNDER
### THE DICTATORSHIP

At four in the morning of April 21, Mikis was wakened by a
phone call.

It was a rightist journalist informing him that tanks were
rolling through Athens and occupying the city. Mikis was not
shocked; for months now, political events had been hastening
towards this disaster. He awakened Myrto, and both burned
whatever documents they thought might be dangerous as possible evidence to be used against him. She and the children
stayed indoors, while Mikis slipped out into the night to go
to his father's house. There, he called a friend, whom he met
later in a nearby home to arrange their next moves. In vain,

he tried to get in touch with a few officers of the Lambrakis Youth, to ask for a mass rally in Syntagma Square, but nothing could be done since every inch of the city and the entire country was now under tight control. The only recourse to action he had was through underground methods. Three days later, he smuggled out, through Paris, the first antidictatorial message to come out of Greece, at a time when any communication with the outside world was absolutely dead. In his message he attacked Kollias, whom he mentioned first, the "foreign locusts," the Americans, and the King, and asked all the Greeks to unite behind the banner on which was written "Freedom," "Democracy," "Greece."[1] "Our country's history" the first resistance manifesto went on, "is great and glorious. We have, tens of times, confronted ironclad enemies, and have been victorious. We realize that the new historic struggle is very difficult and arduous as it is decisive and beautiful, because it will lead to freedom in a crownless, a real, democracy, to national independence, to the patriotic unity of our people, and to a national renaissance."

Right after that, he staged his own coup—he cut his hair, donned an officer's uniform, and went underground. He moved from house to house, especially among rightists, and used various disguises. Once, to get to a secret meeting-place, he was transferred in a truck, covered with gunnysacks. A few days later, April 28-30, the Patriotic Antidictatorial Front (PAM) was created by leftists, rightists, and centrists, but mainly by youths and professionals uncommitted to any party. PAM also printed the first underground mimeographed bulletin, *Nea Ellada* (New Greece), and made its first antijunta declaration on May 29. In early June, Mikis sent out three taped songs, the cycle *Songs for the Patriotic Front*. The music and lyrics were written in his own hand, and he sang the songs while beating out the rhythm with his fingers on a table. In one of the songs, he is accompanied by

[1] For the full English text of the manifesto and subsequent declarations, see Stephen Rousseas, *The Death of a Democracy: Greece and the American Conscience* (New York, 1967), Appendix III, 212-26.

Ioannis Leloudas, one of the founders of PAM. The police heard the songs broadcast over the Greek Communist station "Voice of Truth," transmitted from Bucharest, and thinking they had discovered the culprit to whom belonged the second voice, they beat to death a suspect who, in fact, had nothing to do with the recording. The content and mood of the music are a most realistic and tragic reflection of the situation in their call to the Greeks to rise against the dictators and Texas (the Johnson administration).

The junta, however, waited a month before enforcing the ban on Mikis' music. His Ensemble was performing in Thessaloniki for a highly emotional audience under the threatening eyes of the police, who were awaiting an order from above. The order finally came on June 1, signed by the most Christian Greek of all, the head of the Armed Forces and the American Pentagon's man in Greece, Odysseas Angelis:

## JOINT CHIEFS OF STAFF
## PROCLAMATION NO. 13

I. Taking into consideration the ordinances of the law DMH/1912 on the "State of Siege," which has been enforced by the Royal Decree 280/21 April 1967,

### WE HAVE DECIDED AND ORDER:
### IT IS FORBIDDEN

throughout the Dominion

a. To broadcast in any manner or perform the musical compositions of the Communist Mikis Theodorakis, former leader of the already disbanded Communist organization "Lambrakis Youth Movement" (LYM), which, among other things, was the means of liaison between the Communists.

b. To broadcast or perform the anthems of the various party youth associations which were abolished by our Proclamation No. 8 of 6 May 1967, as these anthems revive political enmities and cause discord among the citizens.

II. Violators will be brought before the Special Military
   Tribunals and will be punished according to the ordinances of the "State of Siege" Law.

Athens 1/6/67

ODYSSEAS ANGELIS
Lieutenant General L.G./J.C.S.[2]

Mikis' response to the banning was to smuggle out new
compositions and to send a score to the International Movement of Young People and Children which he had written
on July 7, 1967. He had heard their request on the "Voice of
Truth," over a transistor while in hiding. A week later, a
court-martial in Athens sentenced him *in absentia* to five and
a half months' imprisonment for having insulted the royal
family in 1966.

The junta, in the meantime, was also passing decrees banning books, magazines, and anything intellectual considered
dangerous to their status, including performances and record
sales. A law passed during the German occupation, for instance, which was intended to protect (impose!) moral, spiritual, and cultural standards of the people, was revived. Seven
ancient tragedies and comedies were deleted from the programme of the Athens Festival, three of which had background
music composed by Mikis—*Phoenician Women, Trojan
Women,* and *Ajax.* A tumultuous outcry was raised by world
public opinion, and systematic boycotting of the festival began throughout the world: Isaac Stern, Eugene Istomin,
David Rose, the Los Angeles Symphony Orchestra under
Zubin Mehta, and the Theatre de France of Jean-Louis Bar-
rault refused to participate, along with the Kiev Ballet, the
Moscow Symphony Orchestra, and the Budapest Symphony
Orchestra. The regime tried to cover up its action and had
Alexis Minotis, husband of the actress Katina Paxinou and

---

[2] This proclamation was circulated in the international press where it
caused a reaction among the artistic world particularly. It inspired the German composer, Paul Dessau, to write a few months later as a tribute to
Mikis, who by that time had been imprisoned, an oratorio for mixed choir,
recitative, and nine instruments, entitled *Armeebefehl 13,* based on the text
of the decree.

the festival's director, give the junta's version of the situation. Minotis, among other things, said: "Since three of the originally scheduled tragedies for this year's Athens and Epidaurus Festivals had music by Theodorakis, the board of directors of the National Theatre, appointed by previous governments, in consultation with the Education Ministry, decided to eliminate them."[3]

During his four months in hiding, Mikis wrote a series of political reflections on the crisis, entitled *We the Greeks*. Then, he drafted a programme of action for PAM, as well as a satirical pamphlet. All were to be confiscated by the security police, however, upon his arrest. In early August, another clandestine group, the Democratic Defence resistance organization, was formed, consisting mainly of intellectuals and professionals who adopted PAM lines, but pursued action within the limits of the law. PAM and Democratic Defence soon began exploring the possibilities for alliance, or at least liaison. As communication between the two groups increased, the police started picking up clues as to the important hideouts. For months they had been looking for Mikis, combing every inch of the city in their search. Because Mikis had to communicate with the other groups, the police finally tracked him down. Too many comings and goings had aroused their suspicions. He was apprehended on August 21 at the home of Mrs. Tsourmas on Prophet Elias' hill, concealed behind the piano as the police burst in. From that date world opinion focused on Mikis' fate at the hands of the colonels. Hundreds of protests, demonstrations, telegrams, statements, and appeals for his safety and release were made.

The composer was bound, pushed around, hit in the stomach with a police club, and attacked with a barrage of filth and curses. He was asked by the officer in charge, "You were wearing a first-lieutenant's uniform?" "Yes, and I regret it because I did not promote myself to a colonel." Infuriated, the police hit him harder, and then led him to a mock shooting in the early dawn, his head covered with a sack. Fi-

---

[3] Testimony cited by *The New York Times,* July 9, 1967, cf. editorial comment on the same subject in *ibid.,* September 5, 1967.

nally he was taken to the "famous" Security Police Headquarters on Bouboulinas Street in Athens.[4]

The myth of Sisyphus began all over again. Twenty years
before, almost to the exact day, he had gone through similar
procedures. Now he knew the routine. But the last thing his
tormentors wanted was to turn him into a martyr-hero. The
false news that Mikis was about to die had brought forth a
barrage of world protest, and so Lambrou, the chief of the
security police, devised a scheme to discredit him abroad and
give the impression that he was not suffering at all. He called
a press conference and summoned a junta supporter, the
editor of *Eleftheros Kosmos,* Savvas Konstantopoulos, who
was a former leftist and whom Mikis had known for years, to
pose for a photograph with Mikis holding his arm in a
friendly fashion. Konstantopoulos remarked that nobody was
satisfied with the present situation, that the world should
help them get rid of this mess, and that democracy must return. Mikis could not help finding such statements from
Konstantopoulos amusing, and so he was photographed not
only with Konstantopoulos holding his arm but smiling. The
mission accomplished, he was thrown back into his cell; and,
the next day, the front pages of the Athenian newspapers carried a photograph of Mikis smiling at Konstantopoulos. The
same picture was reprinted throughout the world.

The screams in the security police prison never ceased.
At every hour of the day or night, the cries of pain tormented
him. To counterbalance this and from his own fear that his
turn was coming, he began composing melodies and verses.
In his despair, he protested loudly to the head of the police
that he at least be given some music paper on which to write.
Ten days later, he was given some staves. Thus, he composed thirty-three pieces from September 2 to October 17, and
set the music to fifteen of them with the title *Sun and Time,*
describing his situation and fear that he might never see the

4 Mikis' arrest and imprisonment so moved his fellow musicians, such as
Paul Dessau, that the French composer F. Thomas set J.-C.Rivat's lyrics to
music, with the title "Theodorakis," which was sung by Giles Dreu. The
Yugoslav composer, Vojislav Kostic did the same for a poem by Ljubomir,
"A Ballad on Theodorakis."

sun again. Several of these songs, with the help of a policeman and the underground, were smuggled out of Greece and handed to the *Guardian* in London on October 30.

Two weeks later (November 15), the trial of thirty-one members of PAM began. The special military tribunal that had been set up consisted of five judges, four of whom were field-grade army officers. Presiding was a Supreme Court judge who had been given an army rank for the duration of the trial. The thirty-one were charged with having set up a clandestine network for the transmission of messages and subversive slogans and with having published antigovernment pamphlets and a news bulletin called *Nea Ellada*. Mikis, as leader of the group, was charged with defaming the government to foreign embassies and newspapers through the Patriotic Front and his resistance manifestoes and with planning to overthrow the regime, a crime that could result in the death sentence. As if these charges were not enough, he was also accused of having publicly insulted the royal family, of impersonating an army officer, of having been a leader of the Lambrakis Youth, and of having publicly declared, in November, 1966, that a dictatorship was in the making. It was decided not to try him with the others because of "certain formalities" that had to be fulfilled before bringing him to court. He was transferred to another cell in the security police station.

There, as the prisons were packed with new arrivals, most of them women apprehended for antiregime activities like delivering leaflets or spreading antidictatorial slogans, he encountered a young girl who had just started composing a long poem. She handed it to the composer, introducing herself with the pseudonym "Marina." Mikis was very impressed with the poem and asked her to send it to him, when completed, as soon as possible and under any circumstances. He received the work, entitled "State of Siege," a few days later, while "Marina" was on trial.

As the trial of the thirty-one started, the police spread a third lie that Mikis had given in to them and betrayed his co-fighters. When this reached Mikis, he requested that he be judged along with the others. His request was denied. The word was passed along that he was very ill and could not be brought to court, but, of course, no explanation of the nature of the illness was given. Instead, the Minister of Public Order, Paul Totomis (who had been educated in the United States), said that he was to be tried separately.

Mikis was determined to stage a hunger-strike.[5] Looking through the keyhole of his cell door, he saw his friend Andreas Lentakis[6] being returned to the adjoining cell. In a taped message smuggled out by the underground later, the composer described these days in the police station:

> I was kept in adjoining cells with Andreas Lentakis, who was a member of the Executive Committee of the Lambrakis Youth. Using a code, we used to communicate by knocking on the wall, thus breaking down the isolation. With the "tac-tac," on the wall, Andreas would describe to me all that the police were making him suffer. When I began my hunger strike, I informed Andreas of it through the wall. He passed the news on to the other cells, all of which wished me good luck and courage. He then gave me his final advice: that I should drink water with sugar in it. He informed me that he would manage to get some pills so that I would not become exhausted too quickly. And on the news went with this special code through the wall, up until the very moment when I began to lose my senses. I tried to communicate my message, but in vain. I realized suddenly that, all at once, I had lost my strength and was in danger. Then I lost consciousness completely.[7]

[5] A personal letter from Senator Robert F. Kennedy was sent to the Greek Ambassador in Washington, in which he said that Theodorakis should be allowed to stand trial and present his case in a public hearing.

[6] Andreas Lentakis was a doctoral candidate in Archaeology at the University of Athens. After three years of imprisonment, he was liberated by the junta, but still suffers the effects of brain damage caused by the severe tortures. The treatment he received at the hands of the dictators was used as evidence at the hearings of the Human Rights Commission in December, 1969.

[7] In this manner, tapping on the wall with a code, and under these circumstances, Lentakis informed Mikis that he had stolen from his files the original manuscript of *Axion Esti* to place it in the library of the Lambrakis Youth Centre. Months later (June 26), Mikis wrote the lyrics and the music to the song cycle *Songs for Andreas,* describing the tragic hours in the Security Police station.

On the tenth day, he was taken to the military hospital, Aghios Pavlos, in a coma. The prosecutor, to smooth matters over, said at the trial that Mikis had been only a Communist pawn, used as a figurehead because of his popularity as a composer. Mikis, after his recuperation, sent a letter to the prosecutor, in which he asked to be allowed to go to trial, but again he was not permitted. "He might die if we forced him to come to court," announced the prosecutor. The authorities were obviously afraid that he would expose their lies.

In the meantime, all the accused insisted that they had complete faith in Mikis, while describing their tortures by the police. On November 17, the trial ended, and most of the accused were found guilty of having aided the composer in his hiding and for working with him in the underground Patriotic Front. Among them were people from all walks of life and political affiliations: Mrs. Tatiana Milliex, a Greek-born author who lived in Cyprus; George Loulis, a former Centre Union deputy; Mrs. Sylvia Akrita, widow of the Minister of Education under Papandreou; the United Democratic Left deputy, Kostas Fillinis; four journalists, writers, actors, as well as Mrs. Tsoucalas, wife of the author; Kalliope Doxiades, daughter of the city-planner, Constantine Doxiades; Yiannis Leloudas, Kitti Arseni, and the girl, "Marina," and many more. Some escaped, like the United Democratic Left deputy, Antonis Brillakis. Some were later released, but twenty-three were condemned, two to life-imprisonment, and the rest for as much as fifteen years. "Marina" was sentenced to the women's detention of Averoff prison. Mikis' trial was set for January 17.

Meanwhile, on December 13, the King staged a counter-coup against Papadopoulos in Larissa, halfway between Athens and Thessaloniki. It was a futile gesture, lacking both in understanding of the junta's power and in popular support. The King was forced to flee within a few hours, together with his wife, children, the Queen-Mother, Prime Minister Kollias, bodyguards, and household to Rome, where he has resided ever since. No one remained to challenge Papadopoulos. Forty days later the dictator theatrically announced a partial amnesty, promising that Mikis, too, would be released. He wanted him to "write a song for the revolution." The composer wrote revolutionary songs continuously—but against Papadopoulos.

At the same time Mikis' bouzouki ensemble, composed of Maria Farantouri, Antonis Kaloyiannis, the pianist Yiannis Didilis, and the bouzoukis, was touring the capitals of the world, performing his new songs as well as earlier ones, as Mikis had requested from his hiding. Through the emotional participation of the foreign public, the bouzouki began to gain another favourable climate, this time outside Greece. The mobbed debuts became demonstrations against the dictators, while Greeks of all parties were united in attending and singing his songs. The bouzouki even conquered some foreign columnists. Robin Denselow, writing for *The Guardian,* said: "They [the bouzoukis] provide an excellent introduction to Greece's other revolution—the establishment of an extraordinary new popular music form."[8]

On Christmas Day, 1967, Mikis was transferred to the Averoff prison in the heart of Athens. At first, he was thrown into a section where common criminals—thieves, drug addicts, murderers—were being held. Then, he was transferred to another sector and allowed to consort with other prisoners as well as the thirty-three of the Patriotic Front. He began even more feverishly to compose and perform with the other prisoners. Mikis always managed to receive and smuggle out material. A cleaning-woman hid in her breast "Marina's" poem "State of Siege,"[9] along with several messages. He began sketching the composition there. Mikis' arrival in the prison was celebrated by the others, and, on January 1, 1968, he sang the songs of *Sun and Time* for them, rapping

[8] Robin Denselow, "The Theodorakis Ensemble," *The Guardian,* February 29, 1968.

[9] The poem, 150 lines, free verse, and divided in three parts, was rewritten in the Women's Prison Branch of Averoff in November-December, 1967. The theme of the poem is most tragic in the sense that this girl, "Marina," although already heavily tortured and buried alive in the Averoff jail, is constantly compelled to burn up her life for the cause against the dictators, in spite of her inability to cope with its vast dimensions.

objects with his knuckle for the rhythm, while the others followed his singing.

Here again, as he had done in all his previous prison experiences, he created, along with the others, a prison university "Averoff University." Some taught languages or other subjects, as their professions dictated, lectured on the arts and whatever other subject was suggested or permitted by the guards. And, so, the hours passed as pleasantly as possible. The other prisoners gathered pieces of paper and put together, in small pamphlet form, the songs of *Sun and Time,* with an English translation, which in turn was sneaked out of Greece and was reprinted and circulated in Europe.

It was at Averoff that he explored into Seferis more than ever before and composed a song cycle based on the poet's poems, entitled *Mythistorema* (Mythical Story). He was overcome with inspiration. He continued to work on Seferis. The prisoners agreed to celebrate the day of the Epiphany, on January 6, with a new and most powerful composition drawn from Seferis' long poem, "Epiphania," which Mikis entitled *Epiphania Averoff.* Ron Hall of *The Sunday Times,* who was the first to receive this and other works, offered a moving commentary on the plight and spirit of the prisoners who were with the composer. As soon as Mikis had finished the work, the walls transmitted the news in code. The prisoners rejoiced and immediately began the activity. Mikis rehearsed them as much as circumstances allowed, and soon they knew their parts. A "programme" was scrawled out on a piece of paper, headed "WORLD PREMIERE—THEATRE AVEROFF!" signed by forty-three prisoners and dedicated to Yiannis Ritsos and the other political prisoners. An artist drew a portrait of the composer conducting in prison, and another page was covered by a second drawing of a view of the prison from a cell. Mikis conducted the choir and sang the orchestral parts himself, imitating as best he could the sounds of the piano and the bouzouki. In this way, the "première" in Averoff was given, successfully.[10] Both works, the *Mythistorema* and the *Epiphania Averoff,* were

[10] Ron Hall, "The Ballads of Averoff Jail," *The Sunday Times,* February 11, 1968.

secretly sent to Seferis, who was greatly pleased with Mikis' interpretation of his poems. Twenty days later, on January 27, the composer was released, owing to the pressures, demonstrations, and campaigns throughout the capitals of the world.[11] As he was leaving the prison, those who remained behind hung on the cell windows and sang a hopeful song, the last one of the four from the cycle *Mythistorema*. And thus ended his five-month imprisonment, which taught the dictators that Mikis was not as small as they thought and world public opinion would not allow arbitrary acts of their own making. On March 15, the Institute of Civilization in Moscow created "Romiossini," an ensemble of nine artists, which performed Mikis' works in the Soviet Union. And, on April 26, London paid tribute to the composer by performing in their première the two works *Love and Death* for mezzo-soprano, with lyrics written by Mikis and Lorentzos Mavilis, sung by Glenys Louli, and *Oedipus Tyrannus*, an ode for string orchestra. Bryan Fairfax conducted the Polyphonia Orchestra at the Queen Elizabeth Hall. On the same bill were performed works by Mozart and Haydn. The British press praised both of Mikis' works highly.

He was released from Averoff prison, but was placed under house arrest in Athens, where he stayed with his family until the end of spring. Then, he was allowed to spend his summer days in Vrachati, a coastal village in the vicinity of Corinth on the Peloponnese. Here, at last, he found tranquillity and rejoiced in being surrounded by his two children, Yiorgos and Margarita, his wife, and other relatives and friends. He even had a secondhand piano. The horror was somehow dispelled by his life at home, and he found the strength to work on his music. He took up the *State of Siege* he had sketched in Averoff and completed it the first two days of May. He then began the new type of song, the song-river, with the piece of George Photinos, *Our Sister Athina,* completed on May 15. But the screams of his friends, prisoners still being

---

[11] Theodorakis, under a partial amnesty granted that month, had to pay 41,300 drachmas (£550) in fines to cover the reduced sentences he was charged with *in absentia*, and then applied for release.

tortured in the jails, would not leave him. He finished the song cycle *Songs for Andreas* in one sitting on June 26. More texts by modern Greek poets were secretly sent to his residence. One of these, containing *Night of Death, Twelve Laik Songs,* and *For the Mother and the Friends,* by Manos Eleftheriou, he set to music between May 26 and June 30. Then on May 30, the Academy of Fine Arts of East Germany proclaimed him a corresponding member for his musical works and for his actions in defence of human rights in Greece. But Vrachati was not really suited to his creative temperament. He was cut off from the people, and thus cut off from the consuming passion that characterizes his personality and life. In a letter he wrote to a fellow artist in Europe, and channelled through the underground, he expressed his strong desire to work on his music, rehearsing, recording, and performing. "These are my very soul," he wrote. "I lack all these right now, except, of course, if I am to be taken to prison again. Then, this total lack is shared with the sense that one offers something essential to the others; this, too, is a kind of creativity." (July 18).

Lack of musical opportunity, however, was not the only reason that made life difficult in Vrachati. Rumours were spread abroad that he had been brainwashed, not by the regime directly but by their flunky from the right-wing press, Savvas Konstantopoulos, the same man who had appeared at the security police press interview with Mikis the previous year. Through devious means, he had become the colonels' pet theoretician. At this time, in his newspaper, *Eleftheros Kosmos,* he was determined to discredit the composer as a man of politics and a resistance hero. The security police, which had confiscated all Mikis' belongings and those of the United Democratic Left, had found memos addressed by Mikis to the party in 1966. These "interparty memoranda" were turned over to Konstantopoulos, who then published them on May 19 and 21, 1967, without Mikis' approval. (There was no need for such formality under a dictatorship.) The memoranda, among other things, said that the composer, after the conviction of Daniel and Sinyavsky in the Soviet

Union, had denounced the party's interference with intellectual freedom, and declared his dissociation from similar dogmatism among Greek Communists. Subsequently the dictators announced they would lift the ban on his music. This, however, never came to pass. Instead, there followed a highly organized campaign to discredit Mikis for the benefit of the regime's enemies throughout the world, and especially the leftists in Athens. On June 16, 1968, the London *Observer* published a letter by Stamatopoulos, who was in charge of the Press Division at the Ministry of the Prime Minister, and accompanied by comments from the newspaper, accusing Mikis of being unstable in politics, untrustworthy, but withal, a good musician. On July 7, Mikis' furious response to both was printed in *The Observer*, in which he said that, were he as free to defend himself as the newspaper and Stamatopoulos were to discredit him, he would have dealt differently with the lies and accusations they both threw against him. He stated that he had chosen of his own accord the battle he was waging, and he concluded by saying that the talent of music had no value unless one could fulfil at every moment one's duty as a responsible person. A few days later two members of the junta, Vassilios Lambrou and Ioannis Ladas, paid a visit to Mikis in Vrachati to ask him to refrain from making statements. But Mikis confronted both men bravely, remaining adamant in his beliefs, and both left without achieving anything.

Mikis was determined to make known the real state of affairs to the world. When the Dutch newspaper *Telegraph* secretly sent a correspondent to interview him, he openly described his treatment and suffering at the hands of the police. He also thanked world opinion for pressuring the colonels for his release. He then attacked the regime as a disgrace to the nation. At that particular moment, the colonels were especially vulnerable to his words, because they were building up their defences to win the referendum on the Constitution that was scheduled for September 29. Mikis had to be put beyond the reach of the press and world reportage. Thus, on August 23, he was arrested again and, with his wife and children, deported to the isolated mountain village of Zatouna, in the Peloponnese. The primary reason for choosing Zatouna was that it was a stronghold of anti-Communist sentiment and totally isolated from the world. Only one rickety bus a day served to connect the inhabitants with the outside world. Few houses had telephones, and these were only trunk lines connecting them to the nearby town of Dimitsana. Furthermore, the rugged landscape, the rocky outcroppings, and the forests of evergreens rendered escape unlikely, for only those born there and fully acquainted with the area could find their way.

From Vrachati, Mikis was accompanied by a motorcade of state police to a desolate house in Zatouna, completely fenced off from the rest of the village, directly across from the church. Guards were immediately placed all around the house, and the entrance was marked with a cross as if it were infested with plague. In a matter of hours, the villagers knew who their important guest was. They, too, were inconvenienced, as everyone who left for the village or returned had to be checked by the police. It was like going through customs twice a day just to go to work. Half the passengers of the rickety bus were policemen, soldiers on duty changing the guard. Three police booths were set up on the road at a distance of fifty yards from each other, so that no car entered the village without being searched three times.

In Zatouna, Mikis led the life of an outcast. He was permitted no communication with anyone except his wife and children or the police guard. He was not permitted to leave the enclosure except once a day, when, flanked by two policemen, he took an afternoon walk of three hundred yards. The farthest he was occasionally allowed to go was to church on Sunday. "Christian Greeks," after all, could not prevent a man from attending church. Restrictions at the service were eased, and he was allowed to chant in church as he had done as a boy. He could even carry on brief conversations with the village priest on liturgy and music. The priest one day asked Mikis, "Did you compose a hymn today, my son?" to which Mikis replied, "Yes, I did, Father, but it was a march." At the end of the Sunday service, he was walked back to his prison-home. The tiny house had only two rooms, in one of which he kept the ancient secondhand piano he had been allowed to bring with him, as well as his tape-recorder. Day after day, he would sit at the piano, playing and singing to his audience of one, his son Yiorgos, who kept him company more often than the two women of the family. At the end of each recital, the father would ask his son whether he had liked the piece. Yiorgos would smile happily 'and nod his head in approval.

This was the poor child's only happiness. At school, he and his sister were isolated from the rest of the children, lest they hand out secret messages to a child who might serve as an underground carrier of news to the outside world. Both of the children, as well as Myrto, were brutally searched each time they left the house and each time they returned. The police knew Mikis could communicate only through them, since he was not allowed to leave the house at all except for his walk or to register daily at the police station. Myrto had to board the bus for Dimitsana in order to get food for the family. She was accompanied by a policeman to and from Zatouna. He never left her for a moment while she did the marketing. A policewoman frisked her or would make her undress before she went back in the house.

Meanwhile, a hue and cry against the composer's reimprisonment went out from all his supporters throughout the world. Rumours of ill health and mistreatment circulated that the junta was anxious to dispel. A group of representatives from a German television concern was permitted a formal interview in November. Of course, the questions and answers were censored by the authorities, and the film as well. The interview, which finally appeared the following April, was, of course, far from accurate in its reportage. Reports on Mikis' poor health were increased. His tuberculosis, which had always been a problem, flared up once more. He had no access to any medicine, and there was no doctor except Myrto in Zatouna to prescribe treatment. Instead, a "specialist" of another sort arrived to torment Mikis, attacking where he would be most vulnerable, through his son. One December afternoon, Yiorgos was stopped by a new policeman. The man slapped the boy sharply on the face, forced him up against the wall with his hands over his head, and stripped him naked in plain sight of any villager who might pass by, all the while blinding him with the glare of a powerful flashlight beam thrust in his eyes. The child burst into hysterical crying, and, shaking and trembling, fled into the house in a terrible state of shock. His sobs remained uncontrollable for days, and he had to be taken to Athens for treatment. Mikis himself was so shaken by the brutality that he composed a moving song, "My Son Is Nine Years Old," to avoid a breakdown himself. A few days later, when he saw the policeman who had terrorized his son, he reached out and, grabbing him by the lapels of his jacket, said: "So, you are the tough guy who threatens and slaps children! You, hero!" The policeman instantly thrust the muzzle of his machine-gun into Mikis' stomach—such was his hatred for the composer—and was about to pull the trigger had not another guard, seeing the crisis, rushed up to prevent him. Luckily, this man was removed from Zatouna.

As yet, nothing but rumours reached the outside world. Such rumours were easy for the junta to disregard or discredit. But public opinion was mobilizing, demanding facts. A daring Britisher, John Barry, set out to remedy the situation. He decided that he would find a way to get into Zatouna. With information about a round-about donkey trail into Zatouna that police, perhaps because they did not know of its existence, did not guard at all, Barry, disguised as a Greek, made his way to the forbidden village. Although he did not see Mikis, he organized a network whereby he was given a series of tapes of the composer's recent works and two letters, one to the Secretary-General of the United Nations, U Thant, and the other to the Subcommission on Human Rights of the Council of Europe. Subsequently, both letters, or excerpts therefrom, appeared in journals and papers throughout the world, including *The New York Times* (March 16, 1969). It was not until December 12, 1969, that the Council of Europe finally expelled Greece from its membership, after having compiled pages of documentation from the hundreds of tortured victims of the military state.

The sensational story of John Barry's success in reaching Zatouna, as it appeared in *The Sunday Times* (March 16, 1969), incensed the colonels. The guard around the isolated house was tripled. A floodlight was focused on it throughout the night. The authorities took away Mikis' piano and cut off the telephone that had linked him with his father in Athens. There were rumours that a delegation from the Council of Europe would arrive sometime in April. The guards threatened that he would have to pick up his belongings and move to an even remoter area. Mikis was determined to resist. He decided upon the only weapon that would have any effect, a twenty-day hunger strike. He had used this tactic before, and the authorities knew that, if he decided upon such a thing, he would carry it out, even to the point of coma, or death. And, whatever the colonels wanted, it was not to have Mikis die the death of a martyr. As he was about to start the hunger strike, the governor of the district visited the family. Myrto informed him that, if Mikis were to die, she would kill her two children and then herself. As a result of such determination, the piano was returned, although the telephone was not. The composer had long since hidden his tape recorder, knowing it was one of his most vital means of reaching the world.

During this crucial period of protest, Mikis seemed to be in no mood to compose music. Instead, he spent hours filling the pages of a school notebook with a surrealistic drama of the life of the tortured under the junta. The victim he christened Evangelos, "messenger of good news," to give an ironic twist, and the work he called *Exodus*. It opens and closes with the same situation, an almost literal description of the composer's own arrest:

> The soldiers came to arrest me while I was sleeping. They undressed me and ordered me to kneel down. Then they tied my hands behind my back the way the GIs tie their Vietcong captives. When Maria entered, I felt ashamed and asked them to put on my underwear. They put the underwear on me and

khaki trousers. I was barefoot and asked Maria to put on my shoes. As she bent down in front of me to tie my shoes, I whispered to her, "Courage, Maria!"[12]

As the national holiday of March 25 was approaching, Mikis felt a burning desire to work with the most heroic of poems: Angelos Sikelianos' "March of the Spirit." The composer, burning with inspiration, finished the oratorio in a matter of hours. Thus, the bitter days of exile passed that winter for Mikis. The tighter the restrictions, the greater his joy, for he knew what that meant—that people on the outside were trying to do something. His greatest sense of satisfaction came from smuggling out the tapes of music and anti-regime messages, together with photographs. A family friend was permitted to visit them. She, with the help of Myrto and the composer, transported a long tape by sewing it into the hem of her dress. The police, of course, searched her thoroughly, but the tape was not found. In fact, he later confessed, after his release, that he did not know what made him happier—the compositions that he managed to finish, or the opportunity to smuggle them out through the underground, despite the increased guard and hostility of the police. One of the smuggled messages that reached *The Sunday Times* said: "It is necessary, I imagine, to say that all these restrictions, far from disturbing us, fill us with joy. Not, of course, because we are masochists, but because they are a sign that what our friends, who love us, are doing has an impact abroad. In the midst of these conditions, our morale and our faith, far from weakening, are, on the contrary, being sharpened and strengthened."[13]

[12] Mikis Theodorakis, *Exodus*—a dramatic fantasy. The work exists in the original handwriting of the composer and my translation into English. I cannot recall any greater joy in my life than that of April 26, 1970, when I met Mikis in Paris after his liberation at last. He produced out of his bag his prison creations—paper napkins with musical scores, coloured pages with musical analyses—and then he started reading aloud the *Exodus*. His big round eyes turned red. He walked back and forth, gesticulating, and then would sit down again on the chair with emphatic gentleness. I was completely absorbed into the torture-chamber of Evangelos. In fact, I was so carried away by the power of the work that I spent the whole rest of the night translating the work. What else could I do?

[13] Theodorakis, "My Life in Exile," *The Sunday Times*, May 4, 1969.

Such reportage created more uproars from the junta, a new changing of the guard, renewed restrictions, an intensification of the watch. Clearly Mikis' spirit was not defeated. On the tape which was smuggled out his voice comes clear as he speaks to a police officer: "When I see you, I hear inside me the sound of jungle drums. To me, you represent the law of the jungle."

Day by day, pressure increased for his release as well as for more humane treatment for the political prisoners in general. The junta was fast losing any pretence of support from the European nations. For example, a strong petition for Mikis' release by seventy-eight world-famous composers, artists, directors, actors, and other celebrities was signed in London. Among them were Laurence Olivier, Alec Guiness, John Gielgud, Peter Hall, Harold Pinter, and Benjamin Britten. Such a petition, of course, had little effect on the junta. Mikis tried to acknowledge his colleagues' efforts on his behalf as best he could. Realizing that the prime mover in the petition was Melina Mercouri, who at the time was in London, he wrote to her: "We share the same political aims and we have the same dreams for a happier Greece tomorrow. I am very happy, Melina, because I serve such great people and because I have comrades like you and thousands of other resolute fighters. I live for one reason: the resurrection of Greece."[14]

In Zatouna, meanwhile, in spite of their daily annoyances because of their prisoner, the villagers began to overcome their fear and to show sympathy and affection for Mikis. They would gather around the house, when he was playing, in small unnoticeable groups, pretending to be uninterested but anxious to hear more. As the days passed, his spirit remained indomitable, and even the policemen began to like his songs. They could be heard whistling them. That spring, villagers and police together sometimes came and would call to him, "Mikis, play for us *The Survivor* or *I Speak*."[15]

[14] *The Observer*, May 4, 1969.
[15] Both works belong to the song-river type of music and are classified as *The Survivor—Ark. VII*, words by Takis Sinopoulos, and *I Speak—Ark. VIII*, words by Manos Anagnostakis.

Isolated as he was, Mikis somehow managed to keep in touch with the efforts of the various antijunta groups in Greece and abroad. He learned, to his delight, of the partial fulfilment of one of his dreams, that of a unified front, or collaboration between PAM, Brillakis' group (he had escaped in 1967), and Papandreou's PAK, which took place in Rome on April 2, 1969. This agreement did not please the junta any more than it pleased the Moscow-directed Communist group of Kolliyiannis.[16] Thus, in June, he decided to deliver his credo to the Kolliyiannis Political Bureau in a letter. He stated that he would go so far as to accept Karamanlis as a transitional "caretaker." Even though such an expedient could only cripple democracy, it would be much better than the present dictators. In his isolation in Zatouna, he began to review in his mind the problems of antidictatorial action and to see things from a broader perspective. Through underground channels, he gave his explicit opinions to the Italian magazine *L'Europeo* in June. He contended that the present Greek crisis was caused not only by Papadopoulos, but that the real responsibility lay with all the Greeks without distinction. As for his own personal position in the present crisis, and his opinion for the future, he said:

> As for where I stand personally, I shall continue to adhere to the Patriotic Antidictatorial Front, to those of the "patriotic front," as long as it continues to resist the present regime. . . . At this moment, the difference in parties does not interest me. I see only one enemy—the dictatorship. And I have but one objective, its overthrow. . . . My own future, after the fall of the dictatorship, will depend on many factors. Fundamentally, I want to dedicate myself wholly to my artistic activities—to my music. Only when I see that I cannot do otherwise, as at the present moment, will I turn to political activity.[17]

Mikis saw the fate of Greece squashed between the two great powers—the United States and the Soviet Union. In an

[16] The climate for unity was more favourable now that the European Parliament, a very important body of the Common Market, finally condemned and made a strong appeal to the Greek junta on May 7 about the measures of oppression, the abolition of parliamentary life, etc.

[17] N. Minuzzo, "Interview with Theodorakis," *L'Europeo*, June, 1969.

open letter to both President Nixon and President Podgorny of the Soviet Union, which he sent in July, he held both powers responsible for the present situation in Greece. He maintained that the geographical position of Greece added to the rivalry of the two, and that this rivalry had had catastrophic results. Both presidents should not consider Greece only as a strategic spot but as a living country, with a brave and vital people possessing a rich history. Such assertions infuriated the Moscow-line Greek Communists; the composer, however, was not to deviate from his stand. He had found his own position.

Much of that summer of 1969 was spent on re-evaluating his own political stand and focusing on the contemporary situation, as well as trying to keep in touch with the Greek underground. He felt a desperate need for more poetry, the new writings of the young people. One of his letters on this need was smuggled out of Zatouna. He wrote to a fellow-artist—who, for the sake of his safety, must remain anonymous —that he needed "poetic texts. If it is possible, modern, today's, burning. I contemplate composing, if possible, fifty 'Arkadies.' " Whatever poetry he received from here and there that could inspire his mood—poetry dealing with modern, burning themes—he set to music. In this way, he composed eleven works, song cycles, song-rivers, and metasymphonic pieces.[18] They were called "Arkadies I-XI," marking symbolically the place, the events, and the times. If he had no poetic texts, or they did not inspire him, he wrote his own verses, such as *On the Mountains of Arkadia (Ark. I)*, just after he had arrived in Zatouna. Another example is *Thou-*

[18] He had finished the song cycles *For the Mother and the Friends—Ark. III,* lyrics by Manos Eleftheriou; *The Vows of Kalvos—Ark. IV,* a nineteenth-century Eptanissian poet whose centennial of death was celebrated that year by everyone but the junta and whose subjects were drawn from the 1821 Revolution against the Turks; the grand oratorio *March of the Spirit (Ark. V)* by Angelos Sikelianos, and continued the song-river type creation with his own poem *Thourion (Ark. VI); The Survivor (Ark. VII)* of Takis Sinopoulos; *I Speak* and *Charis 1944 (Ark. VIII),* both of which make up one work set to the poetry of Manos Anagnostakis, and *The Exile's Mother (Ark. IX)* by Kostas Kallantzis, and *The Three Brave Ones, (Ark. XI)* drawn from a poem by Notis Pergialis.

*rion (Ark. VI)*, where he calls upon the dead poets of Greece as well as the living to help the people fight the dictators for the regeneration of the land.

His musical work, as seen in the *Arkadies,* and his trials as an exile in Zatouna were punctuated by a dramatic event. On September 22, 1969, Kostas Stergiou, the notorious head of the police in Zatouna, whom Mikis described as a "dragon with a helmet," burst into the house, saying, "My name is Kostas Stergiou. I am here to interrogate you!" He began to search Myrto and the children thoroughly; they were to be taken to Athens. Meanwhile, he pushed Mikis into the kitchen and locked him in. On the music sheets of the song-river he was composing at the time, *I Had Three Lives (Ark. X)* , Mikis wrote: "Myrto, Margarita, and Yiorgos are departing for Athens. Lieutenant Kostas Stergiou has been searching them from 8:30 to 12 noon. I was locked in the kitchen and wrote this song. Only in this way did Stergiou save his life, and I escaped going to jail."

The junta, after the escape of another famous political prisoner, George Mylonas,[19] from his island exile of Amorgos, was determined to tighten its security measures. Thus, Mikis was transferred to the Oropos military concentration camp, thirty-seven miles northeast of Athens, on the sea facing Euboea Island, on October 19, 1969. His sudden transfer also reflected the disagreement between the various members of the junta. Those behind Papadopoulos were willing to weigh the pressures and the issue. The others, much tougher, acting against the wishes of the Premier, wanted stricter treatment of the prisoners and a rigid dictatorial regime. Mikis' transfer could be interpreted as a victory for the anti-Papadopoulos clique that followed Ioannis Ladas and the notorious chief of the army policy, Dimitrios Ioannides.

Strange as it may seem, life was more pleasant for Mikis in the Oropos concentration camp than in the rugged mountain village, even though he was permitted only ten-minute visits from his family once every three months. He was no

---

[19] Mylonas was a former Minister of Education under the Papandreou regime.

longer isolated from his fellow-man; at least, he could converse, exchange ideas, read books, and find responsive souls
among the other prisoners. There was nothing more black to
Mikis' gregarious spirit than isolation, whether it was that
of the Bouboulina Security Prison, the seaside hamlet of
Vrachati, or the exile in Zatouna. As he had expressed a year
earlier to a fellow-artist in Europe, he preferred prison, with
the company of others, to solitary house-arrest and isolation.

There was a great spurt of musical activity. The authorities allowed him to form a choral group, as he had done in
previous prisons, which would sing his Zatouna songs, *Arkadies,* as well as much church music. The latter was due to the
presence of a prisoner who had been driven insane by the
tortures he had suffered, the isolation, and the interrogations.
Day and night, the prisoner, Zouzoulas, would go around
chanting Byzantine church music. He had a wonderful voice
and knew all the chants by heart. A communal closeness like
that of the early Christian church developed among the
prisoners, who would often go through the formalities of the
service, processing with banners and books held up like
icons, simulating a liturgy, in order to shake off the withdrawal symptoms of the crazed prisoner and get him to sing
again. Mikis took advantage of his knowledge of the hymns,
many of whose tunes he himself had forgotten, to take down
the notes while Zouzoulas would sing for him. The composer
gave full credit to this man in his *Oropos Notebook* for his
singing of each part he used.

Mikis' six months in the Oropos concentration camp were
to prove one of the most fruitful periods of his creative endeavours. Because he could finally communicate with others,
he began to write down the thoughts and problems that had
occurred to him in Zatouna and throughout his years of imprisonment and exile. Music, the nature and purpose of his
musico-cultural movement, a comparative analysis of the Byzantine church music and the rebetic song were the subjects
he concentrated on, covering pages and pages of any paper
he could lay his hands on, from paper napkins to loose sheets
to a child's school pad.

Once again Mikis turned to the poetry of Seferis. He sketched, wrote, and orchestrated without interruption (January 7-10, 1970) the metasymphonic work *Raven–In Memoriam of E.A.P.*, scored for symphonic and pop instruments, a soloist, and chorus. He dedicated the composition to one of the most talented Greek composers of the twelve-tone technique, Yiannis Christou, who had just died in a car accident.

One day, a prisoner showed him an anthology of Black African poetry translated into Greek. Immediately, the composer sat down to put notes over the syllables. Working ceaselessly through the night to the next morning, he composed three songs of Léopold Senghor and others and sketched three others, all dedicated to Myrto.

The "workshop" of Oropos produced much, but Mikis had to fight another enemy, much worse than the lethargy of prisons—his latent tuberculosis. The months of strain, improper food, lack of heat in Zatouna took their toll. The disease flared up again and began to spread to his other lung, but the prison authorities would not let him see a specialist. His father launched a violent protest to the camp commander, reminding him that, not only would it be a great tragedy for him if Mikis were to die in such a way, but it would create a scandal for the junta. Conflicting reports and news dispatches about Mikis' tuberculosis began to circulate widely in the world press. As a result of such pressure, the commander thought it best to make the great gesture and show Mikis as perfectly well. Foreign correspondents, who had been denied any information all this time, were permitted to go to the camp, as were Mikis' own family. But the concession was only a mockery. All they could do was look at him from a great distance as he strolled in the prison yard. It is not exactly possible to detect anything of a person's health at a distance of three hundred yards. On February 6, Mikis was dutifully reported to be well in subsequent press releases. Nevertheless, when the International Red Cross requested permission to see him, the Minister of Defence refused.

As pressure from various groups and individuals concerned with Mikis' plight and health began to build up in intensity, the hard-line faction within the junta reacted with typical brutality. In early December, the police, authorized by the extremists in the government, committed an unbelievable act of vandalism by breaking into the Columbia Recording Company warehouse and smashing all seventy thousand of Mikis' recordings that had been stored there since June 1, 1967. As a further indication of the regime's attitude toward art, music, and recording, the fanatic Ioannis Ladas, General Secretary of the Ministry of the Interior, spoke at a ground-breaking ceremony for a new Music House in Kalamata, on February 2, 1970. He demanded "State action to discipline the Greek artists who imitated the decadent imported music composed by drug-addicted hippies—music of decay, senility, and decomposition."[20] The ex-colonel and most "Christian Greek" continued: "Does art serve society when it praises pessimism and obscenity, when it brings lewd thoughts to the mind, or when it extols the deniers of values, such as the Communists?"[21]

A wave of reaction, which had begun the year before, spread round the world. In France, Chile, Yugoslavia, Italy, Scandinavia, the Soviet Union, Poland, India, England, Canada, and the United States, committees were formed, whose sole purpose was to protest the treatment of the composer and to demand his release. These committees had turned Mikis into a symbol of the worldwide resistance to the colonels' regime. At the same time, the Russian composer Shostakovich suggested the formation of an international committee of artists for Mikis' release. The Swedish representatives at the Commission on Human Rights submitted an official appeal to the Greek Foreign Minister, Panayiotis Pipinelis, signed by 25,135 scientists, artists, and others.

---

[20] Covered in *New York Times* February 3, 1970. Ladas also had wanted to show Americans how they should carry on the Vietnam war until the ultimate victory. This "dissertation," *The Vietnam Question and the Contribution of the Americans to the Idea of Freedom,* he published in the winter of 1969.

[21] *Ibid.*

In the United States, scores of senators, representatives, newspaper columnists, artists, and intellectuals in general joined in the pressure for Mikis' release. Groups in colleges that had made isolated protests now consolidated their efforts by forming the Committee of Academicians and Artists for Mikis Theodorakis along the same lines that a similar committee of professors and economists had been formed to effect the release of Andreas Papandreou in 1967. This committee obtained either participating or supporting signatures from such notables as Leonard Bernstein, Pete Seeger, Arthur Miller, Edward Albee, Arthur Schlesinger, Jr., Abram Chasins, Harry Belafonte, and others. Among the senators and representatives who supported the committee's efforts or protested before Congress were Claiborne Pell, George McGovern, Eugene McCarthy, Charles Goodell, and Donald Fraser. Participating colleges and universities—City College, Hunter College, and Queens College of the City University of New York; Cornell University; Massachusetts Institute of Technology; Upsala College; and Wesleyan University—sent letters to the composer, officially inviting him to their campuses to lecture or give courses. Members from City College also filed a petition with the immigration authorities that Mikis be classified as a non-immigrant, so that he might be granted a visa.[22]

The concerted effort of the Committee of Academicians and Artists for Mikis Theodorakis made quite an impact on the junta. It was one of the most effective committees formed on Mikis' behalf, for its purposes went beyond the immediate political issues to the artistic level. Because it was particularly interested in bringing to public attention the works of the composer, it sponsored concerts and lectures as tributes to him, such as the one at Hunter College on December 9, 1969, bringing Maria Farantouri from England to sing the composer's most recent songs and play the tapes smuggled out of Greece by the underground. One of these was *Epi-*

[22] This petition was sustained by formal acknowledgment on February 3, 1970. See detailed description of the Committee's work in the *New York Times* article by Henry Raymont, April 15, 1970.

*phania Averoff*, which was presented to the public for the first time since its "première" in the prison.

All this time, there had been no direct answer from the composer, although he was receiving secretly some information as to what was going on. In January, he himself made an appeal to all political prisoners not to rely on the various politically oriented groups and parties to assist them. Such parties had never succeeded in achieving anything constructive in the past; it was not likely that they would do so now. The prisoners could accomplish much more, Mikis suggested, by staging a universal, lengthy hunger strike simultaneously throughout Greece for the abolition of all prisons and concentration camps. This appeal of Mikis did not please the Kolliyiannis Communist group, which violently disagreed with the composer's ideas, accusing him of straying from the orthodox party line.

The colonels continued to arrest or imprison anyone guilty of singing or possessing Mikis' songs. They even condemned those who were out of the country. One such was the Italian Michel Garouffi, who, on a visit to Greece in 1968, had sung one of Mikis' songs in public. He was condemned *in absentia* by a military tribunal in Athens to four years' imprisonment on March 6. Two days before that, the Cyprus Government, observing the demands of the Greek junta, prohibited the public showing of the film *Z*, because "it would not serve the public interest or the international relations of the republic."[23]

Then, the colonels directed their attack straight at the composer. On March 5, he was summoned, together with the poet Kostas Varnalis, to the police station to answer to the charge that, at a public gathering, in November, 1966, both had warned the Lambrakis Youth to get ready to confront the dictatorship that was forthcoming. The composer requested a twenty-four-hour delay to consult his lawyer and study the warrant. But the trial was not carried out; for, in the meantime, the junta had to deal with pressing issues.

---

[23] *The Times*, March 4, 1970.

On the world scene, things were not going too well for the junta. They had lost tremendous face by Greece's ouster from the Council of Europe. Furthermore, in spite of the tight security around Oropos prison, Mikis was getting news of the activities of the various groups and committees that were trying to help. In March, he composed a letter to the Committee of Academicians and Artists for Mikis Theodorakis, which, however, as it had to be sent by roundabout, secret underground hands, the Committee did not receive until April:

> The fact that this spirit comes from the very heart of the U.S.A. fills me to overflowing with the most unimaginable hopes for the very future of man.
>
> I thank you because you are humane and because you are Americans. On the ruins of the relations the tanks and chains have created between the U.S.A. and Greece, let us make an oath to hammer out a genuine friendship which must unite our two peoples.[24]

On March 9, Mikis was awarded the Anthony Asquith Prize in London for his score of Z, a prestigious honour for an artist. Coincident with this event, the film itself was creating its own following of rebels against the junta because of its worldwide success.

As a result of the international furore over the composer's deteriorating health, he was sent to the Sotiria Sanatorium on March 18 for a checkup. It was clear that his tuberculosis had flared up again, and that he needed a specialist. But pressure from the extreme right-wing factions in the junta forced him back to Oropos prison.

It was on March 25 that Mikis drafted a letter directed to all the antijunta groups, particularly to the leftists, to isolate the factionalists of the Kolliyiannis Communist group. In his letter, which was not made public by the National Council of PAM until the day after his release in Paris, he stated his reasons for the boycott. He had no recourse but to denounce the Moscow-oriented Kolliyiannis group for succumbing to personal animosities rather than rising to a broader unity for the

24 *The New York Times,* April 5, 1970, covered the incident.

popular progressive movement. It was destroying the anti-junta unity of the Greeks. Therefore, he appealed to all the progressive, socialist, and Communist forces to back the programme and struggle for unity advocated by PAM in accordance with the ideas of Lenin.[25]

In March and April, 1970, everything came to a head in Greece. The most tragicomic trials in history were being staged. Thirty-four of the most brilliant intellectuals in the nation were on trial for their participation in the underground Democratic Defence. The widely publicized open-door policy to the press resulted in such adverse publicity for the Greek regime that, after two days, the rest of the proceedings were carried on in secret. On April 11, the trial ended. Two university professors, Dionysios Karayiorgas and George Mangakis, were given life sentences. The sentence of the latter was commuted to eighteen years in jail. Nineteen of the thirty-four were condemned to from three to eighteen years' imprisonment. Among those who received the longer penalty was a French journalist of Greek origin, Jean Starakis. The fear that Karayiogras and Mangakis might be killed, as well as the danger to a French citizen, caused the arrival on the scene of the flamboyant Jean-Jacques Servan-Schreiber, whom Greek students in Paris had petitioned to intervene.

At this point, the colonels began to feel as if their backs were against the wall. Their "image" was at its nadir. The pressure for Mikis' release, coupled with the world outrage at the trial of the thirty-four, had placed them in an almost inextricable position. There was only one thing to do: make a dramatic gesture. The colonels could not afford to lose United States support, and they were beginning to feel pressured even there. After all, what was more important, the life of a human being or a new tank? It was decided to make a kind of amnesty: 333 prisoners, including Mikis, would be released. This magnanimous gesture was scheduled to take place before the third celebration of the coup. The colonels had learned something from their American public-relations

25 Excerpts from the letter were published in Le Monde, April 15, 1970, and in L'Express, April 20-26, 1970.

assistants about timing. The American Ambassador, Henry Tasca, called on Myrto to express his sympathy. In reality, he had been pressured by groups at home, as well as by U.S. congressmen, to make a gesture for the composer's release.

All the noise and publicity, however, had not helped Mikis' health. It was steadily deteriorating, and the colonels decided finally to send him to a specialist at the Sotiria Sanatorium once again. On the morning of April 12, an official representative of the junta, accompanied by Myrto, who had been called in, was shown to Mikis' room at the sanatorium: "Are you happy to stay here, or would you like to go to Paris?" the official asked. Mikis turned to Myrto: "Do you want me to go?" "If I want you to go! . . ." Tears accompanied her reply.

### LIBERATION AND AFTER:
### THE POLITICS OF UNITY

Monday, April 13, 1970, was Theodorakis Day throughout the world; the most difficult prisoner, the greatest Greek celebrity, was released, after three years of captivity, and arrived in Paris for medical treatment. Front-page columns and photographs, and, in some instances, whole pages, were devoted to the outstanding event. Even in Greece, news of Mikis' liberation became known.

A Lear jet hired by the Secretary-General of the French Radical Party, editor-in-chief of *L'Express*, and author of the controversial book *The American Challenge*, Jean-Jacques Servan-Schreiber, flew Mikis from the former Athens International Airport, acquired by Onassis when he bought Olympic Airways, to Le Bourget outside Paris. An ambulance waiting at the airport pushed its way through hundreds of exiled Greeks, and Frenchmen, who had come to greet him and took him to a private clinic in Paris. There, he was examined and operated upon by lung specialists using the latest scientific equipment and methods.

While Mikis was in the hospital, the involvement of Servan-Schreiber in the former's release created quite a stir in Europe. But the publicity created by Schreiber's role in the

affair had certain results: For one thing, the French government jumped in to take some of the credit for Mikis' release;
Gaullist newspapers accused Schreiber of taking credit where
it was not due. The French Parliament debated the Theodorakis issue for two days, and finally the matter became one
of local parliamentary polemics, for Schreiber, belonging to
the opposition Radical Party, went again to Athens to seek
the release of more prisoners. Foremost among these was the
French citizen and journalist, Jean Starakis.[26] The French
Government was thus forced to intervene through its ambassador in Athens and to request Starakis' release. The Greek
regime gladly returned him in a move calculated to win
France's vote in the forthcoming meeting of the Council of
Europe concerning the violation of human rights in Greece.
It was, however, a gratuitous gesture, for the French Government was the only European government which supported
the junta with guns, heavy arms, tanks, and aeroplanes, thus
competing with the United States in its "generosity."

Schreiber's endeavours had a second positive result—the implication of industrialists and nouveaux riches, such as Onassis, his wife Jacqueline, Stratis Andreadis (shipowner and governor of the Commercial Bank of Greece), Tom Pappas (of
the industrial complex Esso-Pappas in Greece)—the main
backers of the Greek regime, who, Schreiber said publicly,
had helped him in his efforts to free Theodorakis. Onassis and
the rest, however, repeatedly disavowed any involvement.
Subsequently, Onassis, who had just signed an agreement with
the junta in March, 1970, to invest £240 million for the next
seven years, exposed his real beliefs and political credo, in an
interview with Konstantopoulos' *Eleftheros Kosmos* on April
29. He admitted to having met with Schreiber on three separate occasions, and went on to say: "I was informed about the
meeting of Prime Minister Papadopoulos and J. J. Servan-
Schreiber through Professor Ioannis Georgakis (manager of
Olympic Airways). At the third meeting I had with Mr.
Schreiber, I expressed my views on his requests for my inter-

---

[26] Starakis was sentenced to a fifteen-year prison term for his involvement
with the resistance organization, Democratic Defence.

vention in the release of Theodorakis and other political prisoners. I told him not to take advantage of the Greek Premier's generosity and kindness. 'You must be crazy to ask for the release of those who have been convicted by Greek court decisions. To release those who planted bombs! . . .' Mr. Schreiber, above the freedom of individuals stand the freedom and independence of our nation. When these two are endangered, it is justifiable to sacrifice some of the people's freedoms. We, the Greeks, cannot tolerate any intervention which hurts one's feelings for the freedom of the nation. I cannot understand why you are in such a rush. You are acting like a bull in a china shop."

The junta, on its part, responded on April 29, 1970, to the agitation aroused by Schreiber, with a statement that, in its meeting with the French political leader, nothing was said about either the regime's feelings toward Mikis Theodorakis or any radical points that could persuade Papadopoulos to hand over to Schreiber Theodorakis' fate. The statement, however, concluded by saying that Schreiber had promised to speak in favour of the regime at the April 15 meeting of the Council of Europe in Strasbourg. Schreiber declared in an interview with *Le Monde* on April 14 that he would go to Strasbourg and reveal "the root of the problem—the American CIA and the U. S. military machine, and that it was not the colonels who were to blame for what was happening in Greece." Servan-Schreiber went to Strasbourg indeed, but he was not successful; for all the member nations, except France and Cyprus, had decided to condemn Greece, and he was therefore not received.

In one of his many statements about Mikis, Schreiber asserted that the composer had told him on the plane that he no longer had any Communist affiliations, and that he would abstain from any political activity while in France. The world shook and awaited the moment until Mikis got better to hear what he had to say to all these provocations. The composer, however, had so far remained silent, except for a note he had sent to Schreiber, asking him, as he was going back to Greece with other French personalities to try to free Starakis, to urge the release of Yiannis Ritsos, exiled once again a few days earlier, Manolis Glezos, a Resistance fighter, and several others. Mikis was still under his doctor's care and was recuperating steadily. Myrto and the children, until then, had not been allowed to leave Greece.

After sixteen days in the hospital, Mikis emerged from his silence, not only to answer the statements Schreiber had made and the critical rumours that were circulating around his own political views, but to mark his return to the political fight. On April 29, at a conference in the Hôtel du Palais d'Orsay, he proposed a concrete programme of struggle against the colonels. The conference room was packed with reporters, photographers, television and radio crewmen, and politicians; at the table sat artists such as Yves Montand, Melina Mercouri, Georges Moustaki, and others, as well as representatives from the three main resistance organizations, Andreas Papandreou's PAK (Panhellenic Antidictatorial Movement), Democratic Defence, and PAM. The political position he advocated was sharply at odds with Servan-Schreiber's statement, and he declared that Schreiber had been wrong to pin his hope on persons like Onassis, "an enemy of the people." He maintained that he had not entered into any agreement with anyone to refrain from political activities. "I am picking up my activities at the point where they were interrupted at dawn on August 21, 1967," he said. Then he made a long statement, in effect a political manifesto, in which he called for the creation of a united front. He called it the National Resistance Council, which would consist of all those who were against the junta—leftists, centrists, and conservatives—in order to depose the colonels by whatever means possible. The National Resistance Council could be headed by Andreas Papandreou, or by some other dedicated and able person, who might still be in prison. Mikis himself, however, made no claims to leadership.

He presented a nine-point programme for political action which would be endorsed by all the Greeks, finally united, after the overthrow of the junta. Among other things, it called for the formation of a government of national unity;

the abolition of the 1968 Constitution, and of all legal, political, and economic measures passed by the junta; the restoration of all freedoms; and free elections, with the participation of all parties. He advocated the creation of a constituent assembly to determine the role of the palace in the future life of the nation as well. He then answered questions from the press.

In reply to Schreiber's statement that he was no longer a Communist, Mikis had said: "Since I joined the Communists, this same question has always been posed to me. I do not know why, every time that something happens, a fog is created around me, and a statement, an avowal, must come forth to clear the situation. My story, in brief, is as follows: I have been a member of the party since 1943, and I cannot remember having been expelled. There was confusion created—and as you see, my French is not perfect—by my friend J. J. Servan-Schreiber, and I must explain myself. We did, indeed, discuss on the plane the crisis within the Greek Left. In *Le Monde*,[27] there are two statements, one of which was Schreiber's, and the other in which I declared my stand against the Greek Communist Party in exile. Perhaps it is the fact that I stated I do not belong to that faction which Mr. Schreiber took to be my position vis-à-vis the Greek Left. My criticism of Moscow and the GCP wing only confirms my loyalty."

To an American correspondent who asked whether he was planning to apply for a visa to go and lecture on campuses in the United States in response to the invitations of several colleges, he said that this declaration of his party loyalty could render him ineligible for a visa, unless the State Department ordered an exception.[28] His appearance and political statements at the Hôtel du Palais d'Orsay came at a most critical time, when his wife and children had applied to the Greek regime for a permit to go to Paris. He said that he did not

27 *Le Monde,* April 15, 1970.

28 Up to this writing, the State Department has made no exception. As a result, the Lincoln Centre Repertory Theatre was forced to cancel the commission it had given Mikis for a new score for *Antigone,* because he could not come and work with the company in New York. Another version was premièred on May 31, 1971.

wish to place his personal interests above the interests of the people: "My children are ready for sacrifice and are in agreement that their father should continue the struggle."

The junta immediately took measures against Mikis' family and rejected their application to leave the country. They prohibited as well the departure of George Seferis and the scholar Konstantinos Dimaras, who had been invited to lecture before various European literary associations. Surveillance increased throughout the land, and a closer watch was imposed on Mikis' family. But Mrs. Schreiber and her secretary got into contact with Myrto and told her about a plan for her and the children's escape organized in Paris by Mikis, five Frenchmen, and a network of Italian boatmen. Myrto kept strict silence, telling no one in her family, as she prepared two bags for a weekend picnic, just as she had done on the previous two weekends. On Saturday, at 4 P.M., she and the children got into a car that had just stopped outside their home in Nea Smyrne and whose French chauffeur drove to the seashore west of Athens, near Corinth. Two hours later, Mikis called his father to see how the children were doing. His father, who knew nothing of the plan, told him that they had just left for a picnic. Mikis was glad to hear about the picnic, for he knew that Myrto and the children were on their way to escape.

At midnight, the family took a boat and, for twenty-two hours, travelled on tempestuous seas. Spotted twice by the Coast Guard, they had to change course, first heading towards Turkey and then to a deserted beach in Italy, near Messina. Servan-Schreiber's wife was waiting there in her car, and drove them to Gratz, from where Schreiber's plane took them to Paris. Meanwhile Mikis and Schreiber were fervently discussing ways to help those in Greece who opposed the Greek regime and were still in prison at a rally at the Left Bank Mutualité auditorium. Suddenly Professor Paul Milliez, a physician prominent in humanitarian causes, burst in to announce Myrto's arrival. Immediately Schreiber, flushed with excitement and success, urged all present to perform concrete deeds, such as Myrto's escape, instead of just talking and criticising the Greek regime.

The Greek authorities, outraged, bit their tongues in self-reproach as the family rejoiced in Paris over the end of their three years of suffering and oppression. From May 11 on, they organized their lives in the same apartment they had occupied when in Paris ten years before, amidst an outmoded television set, piles of music sheets, newspapers, books, and a rickety old piano, from which music once again began to pour forth day and night, just as it had those earlier years when both parents were students in Paris, and Margarita and Yiorgos were uttering their first infant cries. Now, to all this clutter were added constant crowds of people—artists and revolutionaries organizing the resistance and practising new songs.

Mikis, strong, free, and healthy, took up anew his two lifelong occupations, resistance and music. Liberation brought out the two distinctive elements of his personality—his seriousness of purpose in life's struggle against oppression and his vitality and childlike exuberance. Now more than ever, he perceived the weight of his responsibilities in the crucial problem of uniting the various factions among the Greeks in their fight against the colonels through both his music and his commitment to the Patriotic Antidictatorial Front. The problems and the issues he had to encounter were many and at odds with one another: the junta, the Greek Left, the position of Greece in the international political arena, and the cultural demands of music and the arts, which had been paralysed by the military and forced into silence or emigration.

The schism within the Greek Left dated back to February, 1968, when two factions claimed leadership—the one headed by the Political Bureau of the Greek Communist Party, exiled since 1949 and Moscow-oriented, and the other by the Central Committee of the Greek Communist Party of the Interior, as it came to be called. In August of the same year, all those leftists, including Mikis, Manolis Glezos, Antonis Brillakis, and others, who opposed the intervention of the Warsaw Pact nations in Czechoslavakia, were severely criticized and condemned by the Political Bureau. Mikis had attacked the Political Bureau of Kolliyiannis in March, 1970, and now, upon his liberation, he could confront them unpressured. In an interview with *Le Monde* (April 30, 1970), in which he accused the Kolliyiannis group of obstructing the people's struggle against the junta, he appealed to the other European Socialist parties to let the Greek Left solve its own problems. At the same time, he requested that they end their diplomatic, commercial, and technological exchanges with the junta.

While Mikis was criticizing the Political Bureau and Moscow, as a first step, Kolliyiannis' party through the radio "Voice of Truth," pamphlets and official newspapers, rallies, and gatherings began to denounce the "dissident son" or the "maverick" Communist, as a reporter of *Christian Science Monitor* called Mikis.[29] Persistent "rumours" circulated that perhaps Theodorakis had been set free as a result of some sort of "deal" with the colonels. And so reproaches and accusations mounted, first on a personal level and then on political and organizational matters.

In May, 1970, he began a world tour for the resistance, which he linked to musical performances and debuts of new works. He set out plowing the world's capitals, starting with Italy and Yugoslavia, then on to the Scandinavian countries, the Soviet Union, England, the United States, Egypt, reaching as far as the Sudan and Chile. On May 13, in Belgrade, where he had been invited by the Union of Yugoslav Composers, he met with Tito and other leaders, with whom he discussed the Greek issue and the crisis in world Socialism. There, he stated that he openly disagreed with Andreas Papandreou's persistent exhortation for an armed struggle in Greece. Mikis expressed the view that the overthrow of the junta could be achieved by first uniting all the Greek forces opposed to the colonels; then, in the absence of any alternative, and if the people desired it, armed struggle would follow. Kolliyiannis remained silent. Moscow had many times in the past indicated its condemnation of any of Tito's dealings. The Greek junta, though, protested to Tito for having met with Theodorakis. Then the junta was startled as the composer visited the

United States to attend the World Youth Assembly at the United Nations from July 8 to 14. There, the composer was welcomed by the youth representatives of all the countries. But, as the junta had sent a group of young boy scouts to represent Greece, Mikis, after violently attacking the regime, departed from the Assembly in protest against having to sit at a U.N. meeting along with representatives of a tyrannical regime, which did not represent the people. While he was in New York, he appeared at a public gathering, organized by the American Committee for Democracy and Freedom in Greece, along with Arthur Miller and Pete Seeger, at which all three directly blamed the United States for the situation in Greece.

Shortly thereafter, Mikis was invited by the Union of Soviet Composers to visit Moscow as "an artist and a fighter." He declined the invitation, however, unless he could be invited as the President of the National Council of the Patriotic Front (formed in October, 1968, in Athens). Moscow agreed, but when he landed in the Soviet capital no government officials were at hand to greet him. He stayed there from August 17 to 25 and, before leaving, appointed as PAM representative the guerrilla leader of the Resistance and the Civil War, Markos Vafiadis, who was obviously not with the Kolliyiannis party.

Gradually, Mikis began ignoring the bureaucratic and dogmatic quarrels of the Greek leftists, for they were delaying and damaging the common struggle against the junta; instead, he carried on his own programme of unification of all sides, forces, and issues through PAM. First, together with other PAM members, he started a serious weekly newspaper, *Eleftheri Ellada* (Free Greece), a printed version of the hitherto mimeographed bulletin of PAM in Rome, *Eleftheri Patrida* (Free Country). The latter had been circulating since September, 1967, and the title was deliberately taken by the Kolliyiannis group, who put out a newspaper in London, beginning in 1967. Mikis wrote the editorial for the first issue of *Eleftheri Ellada*, in September, 1970, calling for unity.

The composer has written a number of articles, and made numerous public statements, on his political positions and opinions on how to organize the Greek resistance and what he thinks could be the future political life of the country. One such article appeared in the October, 1970, issue of *Poreia*, a review started in 1967 by the Greek students in Paris, the group that had asked Servan-Schreiber to go to Athens for the trial of the thirty-four of the Democratic Defence in April, 1970. Mikis explained his "politics of unity." All the forces opposed to the junta should have as their common denominator a "national and anti-imperialist" character, with three principal aims: the overthrow of the junta; the restoration of democratic rights and freedoms; and national independence. He made four proposals: first, unity on the part of the leaders, who would create the National Resistance Council; secondly, coordination and unity of action; thirdly, planning and organizing of new phases of struggle, especially the drastic phases of struggle; and fourthly, massive-resistance mobilization. Unity on the part of the people should be achieved by three means: a period of struggle for the overthrow of the junta; a transitional period involving a constituent assembly; elections; and, finally, a period of democratic development, whose ultimate aim would be the National Renaissance.[30]

The period between the writing of the article and the time when a step towards this unity was achieved, was marked with a variety of statements, interviews, meetings, and quarrels. In February, 1971, four resistance organizations formed the National Resistance Council (EAS) in London, which Mikis had proposed and worked for since his liberation. The organizations that participated were the Patriotic Front, led by Mikis, the Democratic Defence, represented by George Mylonas, the former Minister of Education under George Papandreou, the Defenders of Liberty, consisting of ousted army officers and represented by Dimitrios Opropoulos, and the Free Greeks, a group of royalist officers who helped the King in his abortive coup of December, 1967, and of whom more than fifty have

---

[30] Mikis Theodorakis, "On a Few Basic Problems of the Resistance," *Poreia*, October 16, 1970, 2-14.

been confined and exiled in isolated villages. Andreas Papandreou had disagreed with such a coalition in early December of 1970, stating that he was opposed to the King, and did not sign the EAS agreement. The GCP of Kolliyiannis, in spite of its preaching of unity, has never participated in a collective body, for, it seems, it wants unity only behind its own leadership. It must be said, however, that the GCP, although outlawed, is a political party, and none of the parties (ERE, Centre, EDA) have committed themselves as such against the regime. This is because the parties are forbidden to meet and act as organizations in Greece. EAS made its first public appearance at a rally in Düsseldorf, West Germany, on May 2, 1971. Representatives of the participating parties were George Mylonas of the Democratic Defence, Mikis of PAM, and George Voloudakis of the Free Greeks and the Defenders of Liberty. They were welcomed by the Minister of Justice of North Rhine-Westphalia. Two days later, *Eleftheros Kosmos,* semi-official organ of the junta, published a vitriolic editorial against the group.

Thus far, Mikis' efforts to unite the antiregime Greeks have been fruitful, at least for the drawing up of a common programme of action. He was the first to make the constant desire of the Greeks for unity into a reality. This he did through his fame, through his democratic and middle-of-the-road attitudes and programmes, which could be called those of the New Left of Greece, and, above all, through the power of his music.

Since his liberation, however, Mikis faced more problems than just the political ones. The three years of hardship were bound to have some repercussions on his marriage, and, indeed, Myrto was somewhat embittered and resentful of all she had to go through. Since their first trip to Paris and the birth of their children, she had been forced to give up her science and all her plans for a career, to become a housewife. Neither motherhood nor Mikis' music, politics, and the whirlpool of the latest events she had to live through could fulfil her desire for achievement. She had worked so hard during her youth and student days to create her own personality and accomplish her goals. And, now, upon her return to Paris ten years later, she was faced with the past and her shattered dreams. She found all her research work done at the Hospital Curie lying in dusty shelves and had to burn them. Each page was a reminder of the future she had dreamed of. Mikis had to admit to himself that he was responsible for Myrto's giving up all her youthful ideals and plans of becoming a scientist and a liberated woman.

Mikis' problems also extended to his artistic career, as was only natural. During the three years of captivity, he had produced a great quantity of written material and compositions. He wanted to keep his art at the forefront of his political struggle and fight the dictatorial culture imposed upon his people. Consequently, his musical creations and performances were bound to take that direction. The first of these, and most electric in its excitement, took place in Albert Hall in London on June 29, 1970. Before an enraptured audience of seven thousand, he directed the official premiere of his *magnum opus*, Angelos Sikelianos' *March of the Spirit (Ark. V)* .

The evening had been organized as a political event by the local committee against the dictatorship in Greece. Nothing could have been more suited to public protest against the colonels than this powerful combination of music and poetry, rooted in the conviction that the Greeks, and all peoples, must fight to "lift up the sun out of the mud," the sun of freedom.

Throughout the summer and fall of 1970, the composer gave concerts with his ensemble, declaring, with his introductory words and music, his determination to resist the dictatorship. At every concert, he urged the people to commit themselves to the common cause. In Moscow, the Komsomol Youth gave him the Order of Lenin on August 25; in Denmark, the University of Copenhagen conferred upon him the honorific title of distinction in the arts on October 12; the Italian "Club Valantino" gave him a Golden Award for his film scores at the closing of the year; while the University of Orkus acknowledged him as "Artist of the Year 1970," on January 28, 1971. That same month, he collected various unit-songs and composed new ones, thus creating his most harmonious cycle, *Songs of Strife*, sung by four singers and himself. Three of the poems were written by Alekos Panagoulis, who has been sentenced to death for his abortive attempt to assassinate Premier Papadopoulos in 1968. One of them is dedicated to Nikiforos Mandilaras, a strong defender of Papandreou at the Aspida trial, and the junta's first victim, killed during the early days of the coup.

In spite of the success and wild enthusiasm which his concerts have aroused, Mikis still has not solved the more crucial problem of which direction to take with respect to his musical movement. What kind of movement can it be, if the public is composed only of foreigners or Greek exiles? To seek Greece in other lands is an absurdity.

In Greece itself, however, a favourable breeze has begun to blow after four years. No matter how strict the dictatorial measures taken against those caught listening to his music, the people, largely through European radio broadcasts, are able to keep in contact with Mikis' music. Also, hundreds of travellers visiting Greece from abroad bring in tapes or recordings. Much as it would like to, the junta cannot check on all these persons.

To what extent the composer's affection for his land and people is returned was made poignantly clear at the funeral of George Seferis, the Nobel laureate, whose influence on Mikis' work was tremendous. The five compositions, *Epiphania*, *Mythistorema*, *Epiphania Averoff*, and *Raven—In Memoriam E.A.P.*, and *Mythistorema–XV*, are testament enough to the special bond that existed between them. Yet, when, upon hearing of his death, Mikis, from his exile in Paris, requested permission from the junta to attend the funeral, the colonels refused; for, "most Greek of Greeks" though they may be, they chose to ignore the death of one of Greece's fairest sons. But they could not check the people. Young and old, from all walks of life, thousands marched solemnly together in homage to this patriot who not long before had bravely spoken out against the darkness that had befallen their land. And, as if of one accord, they burst out singing the *Epiphania* and then the national anthem.

This book was already in press when Mikis, while on a tour with his Ensemble in Melbourne, Australia, announced on March 5, 1972, that he was no longer a member of either of the two Communist parties of Greece—the party of the Exterior headed by Kolliyiannis in Moscow, or the party of the Interior in Greece—and that from now on he would dedicate himself entirely to the interests of the nation. He said that he was disillusioned with both Communist parties since the schism in 1968, and also with the Soviet Union's intervention in Czechoslovakia, as well as the general ideological crisis within the Socialist world. He hopes to create a New Greek Left, a movement that will attract the healthy members of both parties and respond more directly to the immediate needs of the working-class people. Thus, a new era is inaugurated for Mikis.

# Appendix I

# The Works of
# Mikis Theodorakis, 1939–71

*EXPLANATION OF ABBREVIATIONS*

| | |
|---|---|
| BBC | British Broadcasting Corporation |
| BP | Ballet de Paris |
| EC | Elliniko Chorodrama |
| EIR | National Broadcasting Corporation |
| EME | Greek Music Publishers |
| EPON | United All-Greek Youth Organization |
| ETE | Greek National Theatre |
| KOA | State Orchestra of Athens |
| LSO | London Symphony Orchestra |
| MT | Mikis Theodorakis (soloist) |
| ONF | Orchestre National Français |
| RB | Royal Ballet |
| SOP | Symphonic Orchestra of Piraeus |
| TEE | Theodorakis Ensemble in Europe (1970–   ) |
| TEG | Theodorakis Ensemble in Greece (1960–67) |

Letters *A*, *B*, and *C* under "Description" indicate the three categories of song cycles.

Numbers in parentheses indicate number of unit-songs in the cycle.

| Date | Opus | Title | Description | First Performance | Publisher |
|---|---|---|---|---|---|
| 1939 | 1 | Concerto for Violin (lost) | Violin, strings | | |
| 1939–45 | 2 | Songs for Children (uncollected) | Harmonica or other | | |
| 1940 | 3 | Concerto for Piano (lost) | Piano, strings | Tripolis, 1942 | |
| 1942 | 4 | The Lord (Konstantinopoulos) | Oratorio; 4 voices, strings | Tripolis, 1942 | |
| | 5 | Grievous Nature (Theodorakis) | Song cycle; voice, piano | | |
| | 6 | Troparion for Kassiani | Liturgical; chorus a capella | Tripolis, 1942 | |
| 1943–47 | 7 | Resistance Songs (uncollected) | Not arranged | | |
| 1944 | 8 | Sinfonia (Theodorakis) | Oratorio; chorus, strings | | |
| 1945 | 9 | Third of December (Theodorakis) | Oratorio; voice, piano or chorus, strings | Athens (EPON), 1945 | |
| | 10 | Night March Towards Makriyianni (Theodorakis) | Oratorio; voice, piano or chorus, strings | Athens (EPON), 1945 | |
| | 11 | Duo for Violin | Violins | Athens (EIR), 1952 | |
| | 12 | Piano Trio | Piano, violin, cello | | |
| | 13 | Sonatina No. 1 | Three movements; violin, piano | Athens (EIR), 1958 | |
| 1945–48 | 14 | Love and Death (Mavilis, Theodorakis; dedicated to Myrto) | Song cycle (4); voice, piano—1955 arrangement: voice, strings | | Boosey & Hawkes |
| 1945–50 | 15 | The Feast of Assi-Gonia | Orchestra | Athens (KOA), 1950 | |
| 1946 | 16 | Sextet for Flute | Flute, piano, strings | Athens (EIR), 1952 | |
| | 17 | Oedipus Tyrannus | Orchestra—1955 version: strings | Athens (EIR), 1958 | Boosey & Hawkes |
| 1947 | 18 | Margarita (Vrettakos) | Oratorio; chorus, orchestra | | |
| | 19 | Greek Carnival | Orchestra—1953 arrangement: ballet suite (Rearranged as Le Feu aux Poudres) | Rome (EC; choreography: Manou), 1954 Paris (BP), 1958 | |
| 1948 | 20 | Elegy and Threnody for Zanos | String orchestra | Makronissos (by prisoners), 1949 | |
| | 21 | Passacaglia on a Theme from the Islands | Orchestra; 1952 arrangement | Athens (EIR), 1958 | |
| | 22 | Preludio-Penia-Choros | Percussion, strings, celesta | Athens (EIR), 1957 | |

| Date | Opus | Title | Description | Premiere/Publication | Publisher |
|---|---|---|---|---|---|
| 1949–50 | 23 | First Symphony | Three movements; orchestra | Athens (KOA), 1954 | |
| 1950 | 24 | Five Cretan Songs | Song cycle (5); chorus, orchestra | Chania, 1950 | |
| 1950–51 | 25 | Five Soldiers—Theme and Variations (*Theodorakis; lost*) | Symphonic poem; voice, piano, orchestra | | |
| 1952 | 26 | Orpheus and Eurydice | Ballet music | Athens (EC; choreography: Manou), 1952 | |
| 1953 | 27 | Barefoot Battalion | Score for film | American (Tallas), 1953 | |
| | 28 | Eva | Score for film | Greek (Plyta), 1953 | |
| 1954 | 29 | The Circle | Song cycle (6); voice, piano | Athens (EIR), 1955 | |
| | 30 | Suite No. 1 | Four movements; piano, orchestra | Athens (KOA), 1957 | |
| | 31 | Sonatina for Piano | Piano, orchestra | Paris, 1955 | |
| 1955–58 | 32 | Poèmes d'Eluard | Song cycle I (4), II (6); voice guitar, oboe, strings | | |
| 1956 | 33 | Erophili | Ballet music | Athens (EC; choreography: Manou, Tsatsou), 1956 | |
| | 34 | Suite No. 2 | Chorus, orchestra | Paris (ONF), 1956 | Boosey & Hawkes |
| | 35 | Suite No. 3—The Insane Mother (*Solomos*) | Five movements; soprano, chorus, orchestra | | |
| 1957 | 36 | Ill Met by Moonlight | Score for film | British (Powell), 1957 | |
| | 37 | Block No. 40 | Ballet music | Athens (EC; choreography: Tsatsou), 1957 | |
| 1958 | 38 | Le Feu aux Poudres (*see* Opus 19) | Ballet (music expanded) | Paris (BP), 1958 | |
| | 39 | Les Amants de Teruel | Ballet music (arrangement for score of filmed ballet) | French (BP; choreography: Rouleau), 1964 | |
| 1958–59 | 40 | Sonatina No. 2 | Four movements; violin, piano | Athens (SOP), 1967 | |
| | 41 | The Shadow of the Cat | Score for film | British (Gilling), 1958 | |
| | 42 | Antigone | Ballet music | London (RB; choreography: Cranko), 1959 | |

| Date | Opus | Title | Description | First Performance | Publisher |
|---|---|---|---|---|---|
| 1958–59 | 43 | Epitaphios (Ritsos) | Song cycle B (8); voice, pop orchestra | Athens (TEG), 1959 | EME |
| | 44 | Deserters (Yiannis Theodorakis) | Song cycle B (4); voice, pop orchestra | Athens (TEG), 1960 | EME |
| | 45 | Epiphania (Seferis) | Song cycle B (4); voice, pop orchestra | Athens (TEG), 1961 | EME |
| 1959 | 46 | Images d'Antigone (extracts from ballet) | Suite; orchestra | | Boosey & Hawkes |
| | 47 | Politia (Christodoulou, Livaditis) | Song cycle A (8); voice, pop orchestra | Athens (TEG), 1961 | EME |
| | 48 | Archipelagos (Theodorakis, Gatsos, Elytis, Christodoulou, Kokkinopoulos) | Play, song cycle A (12); voice, pop orchestra | Athens (TEG), 1961 | EME |
| 1960 | 49 | Faces in the Dark | Score for film | British (?) 1959 | |
| | 50 | Myrtia | Score for film | Greek (Karayiannis), 1960 | |
| | 51 | Honeymoon | Score for filmed ballet | British (Powell; choreography: Massine), 1960 | Cavendish Co. |
| | 52 | Phoenician Women (Euripides) | Theatre music | Epidaurus (ETE; Minotis), 1960 | |
| | 53 | Axion Esti | Pop oratorio, three parts; pop singer, cantor, reader, mixed chorus, pop and symphonic orchestra | Athens (MOA, TEG), 1964 | EME |
| 1960–71 | 54 | Isolated Unit-Songs (various hands) | 30 pieces; voice, pop orchestra | Athens (TEG), 1960 | |
| 1961 | 55 | Ajax (Sophocles) | Theatre music | Epidaurus (ETE; Mouzenidis), 1961 | |
| | 56 | A Neighbourhood: The Dream (Livaditis) | Song cycle A (12); voice, pop orchestra (score for film) | Greek (Alexandrakis), 1961 | EME |
| | 57 | Manolis | Score for film | British (Crosfield), 1962 | |
| 1962 | 58 | Electra (Euripides) | Score for film, also suite; pop, symphonic instruments | Greek (Cacoyannis), 1962 | |

| | | | | |
|---|---|---|---|---|
| 1962 | 59 | Phaedra (adaptation: Liberaki) | Score for film | American (Dassin), 1963 |
| | 60 | Five Miles to Midnight | Score for film | American (Litvak), 1963 |
| | 61 | The Hostage (Behan) | Play, song cycle C (16); voice, pop orchestra | Athens (Trivizas), 1962 EME |
| | 62 | The Ballad of the Dead Brother (Theodorakis) | Musical tragedy, song cycle C (8); voice, pop orchestra | Athens (Katselis), 1962 EME |
| | 63 | Beautiful City (Theodorakis, "Bost," et al.) | Musical revue, song cycle A (8); voice, pop orchestra | Athens (Cacoyannis), 1962 EME |
| | 64 | The Angels' Quarter (Campanellis) | Musical revue, song cycle A (10); voice, pop orchestra | Athens (Karezi), 1962 EME |
| 1963 | 65 | Enchanting City (Theodorakis, Hadjidakis) | Musical revue, song cycle A (8); voice, pop orchestra | Athens (TEG), 1963 EME |
| | 66 | Politia II (Christodoulou, Varnalis, Gatsos, Kokkinopoulos) | Song cycle A (6); voice, pop orchestra | Athens (TEG), 1963 EME |
| 1964 | 67 | Une Balle au Coeur | Score for film | French (Pollet), 1963 |
| | 68 | Little Cyclades (Elytis) | Song cycle B (7); voice, pop orchestra | Athens (TEG), 1964 EME |
| | 69 | Songs for Farantouri (Christodoulou, Gatsos, Livaditis, Stavrou) | Song cycle A (6); voice, pop orchestra | Athens (TEG), 1964 EME |
| | 70 | Zorba the Greek (Kazantzakis) | Score for film | American (Cacoyannis), 1964 |
| 1965 | 71 | The Island of Aphrodite (Theodorakis, Gatsos, Malenis) | Score for film, song cycle A (12); voice, pop orchestra | Greek (Papadopoulos), 1965 EME |
| | 72 | Trojan Women (Euripides) | Theatre music | Epidaurus (ETE; Mouzenidis), 1965 |
| | 73 | The Ballad of Mauthausen (Campanellis) | Song cycle C (4); voice, pop orchestra (arranged for ballet) | Athens (TEG), 1966 EME; Holland (choreography: Briër), April, 1971 |
| | 74 | The Ballad of Romiossini (Ritsos) | Song cycle C (9); voice, pop orchestra | Athens (TEG), 1966 EME |

| Date | Opus | Title | Description | First Performance | Publisher |
|---|---|---|---|---|---|
| *1965* | 75 | The Blockade | Score for film | Greek (Kyrou), 1966 | |
| *1966* | 76 | Lysistrata (*Aristophanes*) | Theatre music | Lykavittos (Synodinou, Volanakis), 1966 | |
| | 77 | Letters from Germany (*Ladis*) | Song cycle *B* (13); voice, pop orchestra | Lykavittos (TEG), 1966 | EME |
| | 78 | The Day the Fish Came Out | Score for film | American (Cacoyannis), 1967 | EME |
| *1967* | 79 | Six Maritime Moons (*Elytis*) | Song cycle *B* (6); voice, pop orchestra | Athens (TEG), 1967 | EME |
| | 80 | The Ballads of Antonio el Camborio (*Lorca*) | Song cycle *C* (7); voice, pop and symphonic instruments | London (Albert Hall), 1970 | EME |
| | 81 | Songs for the Front (*Theodorakis*) | Song cycle *B* (3); not arranged | | |
| | 82 | Sun and Time | Song cycle *C* (15); voice recitative, pop and symphonic instruments | In hiding (MT), 1967 | |
| *1968* | 83 | Epiphania Averoff (*Seferis*) | Oratorio; voice, choir, pop and symphonic instruments | Averoff Prison (by prisoners), 1968 | |
| | 84 | Mythistorema (*Seferis*) | Song cycle *B* (4); voice, pop orchestra | London (TEE), 1971 | |
| | 85 | Our Sister Athina (*Photinos*) | Song-river; voice, pop and symphonic instruments | | |
| | 86 | State of Siege ("*Marina*") | Cantata; two voices, pop and symphonic instruments | London (TEE), 1969 | |
| | 87 | Songs for Andreas (*Theodorakis*) | Song cycle *B* (4); voice, pop instruments | Rome (TEE), 1970 | |
| | 88 | Night of Death (*Eleftheriou*) | Song cycle *B* (10); voice, pop orchestra | | |
| | 89 | Twelve Laik Songs (*Eleftheriou*) | Song cycle *A* (12); voice, pop orchestra | Paris (TEE), 1971 | |
| | 90 | On the Mountains of Arcadia— Ark. I (*Theodorakis*) | Song cycle *B* (6); voice, pop orchestra | | |
| | 91 | In the Market Place—Ark. II (*Eleftheriou*) | Song cycle *B* (9); voice, pop orchestra | | |

| | | | |
|---|---|---|---|
| _1968_ | 92 | For Mother and Friends—Ark. III (_Eleftheriou; dedicated to his mother_) | Song cycle _A_ (6); voice, pop orchestra | |
| | 93 | The Vows—Ark. IV (_Kalvos_) | Song cycle _B_ (3); voice, pop instruments (_see Opus No. 105_) | London (TEE), 1971 |
| | 94 | March of the Spirit—Ark. V (_Sikelianos_) | Oratorio; 3 voices, chorus, pop and symphonic orchestra | London (LSO), 1970 |
| | 95 | Thourion—Ark. VI (_Theodorakis_) | Suite; voice, pop and symphonic instruments | London (BBC), 1970 |
| | 96 | The Survivor—Ark. VII (_Sinopoulos_) | Song-river; voice, pop and symphonic instruments | London (TEE), 1971 |
| _1969_ | 97 | I Speak—Ark. VIII (_Anagnostakis_) | Suite; voice, pop and symphonic instruments | |
| | | Z | | |
| | 98 | | Score for film | French (Costa-Gavras), 1969 |
| | 99 | The Exile's Mother—Ark. IX (_Kalantzis_) | Song-river; voice, pop and symphonic instruments | Radio Moscow (MT), 1970 |
| | 100 | My Name is K.S.—Ark. X (_Theodorakis_) | Suite; voice, pop and symphonic instruments | |
| | 101 | The Three Brave Ones—Ark. XI (_Pergialis_) | Song-river; voice, pop and symphonic instruments | |
| _1970_ | 102 | Raven—in Memoriam E.A.P. (_Seferis; dedicated to Yiannis Christou_) | Cantata; voice, chorus, pop and symphonic instruments | |
| | 103 | Mythistorema—XV (_Seferis_) | Cantata in sketch form | |
| | 104 | Negro Ballads (_Senghor_) | Song cycle _A_ (3); voice, pop orchestra | |
| _1971_ | 105 | Songs of Strife (_Theodorakis, Panagoulis, Kalvos,_ et al.) | Song cycle _A_ (15); voice, pop instruments | London (TEE), 1971 |
| | 106 | Biribi | Score for film | French (Moosman), 1971 |
| | 107 | The Trojan Women (_Euripides_) | Score for film | American (Cacoyannis), 1971 |

# Appendix II

# Manifesto of Music: A Draft Plan for the Reorganization of Greek Music

It is common knowledge that most sectors of our musical life are seriously ailing.

On the whole, the activity of our musical institutions is characterized by a total lack of planning, of judicious consideration of problems, and of coordination. Consequently, the evolution of music in our country follows a fitful and often regressive course.

Even those rare exceptions, those hopeful efforts towards a new beginning, though occasionally successful, have at best met with indifference and silence.

The aim of this brief introduction, however, is not to set forth a documented critique.

The draft that follows consists of *suggestions* that embrace, along general lines, the sum of the manifestations of our musical life.

Addressing ourselves to all Greek composers, especially the younger ones, we invite them to contribute to the elaboration of this draft by submitting counter-proposals, corrections, and, in general, suggestions of any sort. The draft will be completed by the collation and publication of these suggestions in a future issue of *Kritiki*.

If this plan is accepted by the state and by responsible musical circles, and is put into effect, it will provide, we believe, the foundations for a revitalization of music in Greece.

Before the plan is put into effect, a special musical convention, attended by proponents of all musical persuasions and, naturally, by representatives of all musical organizations, should back the draft with its approval and with the prestige of its endorsement:

EDUCATION

*Schools:* The sanctioning and reorganization of musical education at the elementary, secondary, and higher levels.

Teachers and professors of music should be graduates of the State Middle Conservatories.

*Conservatories:* The establishment of a State Advanced Academy of Music in Athens.

The establishment of two State Middle Conservatories (one in Athens and one in Thessaloniki).

Teaching in the private conservatories—which should continue to function—by graduates of the State Middle Conservatories or the State Advanced Academy of Music.

The establishment of a chair of Musicology at the University of Athens.

*Popular Education:* The creation of a musical movement, with its headquarters in the municipalities, communities, cultural clubs, labour unions, etc. (Public concerts and lectures—choirs, mandolin orchestras, etc.)

The establishment of contacts with the international movement of the *Jeunesses Musicales,* aimed at developing the musical culture of Greek youth.

SYMPHONIC ORCHESTRAS

Studies and solutions of the difficulties of the State Orchestra of Athens and the Symphonic Orchestra of Northern Greece.

The establishment of independent symphonic orchestras for the National Broadcasting Corporation and the State Opera.

Programming: (a) Performance of Greek works and international modern music; (b) participation of Greek soloists (concentrated effort to promote new soloists); and (c) exchange with, or recall of, foreign soloists, conductors, and musical compositions.

OPERA—BALLET

Tours of the Athens and Thessaloniki symphonic orchestras in the provincial centres.

Studies and solutions of the problems of the State Opera.

The need for a second operatic company, with the purpose of organizing regular performances of operettas in Thessaloniki, Volos, Patras, etc.

The establishment of a School of Opera and Ballet in the State Opera.

The sending of young people abroad to study (a) stage direction for opera and (b) choreography.

Programmed presentation of Greek operas and chorodramas.

Commission and proclamation of open competition for the composition of operas and chorodramas.

RADIO BROADCASTING

Study of the musical problems of the National Broadcasting Corporation, which is a basic medium for musical training.

The establishment of a self-sufficient symphonic orchestra.

With regard to the programming of performances, exchanges, etc., the suggestions in the paragraph on symphonic orchestras apply here as well.

Legal protection of intellectual property.

Periodic proclamation of open competition for the composition of musical works.

The establishment of a workshop of experimental music for the study of *musique concrète* and electronic music.

FESTIVALS

*The Athens Festival:* The "Athens Festival" has not yet acquired a character of its own. Besides ancient Greek tragedy and comedy, provision must be made for medieval and modern Greece. (Presentation of modern Greek works—opera, chorodrama, symphonic music, chamber music, etc. Performances of early Byzantine *melos* and liturgies in churches, which are the monuments of Byzantine art, such as the ones at Daphni, Kaissariani, Osios Loukas, etc. Cooperation of the theatre department of the festival for the creation of a musical theatre to put on works from the medieval period and the Turkish occupation. The presentation of modern Greek folk music and culture—songs, dances, etc.)

The need to make use of other places besides the Herodus Atticus Theatre.

*Local Festivals:* Giving moral and material support to the local festivals.

CHURCH MUSIC

It is imperative that a council be called to study the manner in which the Byzantine *melos* is sung in Greek Orthodox churches today. (Should it remain monophonic and hence be rid of the irrelevant harmonization of the Italian influence, or should it accept polyphonic elaboration, and in what manner?)

In this council, church representatives (from the clergy and laity), as well as personalities from the musical world, should participate.

POPULAR MUSIC

Study of the problems and encouragement of popular music. (Qualitative advancement and professional security; radio broadcasts; orchestras in centres of tourism.)

COLLECTION OF MUSICAL AND DANCE FOLKLORE

The need to aid effectively (live material; technical means—tape recorders, film projectors, etc.) the Folk Music Archives of the Athens Academy. Greece is the only country that does not yet have a scientific state-sponsored publication of its popular and folk melodies.

Parallel with the gathering of the rich musical folklore for the study and cinematographic compilation of Greek folk dances, the Athens Academy ought to organize a Folk Dance Archives.

A systematic programme, geared to the needs of our musical life, for sending students abroad at the expense of the state (extended studies).

The need to legitimize scholarships for closely following modern musical movements and musical societies abroad (duration, three to six months).

The essential requirement for the success of the purpose of state scholarships is that the holder of the scholarship, upon his return to Greece, be able to find work related to his field of specialization without difficulty.

PUBLICATIONS

If the Textbook Publishing Company* is to continue functioning, it must include in its publications elements of music theory and harmony, melodic exercises, collections of songs, etc.

For the publication of modern Greek musical works (scores, compositions, etc.), as well as those on theory, it is imperative that a specialized publishing house be established by the state.

This same house could undertake the publication of a music journal.

MIKIS THEODORAKIS
ARGYRIS KOUNADIS
YIANNIS XENAKIS
YIANNIS A. PAPAIOANNOU
DIMITRIS CHORAFAS
PHIVOS ANOYIANNAKIS

* State-owned firm.

# Appendix III

# The Manifesto of the Lambrakis Youth: A Ten-Point Programme of Action for Greek Youth

We, the young men and women of Greece, desire:

(1) Greece to be Free, Independent, Unfettered, Sovereign; the youth of Greece, free and [undivided], to act creatively for a happy and peaceful future.

(2) A Greek Foreign Policy—unprejudiced and unhampered, one and equal in its relations with all the peace-loving peoples of the world; with [as] criteria the national interest, the defence of peace, and the People's rights; our country to be a bearer of peace and constructive cooperation in the Balkans.

(3) Greece without foreign military bases, relieved of humiliating military agreements, neutral; able, on her own, to judge international events and take stands compatible with the interests of the Greek People, Democracy, Peace, and Humanism.

(4) A free and independent Cyprus, [associated] with a free and independent motherland.

(5) A National Economic Policy. The abolition of privileged foreign monopolies; the nationalization of basic foreign companies; the abolition of all those economic agreements that are contrary to the national interest; free trade and loans with all, provided the interests of the People are observed.

(6) A National Renaissance. To turn our backs on the past—and whatever divides us—and proceed wholeheartedly towards the future that must unite us. The application of democratic principles to all aspects of political and social life. The restriction of the Palace. The equality of all citizens before the law. The abolition of security clearance papers. The legalization of the KKE [Greek Communist Party]. The declaration of a general amnesty. The unity of all the democratic-constructive forces of our people, regardless of political persuasion, in a massive Patriotic Front to deliver our country from the mire of misery and deprivation. Our criteria, henceforth, will be the belief in, and contribution to, the ideal of national renaissance on the part of all.

(7) Patriotic Reform. The formulation of a long-range programme of economic reform based on the national budget; systematic exploitation of the natural resources; utilization of our potential resources; creation of essential units of heavy industry; development of light consumer industry; completion of the electrical and transportation networks of the country; reduction of military expenditures. Slowly to enter the twentieth century and evolve, as fast as possible, from an underdeveloped country to a developed and modern state.

(8) The state machinery, the armed forces, and the state and city police to be in the service of the people and the nation.

(9) Elimination of inequality in the distribution of our national wealth; elimination of the vast discrepancies between the countryside and the city; equal opportunity for all Greek youth; the Greek people to be master of their own household. We believe that the major producers of the country's wealth are the working and agrarian classes—plagued by underemployment, unemployment, migration, substandard housing, starvation, chronic malnutrition, inadequate clothing, illiteracy, and underdevelopment. In compensation for their great contribution, they receive only crumbs; and they exist on the fringes of modern civilization. Life in the villages, where there are no roads and no electricity, is a century behind the times. We demand radical measures for the rapid betterment of the working and agrarian classes. Work for all. Better wages for the working youth. Free vocational training for the young workers. The abolition of child labour. Protection of agricultural produce. Schools of agriculture. Electricity and roads for all the villages. New housing in the boroughs and in the villages.

(10) We believe in the Greek folk culture. We believe in the Greek literary and artistic tradition. We are proud of the Greek creators, scientists, writers, artists. We want—with Education, Science, Culture, and Athletics as our weapons—to train the younger generation in ac-

cordance with our national tradition and heritage of humanistic civilization. We want to see our country abound with schools, universities, laboratories, libraries, concert halls. theatres, museums, athletic stadiums and playgrounds. We envision a bright Tomorrow filled with constructive deeds and songs, filled with humanism, culture, and creativity!

# Selected Bibliography

## BOOKS

ADAMOS, TAKIS. *The Resistance Folk Song*. (Anthology and study in Greek.) n.p., 1964.

[ANONYMOUS.] *To Arms! To Arms!: A History of the National Resistance*. (In Greek.) Athens, 1965.

[ANONYMOUS.] *Verité sur la Grèce*. Lausanne, 1970.

ARAVANDINOU, NINA. *Fifty Greek Dances*. (Bilingual musical collection.) Athens, 1940.

Athènes-Presse Libre. *Le Livre noir de la dictature en Grèce*. Paris, 1969.

BAUD-BOVY, S. *Études sur la chanson cléftique*. Athens, 1938.

BECKET, JAMES. *Barbarism in Greece*. New York, 1970.

BIRTLE, BERT. *Exiles in the Aegean*. London, 1938.

CHURCHILL, WINSTON. *Closing the Ring*. Boston, 1951.

————. *Triumph and Tragedy*. Boston, 1953.

COUBARD, JACQUES. *Mikis Théodorakis, ou la Grèce entre le rêve et le cauchemar*. Paris, 1969.

The Council of Europe. *The Greek Case: Report of the Human Rights Commission*. 4 vols. Strasbourg, 1970.

*Elliniko Chorodrama, 1950–60*. (Anniversary album of E.C., with 20 photographic sketches and illustrations from Theodorakis' four Greek ballets.) (Bilingual.) Athens, 1961.

EUDES, DOMINIQUE. *Les Kapétanios: La Guerre civile grecque de 1943 à 1949*. Paris, 1970.

FORMOZIS, P. E. *Contribution à l'étude de la chanson et de la musique populaire grecque*. Thessaloniki, 1938.

LAGDAS, PANOS. *Aris: The First in the Struggle*. (A biography of the guerrilla leader Aris Velouchiotis, with a contribution by Mikis Theodorakis.) (In Greek.) Athens, 1964.

LEGG, KEITH. *Politics in Modern Greece*. Stanford, Calif., 1969.

LENTAKIS, ANDREAS. *The Neo-Fascist Organizations Among the Youth: A Study*. (Preface by Mikis Theodorakis.) (In Greek.) Athens, 1963.

MEYNAUD, JEAN. *Les Forces politiques en Grèce*. Études de Science Politique No. 10. Montreal, 1965.

————. *Rapport sur l'abolition de la democratie en Grèce.* 2d ed., vol. 1. Montreal, 1970.

PAPANDREOU, ANDREAS. *Democracy at Gunpoint: The Greek Front.* New York, 1970.

PENTZOPOULOS, DIMITRIS. *The Balkan Exchange of Minorities and Its Impact Upon Greece.* The Hague, 1962.

PETROPOULOS, ELIAS. *Rebetic Songs: A Folklore Study.* (Anthology of lyrics, with a glossary and photographs.) (In Greek.) Athens, 1968.

ROUSSEAS, STEPHEN. *The Death of a Democracy: Greece and the American Conscience.* New York, 1967.

STAVRIANOS, LEFTEN. *Greece: American Dilemma and Opportunity.* Chicago, 1952.

STRATOU, DORA. *The Greek Dances: Our Living Link with Antiquity.* (Illustrated.) Athens, 1966

SYNADINOS, TH. *History of Greek Music, 1824–1919.* (In Greek.) Athens, 1919.

THEODORAKIS, MIKIS. [Dinos Mais, a pseudonym.] *Siao.* (Poems.) (In Greek.) Tripolis, 1942.

————. *On Greek Music.* (Essays, articles, and speeches from 1949 to 1961.) (In Greek.) Athens, 1961.

————. *The Ballad of the Dead Brother.* (A play, with lyrics, musical illustrations, and an epilogue.) (Trans. George Giannaris.) Athens, 1962.

————. *The Lambrakis Youth Manifesto: Who Are We? What Do We Want? Why Do They Fight Us?* (In Greek.) Athens, 1966.

————. *Conquistare la libertà.* (Political-cultural pieces from 1961 to 1967, compiled and trans. by Aldo de Jaco.) Rome, 1968.

————. *Exodus.* (A dramatic fantasy in MS.) (In Greek.), 1969.

————. *Fem meter fra min celle.* (An Anthology of songs, with a biographical sketch. Trans. into Danish by Ole Wahl Olsen and illus. by Minos Argyrakis.) Copenhagen, 1970.

————. *Canzoni in esilio: Nos. 1, 2.* (An anthology of songs, with musical notations and a biographical note.) Milan, 1970.

————. *Journal de Résistance: La Dette.* Paris, 1971.

TSOUCALAS, CONSTANTINE. *The Greek Tragedy.* London, 1969.

ZAKHOS, EMMANUEL. *Poésie populaire des grecs.* (Bilingual anthology and study.) Paris, 1966.

## ARTICLES AND INTERVIEWS

*Akropolis.* Report on the Lykavittos Festival: September 3 and 4, 1966.

ANAGNOSTAKI, LOULA. "One Step of Greek Dramaturgy," *Epitheorisi Technis,* no. 90 (June, 1962).

ANDEINOS, X. "Theodorakis in Chile," *Eleftheri Ellada,* June 24, 1971.

ANOYIANNAKIS, PHIVOS. "On the Rebetic Song: Brief Arguments on General Contents," *Epitheorisi Technis,* no. 79 (July, 1961).

————. "Art Pop Music: A Movement," *Epitheorisi Technis*, no. 118 (October, 1964). (Interview.)

ANTONIOU, ANTONIS. "A Labourer on the Laik Song," *Epitheorisi Technis*, no. 76 (April, 1961).

ARKADINOS, VASSILIS. "The Rebetic Song," *Elefthera Grammata*, nos. 1–2 (1948).

————. "The Laik Song and Light Music." *Elefthera Grammata*, nos. 7–8 (1949).

*Avghi*. A critical comment on Theodorakis: November 1, 1962.

————. Comment on *The Ballad of the Dead Brother*: February 17, 1963.

————. Report on the banning of Theodorakis' music and his musical-cultural activities with the Lambrakis Youth: February 19, 1966.

————. Report on threats to Theodorakis: July 12, 1966.

BARRY, JOHN. "The Plea of a Political Exile," *Sunday Times*, March 16, 1969.

————. "Commentary on the *March of the Spirit*," *Sunday Times*, June 28, 1970.

BITHIKOTSIS, GRIGORIS. "Letter to Theodorakis," *Athinaiki*, April 20, 1964.

BLAND, ALEXANDER. "Greek Songs and Dances," *Observer*, April 28, 1968.

CHRISTIANOPOULOS, DINOS. "The Mother Figure in the Rebetic Song," *Tachydromos* (Alexandria, Egypt), September 5, 1954.

————. "Hadjidakis: The 'Sympathetic' Debaser of the Rebetic Song," *Drasis*, July 11, 1960.

————. "Historical and Aesthetic Formation of the Rebetic Song," *Diagnosis*, no. 1 (January, 1961). (An anthology, with a bibliographical note.)

CRISP, CLEMENT. "Saville-Theodorakis Ensemble," *The Financial Times*, April 23, 1968.

DANIILIDIS, D. "To the Memory of Eva Sikelianou," *Eos*, nos. 103–107 (1967).

DENSELOW, ROBIN. "The Theodorakis Ensemble at the Scala," *Guardian*, February 27, 1968.

*Dimokratiki Allaghi*. "A Plebiscite for the Laik Song at AEK," July 5, 1966.

————. Report on the Lykavittos Festival, September 3 and 4, 1966.

————. Report on the seminars at the Musical Association of Piraeus, January 27, 1967.

ELLISON, ELIZABETH. "Moving Tribute to Greek Poetry and Music," *Morning Star*, October 2, 1968.

ELYTIS, ODYSSEAS. "Poetry and Music," *Epitheorisi Technis*, no. 118 (October, 1964). (Interview on *Axion Esti*.)

*Epitheorisi Technis*. "The Theodorakis Case," nos. 97–98 (January–February, 1963). (Editorial.)

————. Documents on censorship: no. 109 (January, 1964).

*Epoches.* A series of articles on the Greek musical crisis by various authors: nos. 33–48 (January, 1966–April, 1967).

*L'Express.* Report on Theodorakis' release: April 20–26, 1970.

*Le Figaro.* Comment on censorship: January 28, 1966.

GALILI, SERGE. "Mikis Théodorakis," *La Presse Nouvelle,* February 9–15, 1968.

————. "Les Bouzoukis de Théodorakis," *Lettres Françaises,* April 3, 1968.

GEROSA, GUIDO. "L'Orchestra in esilio," *L'Europeo,* January 11, 1968.

GIANNARIS, GEORGE. "The Greek Pop Song in America," *Epitheorisi Technis,* no. 86 (February, 1962).

————. "The Oratorio *March of the Spirit* of Mikis Theodorakis," *Greek Report,* nos. 14–15 (March–April, 1970). (Commentary, with trans. text.)

GOLTZMAN, FRANCES. "Mikis Theodorakis Ensemble at the Place des Arts," (Montreal) *Gazette,* June 9, 1969.

GOODWIN, N. *"Antigone," Musical Courier,* December 8, 1959.

GRANDENNITZ, P. "Artistic Renaissance in Modern Greece," *New York Times,* September 11, 1955.

H. S. R. *"Antigone," Musical Opinion and Musical Trade Review,* December, 1959.

HADJIDAKIS, MANOS. "Interpretation and Position of the Rebetic Song," *Elliniki Dimiourgia,* March, 1949.

————. "There No Longer Exists a Laik Song," *Tachydromos,* July 2, 1960. (Interview.)

————. "Why Censorship Must Be Abolished," *Mesimvrini,* February 1, 1966.

HADJIS, KOSTAS. Letter-essay on laik music, *Epitheorisi Technis,* no. 82 (October, 1961).

————. "The Laik Song," *Epitheorisi Technis,* no. 82 (October, 1961).

HALL, RON. "Mikis Theodorakis: The Making of the Greek Sound," *Sunday Times,* September 3, 1967.

————. "The Ballads of Averoff Jail," *Sunday Times,* February 11, 1968.

HANAHAN, DONAL. "Xenakis: How a Man Defines Man," *New York Times,* March 17, 1968.

HASKELL, A. L. *"Antigone*: Royal Ballet," *London Musical Events,* December 19, 1959.

KARZIS, LINOS. "On *The Ballad of the Dead Brother," Eleftheria,* November 2, 1962.

KAUPP, KATIA. "Le Prisonier d'Athènes," *Nouvel Observateur,* no. 157 (November, 1967).

KAVANAGH, SIMON. "Zorba Composer an Idol in Exile," *New York Post,* August 25, 1969.

KEELEY, EDMUND. *"Axion Esti—The Genesis:* A Commentary," *Poetry*

(Greek number) I, no. 105 (October, 1964). (Text trans. by Keeley and George Savvides.)

KONSTANTOPOULOS, SAVVAS. Comment on censorship, *Eleftheros Kosmos*, January 25, 1966.

———. On the Lambrakis Youth, *Eleftheros Kosmos*, August 2, 1966.

KUZNER, MARTIN. Note on Theodorakis, *New Yorker*, August 15, 1970.

LAVIGNE, RAYMOND. "Un Bouquet de chansons pour Théodorakis," *Nouvel Observateur*, no. 159 (November 29–December 5, 1967).

LENNON, PETER. "Greek Freedom Song Finds Its Way to Paris—and Girl It Was Written For," *Guardian*, November 1, 1967.

M., F. "There, Where the Rebetic Song Spreads Joy and Emotion," *Eleftheros Logos*, December 16, 1952.

———. "Stasera a Modena suona l'orchestra di Theodorakis," *Avanti*, January 3, 1968.

M. M. W. "The Zeybekikos," *One* (English periodical), February, 1955.

MACDONALD, ROBERT. "Theodorakis' Songs Hold Nostalgic Memories," *Scotsman*, April 25, 1968.

MATSAS, NESTOR. "The Laik Song," *Ethnikos Kiryx*, May 11, 1952. (Interview with Tsitsanis.)

*Melody Maker*. "Music for the Heart and Mind," February 24, 1968.

MONDINI, PIETRO. "Folla per Theodorakis," *Paese Sera*, December 28, 1967.

*Montréal Matin*. "Un Poste pour Théodorakis au Canada," April 27, 1970.

*National-Zeitung* (Basel). "Wir wollen frei sein. . . ," October 18, 1967.

*La Nazione*. "Il Complesso di Theodorakis si esibisce al Palazzetto dello Sport," January 2, 1968.

*Ta Nea*. "Theodorakis in London," May 17, 1966.

———. "Protest of the Panhellenic Musical Association," July 21, 1966.

*New York Times*. On the banning of Theodorakis' music from the Athens Festival: July 9 and September 1, 1967.

———. "Man in the News: Composer-Communist," September 5, 1967.

*Newsweek*. "The *March of the Spirit*," July 13, 1970.

NIANIAS, D. Attacks on Theodorakis' music and politics, *Epitheorisi Technis*, no. 146 (February, 1967).

*Observer*. Greek politics and music (a political controversy and a letter by Theodorakis): June 16 and July 7, 1968.

*Panspoudastiki*. Comments on the Little Symphonic Orchestra of Athens (MOA): no. 42 (December, 1962).

PAPADIMITRIOU, V. "The Rebetic Songs," *Elefthera Grammata*, nos. 1–2 (1949).

PAPAKYRIAKOPOULOS, P. I. "On the Laik Song," *Epitheorisi Technis*, no. 83 (November, 1961).

PAUL, DAVID. "Simple Café Songs with a Devastating Effect," *Morning Star*, May 11, 1968. (On the Theodorakis Ensemble.)

PLATANOS, VASSILIS. "Theodorakis' *Romiossini*: Elegiac and Heroic Musical Work," *Ta Nea*, February 26, 1966.

*Politiken.* "Graesk besøg," November 18, 1967.

R. B. M. "The Songs and Dances of Mikis Theodorakis," *Stage*, April 25, 1968.

R. M. "Sadness That Is Greece," *Daily Telegraph*, February 27, 1968.

RIMELL, DAVID. "The Poetry of Greece in Haunting Melody," *Morning Star*, March 2, 1968.

RUTLAND, HAROLD. "The Ballet *Antigone*," *Musical Times*, December, 1959.

SETTIMELLI, LEONCARLO. "Interesse in Italia per la musica greca," *L'Unità*, January 2, 1968.

SIKELIANOU, EVA PALMER. "A Small Selection of the Writings of Eva Sikelianou," *Kainouryia Epochi*, Summer, 1957.

SJOGREN, MARGARETA. "Folkling grekisk jam-session," *Svenska Bagbladet*, January 12, 1968.

SLONIMSKY, NICOLAS. "New Music in Greece," *Musical Quarterly*, LI, no. 1 (January, 1965). (Reprinted in *Contemporary Music in Europe: A Comprehensive Survey*, ed. Paul Henry Lang and Nathan Broder: New York, 1968.)

SOPHOULIS, KOSTAS. "Letter on the Rebetic Song," *Epitheorisi Technis*, April, 1954.

SPANOUDI, SOPHIA. "Tsitsanis," *Ta Nea*, February 1, 1951.

SPERER-DRAKOU, LILY. "The *Axion Esti* of Theodorakis," *Athinaiki*, October 28, 1964.

TEDESCHI, RUBENS. "L'Orchestra di Theodorakis accolta fionfalmente dai giovani de Reggio," *L'Unità*, December 28, 1967.

THEODORAKIS, MIKIS. "The True Object of Mikis Theodorakis: My Dream Has a Name—Greece," *Pictures from Greece*, no. 63 (April, 1961). (Written interview in English with George Leotsakos.)

———. "From the Pop Song to the Pop Opera," *Dromoi tis Eirinis*, July, 1961. (Interview.)

———. "The Thread of Contact Between the Artist and the Public," *Epitheorisi Technis*, no. 82 (October, 1961).

———. Report on the composer's quarrels with the Greek Left, *Avghi*, August 10, 12, and 21, 1962.

———. "The Art of the Conductor," *Epitheorisi Technis*, no. 92 (August, 1962).

———. Interview with Mikis Theodorakis, *Avghi*, February 14, 1963.

———. "Theodorakis Speaks to EDA," *Second Panhellenic Convention of EDA* (official documents), Athens, 1963.

———. On the crisis within the Left, *Avghi*, February 17, 1963.

———. "The Big Story of the Little Orchestra of Athens (MOA)," *Tachydromos*, June 22, 1963. (Interview with George Pilichos.)

———. On the elections of 1963, *Avghi*, October 27, 1963. (Interview.)

————. "In Confrontation with Negation and Challenge," *Epitheorisi Technis*, no. 118 (October, 1964).

————. "The Climate That Gives Birth to the Genuine Songs: Theodorakis—Return to the Roots," *I Genia Mas*, January 15, 1966. (Interview.)

————. "The Composers Against Censorship," *Epitheorisi Technis*, nos. 133–134 (January–February, 1966). (Interviews with Theodorakis, Hadjidakis, and Xarchakos.)

————. "The Intellect-Killing Policy Must Stop," *Ta Nea*, March 11, 1966. (Interview with George Pilichos.)

————. Theodorakis' speech at the AEK athletic stadium, *Dimokratiki Allaghi*, July 5, 1966.

————. Letter of protest for not being allowed to conduct in Piraeus, *Ta Nea*, July 21, 1966.

————. "The Music of the 'Yé-yé's': A National Crime," *Eleftheros Kosmos*, July 27, 1966. (Interview with Angeliki Verykokaki.)

————. "On Musical Seminars," *Dimokratiki Allaghi*, January 27, 1967.

————. Interparty Memoranda of February 23 and 24, 1966, *Eleftheros Kosmos*, May 19 and 21, 1968.

————. "My Life in Exile," *Sunday Times*, May 4, 1969.

————. "Letter to Melina Mercouri from the Underground," *Observer*, May 4, 1969.

————. "Intervista con Theodorakis," *L'Europeo*, June 3, 1969. (Written interview with Nerio Minuzzo, from exile.)

————. Interview on the Greek Resistance, with *Le Monde*, April 14, 1970.

————. "Memorandum on the Greek Communist Party," *Le Monde*, April 15, 1970.

————. Press conference for the world news media at the Palais d'Orsay, April 29, 1970.

————. Interview on the Greek Resistance, with *Le Monde*, April 30, 1970.

————. "Mikis Theodorakis: 'I Am a Symbol of Power,'" *New York Times* Sec. 2, August 16, 1970. (Interview with Don Heckman.)

————. "On a Few Basic Problems of the Resistance," *Poreia*, no. 6 (October, 1970).

————. Appeal for the safety of the Burgos prisoners, *Kommounistiki Epitheorisi*, New Series, no. 9 (December, 1970).

————. Appeal for Angela Davis, *Eleftheri Ellada*, January 28, 1971.

————. Appeal for the Basque prisoners and the Monserrat intellectuals, *Poreia*, no. 17 (February, 1971).

————. "The Problems of the Resistance and the Left," *Kommounistiki Epitheorisi*, New Series, no. 10 (February, 1971). (Excerpts of article published in the *Guardian*, December 31, 1970.)

————. "Three Resistance Tactics," *Eleftheri Ellada*, February 11, 1971.

————. "On the Relations Between Party and Resistance," *Eleftheri Ellada*, April 1, 1971.

————. "The First Aim," *Eleftheri Ellada*, April 22, 1971. (Editorial.)

————. "On the National Resistance Council (EAS)," *Eleftheri Ellada*, May 13, 1971.

————. Theodorakis in Germany, *Eleftheri Ellada*, May 20, 1971. (Report and speeches.)

————. "What Is Our Position in World Affairs?" *Eleftheri Ellada*, July 22 and 29, 1971.

THEODOROPOULOU, AVRA. Musical column in *Kainouryia Epochi*, Winter, 1958.

THORNBERRY, CEDRIC. "Freedom Song from Gaol," *Guardian*, October 30, 1967.

*The Times*. Comment on censorship: January 28, 1966.

TORDAY, SANDOR. "Hedendaagse Griekse Muziek," *Mens en Melodie*, February, 1965.

VASSILAKI, F. "Theodorakis and the King" (a comment). *Akropolis*, March 20, 1966.

VOURNAS, TASSOS. "The Modern Laik Song: First Attempts to Approach Its Roots," *Epitheorisi Technis*, no. 76 (April, 1961).

WACZOW, J. "Laico, Bouzouki: Mikis Théodorakis," *Étudiants du Monde*, XXII, nos. 5–6, 1968.

XENAKIS, YIANNIS. "Modern Tendencies in French Music," *Epitheorisi Technis*, no. 6 (June, 1955).

————. "Problems of Greek Musical Composition," *Epitheorisi Technis*, no. 9 (September, 1955).

YIANNOPOULOS, YIORGOS. "Tsitsanis and Our Laik Song," *Ellinikos Vorras*, June 21 and 22, 1960.

ZORBALAS, STAVROS. "Mikis Theodorakis: The Eagle of Greek Music," *Ellinikos Tachydromos* (Canada), December 21, 1967. (Reminiscences.)

ZORIN, SERGEI. "The Theodorakis Ensemble in Moscow," *Politiki-Ekonomiki Erevna*, Second Series, no. 118 (October, 1966).

# Discography

*The Angels' Quarter.* Kourkoulos, Poulopoulos, Karezi, Seilinos: soloists; choir; Karnezis, Papadopoulos: bouzouki; cond. Theodorakis. His Master's Voice GCLP 7.

*Les Amants de Teruel.* Phillips 432790 BE. Also *Piaf Chansons.* Capitol Records ST 10328

*Archipelagos.* Bithikotsis, Linda: soloists; Chiotis: bouzouki; cond. Theodorakis. Columbia SCDG 2791, 2800, 2818, 2909, 2925, 2926, 2930, 2931, 2932, 3015.

————. Yiovanna: soloist; cond. Hadjidakis. Polydisc 14008.

————. Yiovanna, soloist; Anghelou: bouzouki; cond. Katsaros. Fidelity 7164.

*Axion Esti.* Bithikotsis, Dimitriev, Katrakis: soloists; Mixed Choir of Byzantiou, Theodorakis Ensemble, Little Orchestra of Athens; cond. Theodorakis. His Master's Voice GALP 101–102.

*The Ballad of Mauthausen* and *Songs for Farantouri.* Farantouri: soloist; cond. Theodorakis. ODEON PGCLP 16.

*The Ballad of Romiossini.* Bithikotsis: soloist; cond. Theodorakis. ODEON GCLP 18; Broadside BR 307.

*The Ballad of the Dead Brother.* Bithikotsis: soloist; choral; Karnezis, Papadopoulos: bouzouki; cond. Theodorakis. ODEON OMCGA 14.

*The Ballads of Antonio el Camborio.* Farantouri: soloist; Theodorakis Ensemble; cond. Theodorakis. Polydor 2393.025. (Album also includes *Songs for Andreas* and *Mythistorema.*)

*Beautiful City.* Bithikotsis, Giannakopoulou, Douzos, Kalouta Sisters: soloists; mixed choir; Karnezis, Papadopoulos: bouzouki; cond. Theodorakis. ODEON OMCGA 10.

*Chansons pour Andréas.* Moustaki: soloist; cond. Rostaing. Polydor 2215 003.

*The Circle.* Mantikian: soloist; Chelmi: piano. His Master's Voice 7 ERG 15002.

*The Day the Fish Came Out . . .* Instrumental; musical supervision; Cacoyannis. Twentieth Century–Fox S4194.

*Deserters.* Theodorakis: soloist; Chiotis: bouzouki; Fabas: guitar; cond. Theodorakis. His Master's Voice 7 EGG 2565.

*Electra.* Cond. Theodorakis. Phillips 600508 PR.

*Epiphania.* Bithikotsis: soloist; Karnezis, Papadopoulos: bouzouki; cond. Theodorakis. Columbia SEGG 2600.

————. Moutsios: soloist; arr.-cond. Klavvas. Philips 431 709 AE.

*Epiphania Averoff.* Yves Montand: reader; Kaloyiannis: soloist; Choeur National; Theodorakis Ensemble; cond. Grimbert. Polydor 2675.-037. (Album includes also *Sun and Time.*)

*Epitaphios.* Mouskouri: soloist; cond. Hadjidakis. Fidelity 8910, 8911.

————. Bithikotsis, Thymi: soloists; Chiotis: bouzouki; cond. Theodorakis. Columbia SCDG 2778, 2779, 2780, 2781.

————. Linda: soloist; Chiotis: bouzouki; cond. Theodorakis. Columbia SEGG 2583, 2584.

————. Panayiotou: soloist; Choir of Trikala; cond. Papastefanou. RCA Victor LPMG 6.

*First Symphony.* Symphonic Orchestra of Piraeus; cond. Theodorakis. Delta TS 5001

*Five Years: Mikis Theodorakis (1959–64)*—I, II, III. Anthology of songs; cond. Theodorakis. P.I.—ILPS—14—15—16.

*The Front.* Theodorakis: soloist. (Recorded while in hiding.) Clarté SF 9—7—117.

*The Greek Sound.* Instrumental; cond. Theodorakis. EMI (Columbia) SX6172.

*Honeymoon.* Marino Marini and his Quartet. Durium 45–DC 16640.

*The Hostage.* Theodorakis: soloist; cond. Theodorakis. LYRA 3502. MGM SE–4670.

*The Island of Aphrodite.* Bithikotsis, Farantouri: soloists; cond. Theodorakis; chorus cond. Pernaris. EMI GCLP 12.

*The Island of Azores.* Bithikotsis, Thymi: soloists; Chiotis: bouzouki; cond. Theodorakis. ODEON 45–CGRA 2355.

*Little Cyclades.* Birbili: soloist; cond. Katsaros. LYRA LP 3001.

————. Giannakopoulou: soloist; cond. Theodorakis. His Master's Voice SLPH 20.014.

*Love and Death.* Mantikian: soloist; strings; cond. Theodorakis. His Master's Voice 7 ERG 15004.

*March of the Spirit.* Farantouri, Kaloyiannis, Theocharis; soloists; New Opera Chorus, Gwalia Male Choir; London Symphony Orchestra; cond. Theodorakis. (Album also includes *Oedipus Tyrannus;* Georgiadis, leader.) Polydor 2480008 GU.

*Mythistorema.* Farantouri: soloist; Theodorakis Ensemble; cond. Theodorakis. Polydor 2393.025. (Album also includes *Songs for Andreas* and *Mythistorema.*)

*A Neighbourhood: The Dream.* Bithikotsis, Lydia: soloists; Papadopoulos, Karnezis: bouzouki; cond. Theodorakis. Columbia SCD 9 2929

*Oedipus Tyrannus.* State Orchestra of Athens (KOA); cond. Theodorakis. His Master's Voice SELG 15001.

*Phaedra.* Mercouri: vocalist; instrumental; cond. Theodorakis. UAS 5102.

*Politia.* Bithikotsis, Kazantzidis, Linda, Marinella: soloists; Chiotis: bouzouki; cond. Theodorakis. His Master's Voice 7 PG 2792–93, 2908–10.

*Sonatina No. 1 for Violin and Piano.* Orchestre Radio Symphonique de la R.T.F. de Strasbourg; cond. Bruck. His Master's Voice GBLP101.

————. Kolasis: violin; Papadopoulos: piano; State Orchestra of Athens (KOA); cond. Paridis. Fidelity 8912.

*Sonatina No. 2 for Violin and Piano.* Kolasis: violin; Papadopoulos: piano; State Orchestra of Athens (KOA). Fidelity 8913.

————. Tombras: violin; Tombra: piano. His Master's Voice 7 ERG-15003.

*Songs from Zatouna.* (Anthology 1967–69.) Cünne: soloist; arr.: Géri. Imperial 5C062–24150.

*Songs of Strife.* Theodorakis, Farantouri, Dimitriadou, Karalis: soloists; Arnold: guitar; cond. Theodorakis. Polydor 2445004. (Album also includes *The Vows.*)

*State of Siege.* Farantouri, Kaloyiannis: soloists; cond. Demetriou. Polydor 583 062 and 184 357.

*Suite No. 1 for Piano and Orchestra.* Tod: pianist; Symphonic Orchestra of Piraeus; cond. Theodorakis. Delta TS 5002.

*Sun and Time.* Wilson: reader; Farantouri, Kaloyiannis, Dimitriadou, Pandis: soloists; Theodorakis Ensemble; cond. Theodorakis. Polydor 2675.037. (Album also includes *Epiphania Averoff.*)

*Twelve Laik Songs.* Kaloyiannis, Dimitriadou: soloists; cond. Theodorakis. Polydor 2393020.

*The Vows.* Farantouri, Theodorakis: soloists; Theodorakis Ensemble; cond. Theodorakis. Polydor 2445.004. (Album also includes *Songs of Strife.*)

*Z.* Theodorakis, Farantouri: vocalists; arr. directed by Boutet. BS S 63539.

*Zorba the Greek.* Instrumental; cond. Theodorakis. Twentieth Century–Fox 4167.

# Index

# GEORGE ALLEN & UNWIN LTD

*Head Office:*
*London: 40 Museum Street, W.C.1*

*Sales, Distribution and Accounts Departments:*
*Park Lane, Hemel Hempstead, Herts*

*Argentina: Rodriguez Pena 1653–11B, Buenos Aires*
*Australia: Cnr. Bridge Road and Jersey Street, Hornsby, N.S.W. 2077*
*Canada: 2330 Midland Avenue, Agincourt, Ontario*
*Greece: 7 Stadiou Street, Athens 125*
*India: 103/5 Fort Street, Bombay 1*
*285J Bepin Behari Ganguli Street, Calcutta 12*
*2/18 Mount Road, Madras 2*
*4/21–22B Asaf Ali Road, New Delhi 1*
*Japan: 29/13 Hongo 5 Chome, Bunkyo, Tokyo 113*
*Kenya: P.O. Box 30583, Nairobi*
*Lebanon: Deeb Building, Jeanne d'Arc Street, Beirut*
*Mexico: Serapio Rendon 125, Mexico 4, D.F.*
*New Zealand: 46 Lake Road, Northcote, Auckland 9*
*Nigeria: P.O. Box 62, Ibadan*
*Pakistan: Karachi Chambers, McLeod Road, Karachi 2*
*22 Falettis' Hotel, Egerton Road, Lahore*
*Philippines: 3 Malaming Street, U.P. Village, Quezon City, D–505*
*Singapore: 248c/1 Orchard Road, Singapore 9*
*South Africa: P.O. Box 23134, Joubert Park, Johannesburg*
*West Indies: Rockley New Road, St. Lawrence 4, Barbados*